The Crowded Bed

*An Effective Framework
for Doing Couple Therapy*

The Crowded Bed

*An Effective Framework for
Doing Couple Therapy*

Toby Bobes, Ph.D.,
and
Barbara Rothman, Ph.D.

W. W. Norton & Company
New York | London

For information about permission to reproduce
selections from this book, write to
Permissions, W. W. Norton & Company, Inc.
500 Fifth Avenue, New York, NY 10110

Composition by Ken Gross
Manufacturing by Haddon Craftsmen
Book Design by Susan Hood

Library of Congress Cataloging-in-Publication Data

Bobes, Toby, 1940–
   The crowded bed : an effective framework for doing couple therapy /
Toby Bobes and Barbara Rothman
      p.   cm.
   Includes bibliographical references and index.
   ISBN 0-393-70280-4
   1. Marital psychotherapy. 2. Family psychotherapy. I. Rothman, Bar-
bara, 1934– . II. Title.
RC488.5.B63   1998
616.89'156--dc21   98-22639   CIP

W. W. Norton & Company, Inc., 500 Fifth Avenue, New York, NY 10110
http://www.wwnorton.com
W. W. Norton & Company Ltd., 10 Coptic Street, London WC1A 1PU

1   2   3   4   5   6   7   8   9   0

To our husbands,
Norman and Bernie

Contents

Acknowledgments   xi
Preface   xv

Part I. A Synthesis of Family Therapy Concepts   1

1. Our Basic Treatment Framework: Overlapping and   3
    Interlocking Concepts
    Our Philosophical Stance   3
    Systems Theory   6
    Bowen Theory   7
    Object Relations Theory   8
    Postmodern Constructivism   10
    The Developmental Family Life-Cycle Paradigm   12
    Contextual Influences   16
    Comparing and Contrasting Earlier Models with Postmodern   18
       Thinking

2. Connecting What We Think with What We Do   20
    Methods of Intervention   21
    Guidelines for Assessment and Evaluation of the Couple System   25
    Countertransference: Identifying the Therapist's Own Emotional   30
       Responses
    Identifying and Managing Intense Reactivity of Clients   31

3. Ethical and Therapeutic Dilemmas 33
Therapeutic Responsibility: Some Ethical and Legal Considerations 33
Our Philosophy Regarding Diagnosis and Labeling 35
Indications and Contraindications for Couple Therapy 37

Part II. The Case Study of Laura and Michael 41

4. The Initial Contact—The Couple as a System 43
The First Telephone Call 44
Reframing 44
Individual or Couple Work 45

5. The First Session: The Affair Revealed 48
The Power of Family-of-Origin Influences 50
The Couple's Attraction 51
Focus on Strengths and Instilling Hope 52
Join the Couple System 54
Clarify Each Partner's Perception of Problem 55
Connect Presenting Problem to Family-of-Origin 55
Set the Frame and Boundaries of Therapy 56

6. Family Secrets Exposed 57
Clarification of the Visual Picture of Laura and Michael's 59
  Genogram

7. The Crowded Marital Bed 62
Planning the Next Steps of Therapy 63
Boundaries and the Couple System 63
Boundaries Between Self and Other 64
Object Relations Theory 65
Projective Identification: An Intrapsychic and Interpersonal 67
  Concept of Object Relations Theory

8. The Couple's Dance 69
Punctuate Strengths of Couple 70
Triangular Patterns 70
Loops, Patterns, and Circularity 73
Internalized-Other Interviewing: Creating a Pathway for Change 76
Externalizing Conversations: Creating More Pathways for Change 76
The Art of Questioning 78
Circular Questioning 78
Reflexive Questions 79
Guidelines for Crafting Questions That Generate Change 80

9. Unconscious Agendas   83
   Jennifer Reed's Crowded Bed   *84*
   Belief Systems of Jennifer Reed   *85*
   Containment Versus Disclosure   *85*
   Impact of Countertransference Disclosure   *87*
   Gender Influences   *88*
   Ethnicity and Religious Influences   *89*
   Internal Processing and Musings of Jennifer Reed   *90*

10. The Untouchable Wound   93
    Opening Windows of Vulnerability   *95*
    The Impact of Stories, Secrets, and Myths   *96*
    Grief, Loss, and Healing   *97*
    Secrecy and Shame   *97*
    Exploring the Nonverbal Realm   *98*
    A Psychodramatic Journey with Laura and Michael   *99*

11. The Ripple Effect of Change   104
    Effects of Couple Therapy upon the Children   *106*
    Effects of Couple Therapy upon Family-of-Origin   *106*
    Rituals Relating to the Life Cycle   *109*

12. Endings and New Beginnings   110
    Varieties of Endings in Therapy   *114*

**Part III. Our Step-by-Step Treatment Format with   117
Various Populations**

13. Becoming a Couple in a Mixed Marriage   119
    The Interconnection of Interactions at Different Levels of a System 124

14. A Hispanic Couple with Teenage Children   127
    Grief, Loss, and the Family Life Cycle   *129*
    Ethnic and Cultural Considerations   *132*

15. Crisis Work with a Couple Encountering Multiple Losses at Midlife 135
    Vicki and Bob's Story   *135*

16. A Blended Marriage   140
    Family Composition at a Glance   *141*
    The Ruptured Bond   *144*
    Continuation of Therapy with the Wilder Family   *144*
    The Blending of Therapists' and Clients' Cultures   *148*
    Remarriage: The Blending of Multiple Cultures   *148*

17. Couples Facing Aging, Illness, and Death 151
    A Personal Examination of Loss 153
    Reflections about Self-Disclosure 154
    Family Beliefs and Attitudes about Illness and Death 155
    Vignette 155
    Assumptions Underpinning Our Work With Grief and Loss 156

18. Couples Experiencing Domestic Violence 158
    Overview of Domestic Violence 158
    A Supervision Session 162
    Assessment and Treatment of Domestic Violence: The Model ... 163
        of the Southern California Counseling Center
    Dialogue of Consultation 164
    Therapist's Biases, Prejudices, and Concerns Regarding the ... 166
        Subject of Domestic Violence
    Necessary Knowledge and Skills 166

19. Working with Sexually Distressed Couples 168
    Evolving Paradigms in Human Sexuality 168
    Taking a Sexual History 169
    Mike and Lynn 171
    Sexual Intimacy: A Developmental Task 173

20. Working With the Lesbian and Gay Population: It Starts with 175
    Self-Examination
    Working with Oppressed Populations 178
    Meeting the Challenge: Developing Culturally Sensitive Training ... 179
        Contexts

Personal Reflections 180
Glossary 183
Bibliography 192
Index 199

Acknowledgments

The past two years of writing this book together have been an incredible learning experience for both of us. We have laughed, cried, and struggled, just as most close couples do. As we became more open and frank with each other, our writing also became more authentic and honest. It has been a collaborative journey in the best sense.

The individual clients, couples, and families we have worked with through the years have truly taught us what it means to be therapists and to connect with people on a very deep level. We feel privileged to have been part of their lives.

Our students at Antioch University and supervisees at the Southern California Counseling Center demonstrated courage and risk-taking by sharing their rich life experiences. Their insightful questions and comments generated dialogue that set the stage for the writing of this book.

We have been part of a collegial support group for many years—our "Cuddle Group." We have all mentored, supervised, and been confidantes of one another. Our work at times would have felt isolating and insurmountable without this strong and very personal peer group. We consider ourselves fortunate to have Marsha Jacobs, Nancy Steiny, Janet Taylor, and Susan Brundo as such close friends and colleagues.

We want to thank our colleagues at Antioch University who have generously shared their thoughts and work with us as we evolved professionally—especially David Unger, Keith Rand, and Larry Zucker.

To Susan Munro, our editor and guide, we give our heartfelt appreciation and thanks. Her belief in us, knowledge of the process, and enthusiastic support of our work have made this book possible.

We thank Connie Shafran and George Thomas for their valuable contributions and feedback as we wrote the chapter on domestic violence. Connie and George, Co-directors of the Abuse Prevention Program at the Southern California Counseling Center, encouraged us to describe their model of working with couples and families experiencing domestic violence. Some months following this collaboration, George Thomas died suddenly. We will miss a wonderful friend and colleague. We also thank Marsha Jacobs, Executive Director of the Southern California Counseling Center, for her encouragement to write this chapter involving the Center's abuse program.

We thank Sallyann Roth and Karl Tomm for their personal interest and for providing us with valuable material for our book. We also thank Coral McDonnell of the Domestic Abuse Intervention Project in Duluth, Minnesota. She granted permission for us to use the "Power and Control" and "Equality" wheels in our book. The wheels were developed by battered women in Duluth and are part of the *Power and Control: Tactics of Men Who Batter* educational curriculum.

Philippa Sherman, whom we endearingly know as Fifi, was always responsive and available in providing her organizational and computer skills. She worked tirelessly, patiently, and with great care. We were most fortunate to have her as a vital part of our team and collaborative effort.

J. T. Steiny's wonderful imagination and artistic talent brought wit and irony to our book's cover illustration. We are deeply appreciative.

Jeremy Tarcher helped us to navigate the maze of getting a book published. He gave us good advice at the beginning of our journey.

I (TB) am grateful that I had the encouragement of my dear husband, Norman, and my three daughters, Carla, Julie, and Joanne, throughout the writing process. Their enthusiastic support was comforting and their comments so helpful, particularly when they read versions of the manuscript. Their voices became part of our conversations as the book evolved. I thank Roy and Patrick, my sons-in-law, for their encouragement and continuing interest. I also want to express my appreciation to Rita Lynn, a most valued colleague, for her belief in me and in this project. And to Robert Morris, my gratitude for his support and encouragement throughout my career.

I (BR) express my heartfelt thanks to my wonderful husband, Bernie, and my ever expanding family for their help, devotion, and participation in this book. I'd like to mention the names of my children, in-law children, stepchildren, and grandchildren who have taught me the meaning of family: Ellen and Diego, Jane and Jim, Carli and Andrew, Tibby, Michael, David, Jennifer and Mike, Nick, Casey, Claire, Luke, Dillon, Matthew, Chris, and Trevor. I'd also like to acknowledge the support of my friend, Laurie Burrows Grad, whose advice and guidance were extremely helpful. In memoriam, I wish to express thanks to my colleague and mentor, Jean Faivus, for her love, encouragement, and belief in me.

Preface

The Crowded Bed is a powerful metaphor for all the influences and intrusions upon a couple's life. Each partner brings to the relationship ghosts from the past. Family-of-origin issues, previous relationships, generational legacies, burdensome secrets, and family myths hover in the background. Vying for space on the couple's bed are intrusions from the present—children, in-laws, perhaps former spouses, job demands, financial worries— and more. Perhaps one spouse has brought a third party under the covers, or maybe substance abuse and potential violence have pushed family members into a corner. Spouses who entered marriage with great love, enthusiasm, and expectations may be bitter and disillusioned by the time they enter the therapist's office.

For the beginning therapist, sorting out these factors in a timely fashion and then helping the partners to establish boundaries around their relationship and rediscover traits and behaviors that formed the basis of their initial attraction may seem to be an overwhelming task. If an insurance company or managed care provider dictates a limited number of sessions, the therapist may be tempted to simply patch things up and hope the marriage will hold.

In the pages that follow, we offer students and beginning therapists a framework for working effectively and briefly, though not superficially, with couples. We address the following questions:

- How do couples get beyond the reactivity and blaming that destroy self-esteem and good will?
- How can couples possibly sort out the multiple layers and complexities in their relationships?

- Is it possible to move from impasse to dialogue? Can briefer therapy possibly be effective with couples whose long-term patterns and set responses have been operating for years?
- Can therapists who consider themselves "long-term thinkers" work with couples in a more focused mode?

In Part I we articulate the concepts and assumptions that provide our theoretical foundation. We are convinced that multiple perspectives enhance our understanding of a couple's or family's emotional landscape. Assuming that our readers have been exposed to the major family therapy theories, perhaps in some depth, we simply outline the concepts that we have found most useful in building our multidimensional framework.

Parts II and III bridge theoretical concepts with the practical aspects of doing couple therapy. In Part II we follow a typical case from beginning to end. Laura and Michael are a composite of the many couples we have seen over the years. Jennifer Reed is a composite of us (Toby and Barbara) as people and therapists. She embodies many of our therapeutic experiences as well as the way we think and work. We hope your experience reading this case study will be an interesting and enriching one.

In Part III we address some common and universal themes within our developmental framework. Here we also explore common and pervasive therapeutic issues: ethnicity, the impact of physical illness, domestic violence, and homophobia. In addition, we broaden the therapeutic frame by illustrating the use of a reflecting team and a variety of supervisory arrangements.

In our 25 years of experience as marriage and family therapists, we have learned many lessons about the changes and transitions common to all couples and families. In the pages that follow we will be introducing you to many of the clients with whom we have worked. We have learned from them about ourselves and about what makes relationships fulfilling and gratifying. These experiences have touched us deeply and have often been a catalyst for our own self-examination and personal and professional growth. Here, of course, we have changed their names and circumstances to protect their privacy.

As the health-care situation in our country has changed, it has become necessary to revise our way of working. The challenge has been to adapt our many years of doing long-term therapy to doing briefer but still effective work. Without doubt, changes are required in therapists' application of their philosophy and skills in order to conform to today's health-care situation.

Our framework offers a sharply focused approach that includes both a way of thinking and the clinical skills necessary for effective treatment.

While the ideas are set forth in a linear way, systemic and circular concepts shape our decisions about how to proceed as we track our clients' responses. We focus on the circularity of the couple's patterns and on self-perpetuating and reinforcing behaviors. Once this identification is made, we examine the generational roots of these patterns. This model is a reference point that guides our exploration in a directed, focused way with sensitivity and respect for the couple's struggles.

Briefer therapy and good therapy are indeed compatible. It is possible to sort out the complexities of relationships and to reach new levels of understanding and change in a brief period of time. First, however, we must understand how relationships get stuck and how our usual responses lead to more of the same behaviors. We are conditioned from a very early age to think in a linear way, using concepts such as right and wrong, good and bad, and figuring out "who is to blame." It is typical for each partner to view the other as "the problem." As we study and understand the circularity and patterns of relationships, the big picture emerges. This is the key to creating new alternatives for ourselves and new possibilities for change. Implicit in our theory is the strong conviction that healing and growth occur through understanding the health and strength of the relationship rather than examining its pathology. Our writing is punctuated by the teachings of a number of renowned family therapists whose contributions have shaped our model.

This is a practical guide for students and for therapists working in today's complex health-care arena. We also expect that clinicians will find it a useful refresher. Although it has been written primarily for therapists and those studying to become therapists, it will also appeal to anyone who is in a relationship and experiencing the strain and effects of a crowded bed.

The Crowded Bed

*An Effective Framework
for Doing Couple Therapy*

A Synthesis of Family Therapy Concepts

Chapter 1

Our Basic Treatment Framework: Overlapping and Interlocking Concepts

Our Philosophical Stance

Our philosophical perspective today is a reflection of our journeys as couple and family therapists. When we were novice therapists in the 1970s, family therapy was still in its infancy. Our own training was heavily influenced by psychodynamic theory, with its emphasis upon the intrapsychic realm. Indeed, our entire culture was profoundly influenced by this analytic and scientific way of thinking. We initially responded to the introduction of systems theory and family therapy with mild curiosity and great resistance. If we embraced systems theory with its emphasis upon the interpersonal world, we feared all of our previous learning would become irrelevant.

At the time we were working at the Southern California Counseling Center in Los Angeles. The Director of the Center, Nancy Steiny, had great vision and created a family therapy training program in 1985. Fortunately, we were both in the very first training offered. It was a challenging and exciting turning point for both of us. The shift from linear to circular and systemic thinking was by no means easy. It still seemed much safer to walk into a room with an individual client than to face an embattled couple or a family of six. At times it felt as if we were flying by the seat of our pants! As time went on, our work with couples and families increased. We knew our comfort zone had expanded when we started to encourage individual clients to bring in their partners, children, or entire families.

Working with couples and families stirred up many of our personal relationship issues. Through the increased intensity of this type of work, we began to identify difficult areas in our own relationships. Both of us subsequently sought out couple therapy with our mates. As we delved more deeply into unexplored areas of our own families of origin, our clinical work expanded and deepened.

Meanwhile, as our training continued, we became thoroughly acquainted with the many schools of family therapy. We were soon caught between the old comfortable ways of working and the newer, more challenging models. Gradually, from the vast field of family therapy models we chose particular concepts that now form our theoretical base. In the pages that follow we outline the key concepts and assumptions that underpin our way of thinking. Because of our in-depth exposure to a wide range of models in the field, we have incorporated the contributions of many theorists. As early students of Salvador Minuchin's structural model, we found his language and concepts fascinating. The terms *joining*, *boundaries*, *triangles*, *subsystems*, *enmeshment*, and *disengagement* provided a conceptual framework for understanding the couples and families with whom we were struggling. Mapping the family structure enabled us to form early tentative hypotheses. From Virginia Satir's hopefulness, positive outlook, and humanistic approach, we took the respect, caring, and empathy that are the cornerstone of our work. Her collaborative and focused work was a forerunner of directions our field has taken in the last decade. Carl Whitaker introduced us to the notions of spontaneity and creative use of self in the family system. His modeling gave us permission to be ourselves in the therapy room.

The object relations family work offered a bridge between our early intrapsychic work and the new interpersonal realm. While James Framo and later Jill and David Scharff were the pioneers of object relations family therapy, Murray Bowen was family therapy's major theoretician. His eight interlocking theoretical concepts provided the foundation we were seeking in this rapidly changing field. Further training with Gus Napier and Luigi Boscolo added unique dimensions to our emerging styles.

Our most recent trainings with Karl Tomm, Sallyann Roth, and Harlene Anderson have added new perspectives and depth to our professional work as therapists. The collaborative language systems and narrative approaches offer respectful, empowering language that reflects the postmodern way of thinking. Key concepts such as the client-as-expert, historical life stories, and dialogical conversations characterize these non-pathologizing approaches. Our way of thinking dramatically changed as we began to see ourselves more as collaborators and less as experts. As we immersed ourselves in constructivist theory, the notion of objective reality was replaced by the belief that people construe, interpret, and give meaning to their worlds. The impact of contextual influences became more relevant to our clinical practice. Our perception of what a family or couple is broadened in dimension. Constructivism has encouraged us to adopt multiple lenses in working with people. It teaches that any unit of objective reality, family or otherwise, exists in the mind of the beholder (Efran, Lukens, & Lukens, 1988). As the book unfolds, you will see these concepts in action. As you evolve as a therapist, you also will have the opportunity to see what makes sense theoretically for you and what fits for your unique style.

The contextual factors of culture, gender, race, class, age, ethnicity, and sexual orientation have always existed. What has changed is our identification of the need to explore our own attitudes in greater depth. With our heightened awareness of differences, our lenses have been widened to include the profound influence of these contextual issues upon family life. The narrow middle-class perspective of how families "should be" has become obsolete. Single parents raising children, same-sex couples, blended families, mixed religious, ethnic, and racial marriages, and grandparents raising children are the norm today. We must honor these newer constellations as well as the age-old traditions and loyalties handed down generationally. All levels of systems must be acknowledged and respected by therapists working with families.

Along with our professional changes, contextual shifts were occurring within our own families. Our combined personal experiences included a period of single-parenting, a blended family, children in mixed marriages, and grandparenting. Our work as therapists enhanced our openness to these developmental transitions, and these changes, in turn, enhanced a depth of understanding that we incorporated into our work over time. Collaboration, ongoing inquiry, and the emergence of new meaning became a lived experience both at work and at home.

The Crowded Bed grew out of our collaborative efforts over the years. Our work together as counselors and later as supervisors at the Southern California Counseling Center led to our decision to share private practice offices. This provided an ongoing context for peer supervision and mutual support, as we encouraged each other to venture into previously unexplored areas. Our professional paths paralleled one another. Doctoral dissertations, faculty positions, a multitude of seminars, trainings, and AAMFT (American Association for Marital and Family Therapy) approved supervision designations led to the decision to write this book together. Our philosophical positions grew out of our long talks, musings, and soul-searching along the way. The vignettes and in-depth case studies are composites of the many couples and families we have seen over the years of this journey.

This book is our way of incorporating all that we have learned and experienced. As we synthesize what we know, we hope that students will generate new meanings, new inquiries, and greater collaborative efforts in their own work. For us, this writing experience has given new meaning to our own collaborative coupleship.

Systems Theory

Systems theory is fundamental and underpins our work as therapists. It is a way of thinking that deeply influences our conceptualization of the therapeutic process. *Webster's Dictionary* defines a system as "a regularly interacting or interdependent group of items forming a unified whole." The family is a complex system in which the complete unit is greater than the sum of its parts. We look at how it is organized and view it as a natural social system. We notice the roles of the members of the family, how the individuals negotiate, problem solve, and view the world and their place in it. We also pay particular attention to the interaction of all the family members as well as to their patterns of behavior over time.

Many levels of influence operate simultaneously, affecting individuals, couples, and families. In understanding human behavior, the therapist must take into account the multiple levels of complexity in human systems. Take a young couple, Linda and Jeff, who have just had their first child. Their joy in welcoming this new addition to the family is overshadowed by Jeff's recent disappointment when a hoped-for job promotion went to someone else. The new parents had counted on the promotion to bring them more money and ease the financial strain. Linda had worked for years and was angry that their present predicament would probably mean she would need to return to work sooner than she had hoped. Learned social, gender, and role definitions and patterns influenced her wish to remain home with her child, especially during the early years. Family pressures heightened the couple's tensions, as Jeff's father was quite ill. Managed care influences upon the health-care system filtered down upon this family. Jeff's father had to choose a new doctor because he was no longer able to pay out-of-pocket for private care. Jeff feels caught between the needs of his parents and the needs of his nuclear family. Just from this glimpse at Linda and Jeff, one sees a family system with interdependent parts, boundaries that mark a distinction among the parts, and an organization that is struggling to maintain its equilibrium (Napier & Whitaker, 1978). Clearly, the family is an incredibly complex system in which the complete unit is much greater than the sum of its parts!

TABLE 1-1. *Assumptions That We Incorporate from Systems Theory*

1. The couple or the family is the client.
2. Change in one family member will affect the entire system.
3. Patterns are transmitted from one generation to the next.
4. The focus is upon circular causality rather than linear thinking.
5. The interactional patterns of the family are viewed in the here-and-now.
6. A family is a system with interdependent parts, boundaries that mark a distinction among the parts, and an organization that struggles to maintain its equilibrium.

Bowen Theory

As the major theoretician in the field of marital and family therapy, Murray Bowen had a profound effect. A fiercely independent thinker, he viewed the family as a natural system that could only be understood in terms of the repetitive interactions of its members. His approach may be used to bridge object relations theory and a systems perspective. Bowen encouraged therapists to look at themselves in relation to their own families of origin, feeling that such work would enable them to work more effectively with client-families. We find Bowen's interlocking concepts particularly relevant to the way we work.

TABLE 1-2. *Assumptions That We Incorporate from Bowen Theory*

1. Differentiation of self is both an intrapsychic and an interpersonal concept. An individual distinguishes internally between the rational and emotional parts of self. On an interpersonal level, one distinguishes between self and other. A key aspect of differentiation is the capability to hold onto oneself while in close proximity to a significant other.
2. A triangle forms to relieve anxiety when a two-person system (dyad) becomes intense.
3. The nuclear family emotional system involves partners with similar levels of differentiation. Partners low on the differentiation-of-self scale may produce one or more of the following symptomatic behaviors:
   - Overt marital conflict
   - Dysfunction of a spouse
   - Dysfunction of a child

4. The family projection process is one in which undifferentiated parents unconsciously focus upon the most vulnerable child. This triangulation stabilizes the parents' relationship.

5. Multigenerational transmission process refers to the transmission of emotional processes, patterns, and behaviors over time.

6. Emotional cutoff describes the process by which people distance themselves from their families-of-origin by separating physically and/or emotionally.

7. Sibling position refers to the birth order of children in a family. This often influences their place of power in the family as well as their marital interactions in adult life.

8. Societal regression refers to the collective emotional functioning of society. During times of stress (war, poverty, natural disasters), society functions much like a disorganized family.

Object Relations Theory

Object relations theory addresses the root cause of the individual's behavior by examining early relational experiences with primary caregivers. A basic premise of object relations theory is that all of us have internalized mental representations of people and relationships and that these internal experiences, formed in childhood, provide the framework for perceiving objective reality in adulthood (Scarf, 1987). The infant's relationship with a primary caretaker, generally mother, is the foundation for all later relating. In normal development the soothing and accepting (as well as the frustrating and rejecting) aspects of mother are internalized. All parts are then in interaction within the infant. There are some very painful experiences that are too much to bear; the infant splits off or denies these in an effort to protect him or herself. The unconscious contains these split-off parts until a relationship in later life triggers or activates the old wound. This, then, becomes an opportunity for a reparative experience. People often seek out therapy at this critical time in a relationship.

We find that the most effective way to begin therapy is by focusing on the here-and-now interaction of the couple or family system. We often ask for an elaboration of the presenting situation and any other history that will help us evaluate strengths and coping mechanisms. This is followed by exploration of the internal world of each of the partners. As the work unfolds, we alternate between the interpersonal and intrapsychic dimensions (Scharff & Scharff, 1991). Although we recognize the couple and family as interactional systems, we also view the individual members as subsystems. Because we strongly believe that our pasts are very much alive in our present relationships, we have integrated much from object relations theory. The incorporation of this intrapsychic component gives an additional dimension to our systems base. We therefore view the external couple/family system in dynamic interplay with the internal worlds of each individual.

The concept of projective identification is basic to object relations theory and deserves special mention because it is critical to our understanding of couple dynamics. We will present it here briefly and elaborate further throughout the book as this intrapsychic and interpersonal concept is applied to case studies. According to Carl Whitaker, "There's no such thing as marriage—merely two scapegoats sent out by their families to perpetuate themselves" (Whitaker & Keith, 1981). Each partner comes to adulthood with a set of internal family relationships that strongly influences perceptions, behaviors, and interactions in contemporary relationships. People usually repeat the patterns and behaviors they learned as children. Internal images or disowned aspects of an individual are projected onto another person. The other person unconsciously accepts the projection and behaves as if it were his or her own. Is it any wonder, then, that these internalized aspects of self influence us so profoundly? Inevitable confusions arise. The work of therapy is to help people become conscious of these projections and to understand them in the context of their relationship. In this way spouses learn to separate their individual internal worlds from their actual relationships today. The concept of distinguishing self from other is fundamental to effective therapy. The essence of fulfilling relationships is to have each partner relate to the other as the other rather than as an extension of the self.

TABLE 1-3. *Assumptions That We Incorporate from Object Relations Theory*

1. The child's relationship to any important person in his or her world is taken in and internalized from the moment of birth.
2. All of the child's experiences with parents and significant figures become the child's internal narrative.
3. In the child's earliest units of interaction with others, the feelings or affects are either pleasurable or unpleasurable, good or bad (St. Clair, 1986).
4. If the child cannot tolerate an experience of the interaction (such as rage, rejection, or aggression) the child splits off the unsatisfying aspects of this interaction from experience and represses it from consciousness because it is too painful (Scharff & Scharff, 1991). Thus, splitting is a protective mechanism the child uses to split off unwanted or threatening aspects of the self.
5. Internalized objects and experiences from the past continue to affect present relationships.

6. These internalized objects or images influence us so profoundly that we inevitably confuse them with our actual intimate partner, parent, or child.
7. Projective identification is the process by which internal images or disowned aspects of an individual are projected onto another person. The other person unconsciously accepts the projection and behaves as if it were his or her own.
8. Conscious and unconscious processes occur simultaneously.
9. Change occurs when unconscious processes become conscious and people become empowered to make new choices.

Postmodern Constructivism

During the late 1980s and early 1990s the idea of constructivism became popular among family therapists. Constructivists contend that what we call reality is a personal interpretation, a particular way of looking at the world shaped by language. The therapist is no longer the expert on how a family should be; rather, the family members are the experts. If we give meaning to our lives by the stories we tell about ourselves, it follows that language creates meaning around events and thereby creates reality. The postmodern therapist focuses upon the stories clients tell and collaborative conversations rather than upon the interactive repetitive patterns of the family.

Thus we have moved from therapist-as-expert and outside the system (first-order cybernetics) to a second-order cybernetic view in which the therapist is part of the system that is being observed and treated. Our students are often intimidated by the terms "cybernetic epistemology." Actually, the words sound more complex than the meaning behind them. These terms merely describe the evolution that has occurred in our field. The therapist is no longer an expert on how couples and families should be. The boundaries have been collapsed as a "spirit of collaboration" replaces a "spirit of expertise."

It is important to note the difference between social constructionism and social constructivism because, as Harlene Anderson (1997) notes, each has different implications for psychotherapy theory and practice. Freedman and Combs (1996, p. 27) also discuss the differences between these two concepts. They point out that the move from constructivism to social constructionism marks "... a shift from focusing on how an individual person constructs a model of reality from his or her individual experience to focusing on how people interact with one another to construct, modify, and maintain what their society holds to be true, real, and meaningful." Social constructionism emphasizes the interactional and social processes (Anderson, 1997; Freedman & Combs, 1996).

Narrative Theory

All families have their stories. More often than not, they have been handed down from generation to generation. Families and their individual members give meaning to their lives and experiences through the stories they tell. These stories strongly influence perceptions of self and then determine how we live our lives. As Michael White and David Epston (1990, pp. 13–14) write, "We have considered the proposal that persons give meaning to their lives and relationships by storying their experience and that, in interacting with others in the performance of these stories, they are active in the shaping of their lives and relationships."

It follows that if one can "story" his or her experience, it is also possible to "restory" it. By using "externalization of the problem," White and Epston distinguish between the problem and the person experiencing the problem. Through this linguistic separation of the person from the problem, a person's story, which has become his or her identity, may be rewritten.

It is our strong conviction that people's problem-saturated stories are not who they actually are. Although we are not narrative therapists in the "pure" sense, you will see, as the book unfolds, that the philosophy of narrative therapy permeates much of our thinking as therapists. For us, restorying is a corollary to the reframing process. A young couple entering therapy in crisis will be exposed to the idea of viewing their transitional dilemma as an opportunity for new alternatives. The stories of their constant fighting take on new meanings as the therapeutic conversations unfold. The intensity of their struggle lessens as they expose their vulnerabilities to one another. As a listening environment is encouraged, the clients' stories are indeed reframed.

TABLE 1-4. *Assumptions That We Incorporate from Narrative Theory*

1. Individuals and families give meaning to their lives through narratives or stories.
2. Life narratives determine people's perceptions, behaviors, and interactions.
3. Stories are inextricably interwoven with individual and family identities.
4. Just as these narratives have been written, so they may be rewritten in a therapeutic context.
5. Rewriting one's life story involves externalization of the problem. Simply stated, this means that the personal identity of the person must be linguistically separated from the problem.
6. New stories are constructed that replace the old dominant story.

Collaborative Language Systems Approach

The basic premise underlying this evolving approach to therapy is that problems and their solutions are not fixed situations but rather can be dissolved, changed, and given new meanings through language. The pioneers of this approach, Harlene Anderson and Harry Goolishian (1990) believe that change occurs through dialogue and conversation. The therapist's role concerns the process of therapy as he or she collaborates with clients. Thus the therapists and family together are part of a generative process in which new stories are co-constructed to give new and different meaning to people's lives.

TABLE 1-5. *Assumptions That We Incorporate from Collaborative Language Systems Theory*

1. The therapist and client/family are partners in collaboration.
2. While the therapist guides the therapeutic conversation and process, family members are the experts on their lived experiences.
3. The therapist maintains a "not-knowing," curious, respectful, and collaborative attitude.
4. The therapist invites clients to find the resources within themselves to change.
5. The therapist and family become conversational partners and through language co-create alternative narratives.

The Developmental Family Life-Cycle Paradigm

As you can see, our assumptions span the history of family therapy, from the pioneers Minuchin and Bowen to the postmodern theorists. How do we reconcile these perspectives? Like many marital therapists, we are eclectic, working within a framework that is loose and flexible. As you will see in the extended case of Laura and Michael in Part II and in the shorter cases in Part III, we adapt the framework to each couple's unique history and dilemmas.

Some themes apply throughout our work, providing an organizing perspective. The most prominent is the idea of a developmental family life cycle, which may be viewed as a thread that is interwoven throughout the tapestry of our work. Since all families navigate stages and transitions of the life cycle, this paradigm enables us to focus on family health rather than family dysfunction. This developmental lens is also useful in assessing the family or couple through time. Within each stage of the life cycle are specific tasks that must be accomplished before family members can successfully move on to the next stage. Like Carter and McGoldrick (1989), we assume that families often become derailed as they try to move from one stage to the next. Generally, they enter therapy at these points of transition. A basic life cycle assumption is that when earlier developmental transitions have not been negotiated successfully, subsequent stages are more difficult and chaotic. Our job at this time is to collaborate with the couple or family so that they can resume their journey and get back on track.

TABLE 1-6. *Assumptions That We Incorporate from a Life-Cycle Framework*

1. Specific tasks must be negotiated at each stage of development.
2. Couples or families often seek therapy during transition periods that occur between stages.
3. When early stages have not been negotiated, later stages are more difficult to negotiate.
4. The developmental stages of the individual, couple, and family must be viewed simultaneously.
5. The navigation through developmental stages offers the opportunity to address issues of grief and loss in relation to endings and new beginnings.

Interest in the life cycle of the family evolved naturally out of interest in and research on the life cycle of individuals. In its overall shape the family life cycle corresponds to that of the individual life cycle. Of prime importance to the concept of the family life cycle was the work of Erik Erikson (1950, 1964, 1968). His depiction of individual life stages, as well as the interplay between these stages and the shaping processes of social institutions, challenged the narrow focus of intrapsychic theories of development. Although his work on childhood has been more widely understood than his work on adulthood, in his later years he primarily devoted himself to the study of adult development.

Erikson's (1950) eight stages in the life cycle included a series of conflicts or turning points:

1. Infancy: Trust vs. mistrust
2. Early childhood: Autonomy vs. shame or doubt
3. Play age: Initiative vs. guilt
4. School age: Industry vs. inferiority
5. Adolescence: Identity vs. identity diffusion
6. Young adulthood: Intimacy vs. isolation
7. Middle Adulthood: Generativity vs. self-absorption
8. Senescence: Integrity vs. despair

In each of these stages there are specific tasks that create stresses in the individual, as well as in the family. Although these transitions are often marked by increased vulnerability, gains can be made that enhance ego strength (Erikson, 1950).

The first steps toward a family life-cycle view were taken in the field of sociology by Reuben Hill and Evelyn Duvall in 1948, as they prepared background papers for that year's "National Conference on Family Life." The family was still primarily seen as a collection of individuals, with each person having his or her own developmental tasks, until further work by Duvall in 1950. During a workshop on marriage and family research, Duvall broke down the family life cycle into eight stages and outlined the stage-critical family developmental tasks at each stage (later published in her classic text, *Marriage and Family Development*). Since then, many family therapists have contributed to mapping the family life cycle. Carter and McGoldrick's contributions have been particularly valuable (see Table 1-7). By now the life-cycle framework is commonly accepted in the field of marital and family therapy.

TABLE 1-7. *The Stages of the Family Life Cycle*

Family Life Cycle Stage	Emotional Process of Transition: Key Principles	Second-Order Changes in Family Status Required to Proceed Developmentally
1. Leaving home: Single young adults	Accepting emotional and financial responsibility for self	a. Differentiation of self in relation to family of origin b. Development of intimate peer relationships c. Establishment of self re work and financial independence
2. The joining of families through marriage: The new couple	Commitment to new system	a. Formation of marital system b. Realignment of relationships with extended families and friends to include spouse
3. Families with young children	Accepting new members into the system	a. Adjusting marital system to make space for child(ren) b. Joining in child rearing, financial, and household tasks c. Realignment of relationships with extended family to include parenting and grandparenting roles

Family Life Cycle Stage	Emotional Process of Transition: Key Principles	Second-Order Changes in Family Status Required to Proceed Developmentally
4. Families with adolescents	Increasing flexibility or family boundaries to include children's independence and grandparents' frailties	a. Shifting of parent child relationships to permit adolescent to move in and out of system b. Refocus on midlife marital and career issues c. Beginning shift toward joint caring for older generation
5. Launching children and moving on	Accepting a multitude of exits from and entries into the family system	a. Renegotiation of marital system as a dyad b. Development of adult to adult relationships between grown children and their parents c. Realignment of relationships to include in-laws and grandchildren d. Dealing with disabilities and death of parents (grandparents)
6. Families in later life	Accepting the shifting of generational roles	a. Maintaining own and/or couple functioning and interests in face of physiological decline; exploration of new familial and social role options b. Support for a more central role of middle generation c. Making room in the system for the wisdom and experience of the elderly, supporting the older generation without overfunctioning for them d. Dealing with loss of spouse, siblings, and other peers and preparation for own death; life review and integration

Contextual Influences

At one time, therapists were trained to view families through a one-dimensional lens. It was as if there were a particular way families should be, and if we could adjust them to be that way, the therapy would be on track. In the last two decades, however, therapists have come to realize that the majority of the families we see cannot be tied up into these neat packages. A broader multidimensional framework that encompasses the contextual variables of race, gender, culture, class, ethnicity, and sexuality has emerged alongside cultural pluralism in the United States. As our society has grown increasingly multicultural, the issue of diversity has been recognized and addressed by therapists. Increasing attention is being paid to the importance of therapists' exploring their own cultural identities. Trainees and experienced therapists seek to understand how their cultural experiences and biases impact their clinical work with individuals, couples, and families (Hardy & Laszloffy, 1995; Killian, 1998). Curious clinicians find that family members are eager and willing to teach them about the family's culture. Through this collaborative process, clients and therapists share their expertise.

Contextual influences are threads that run through various theoretical frameworks. Figure 1-1 provides a visual picture of these influences in relation to a family or client couple. We consider these many threads as we listen to clients tell their stories. In Part II and Part III of our book, we apply these contextual themes to the couples and families in our case studies. We notice how the power differential between partners is expressed, as men and women respond with gender notions of who is "weak" and who is "strong." Cultural, religious, and ethnic influences are illuminated in various vignettes.

While considering the multidimensional aspects of every couple and family that enters our offices, we examine the variegated threads of our own lives. How can we, Toby and Barbara, as female, middle-aged, Caucasian, Jewish professionals, relate to male-dominated, young, recently immigrated couples of Italian, Russian, or Mexican origin? Is it necessary to be Black to understand the repercussions from the legacy of slavery in our country? Can a heterosexual therapist successfully treat a gay couple? Our own philosophical position is that any unidentified prejudices interfere with the therapeutic process. Certainly, none of us is without prejudices and biases. What is of paramount importance is that they be identified and acknowledged. If not, clients will feel invalidated and unheard; the prejudices they encounter in everyday life will be reexperienced once again in the therapeutic encounter.

Since therapists' judgments, prejudices, and biases must be suspended, students must learn to identify and contain certain internal responses.

These reactions are addressed and dealt with in supervision, personal therapy, and throughout training. As part of our own self-examination, we discuss, in Chapter 9, the multiple levels of complexity that affect the couple and therapist systems of our case study.

TABLE **1-8.** *Assumptions That We Incorporate from Contextual Influences*

1. Contextual influences are threads that run through the various theoretical frameworks.
2. The contextual influences that must be considered in examining the relationships of couples and families are race, gender, culture, class, ethnicity, religion, and sexuality.
3. It is imperative that therapists acknowledge their own personal contextual threads and examine how these variables affect the therapist-client system.
4. As the similarities and differences of multiple contexts are recognized by the clinician, cultural bridges of connectedness between clients and therapist are facilitated. Likewise, in areas of difference, curiosity and interest in learning about the experiences and perceptions of others encourage new understanding and respect (Falicov, 1995).

Attention to life-cycle issues and contextual influences is basic to our theoretical framework, providing a multidimensional focus to our work with couples and families. A broader and richer tapestry is woven as clients and therapists interact and collaborate on expanding their worldviews.

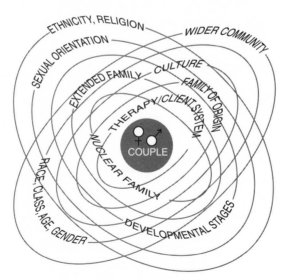

FIGURE 1-1. *Contextual Influences on the Couple*

Comparing and Contrasting Earlier Models with Postmodern Thinking

Our philosophical stance reflects our exposure to a wide range of approaches in the field of couple and family therapy. Rather than seeing these models as distinct and separate, we view them as having many similarities. For example, Murray Bowen's genogram, basically an information-gathering device, is similar to Salvador Minuchin's mapping and Virginia Satir's life chronology. The concepts of boundaries and reframing, originally unique to Minuchin's structural therapy, are now universal concepts that are used by most therapists in the family therapy field. The concept of positive connotation as used by the Milan group and other postmodern therapists was certainly evident in Virginia Satir's work in the 1960s. These are a few examples of the overlap between earlier models and today's views. Our particular paradigm incorporates a blending of the old with the new. While recognizing some of the differences, we also emphasize the similarities.

In the last decade family systems theory has greatly evolved. Therapists as experts outside the system have become part of a collaborative effort within the family system. In other words, second-order cybernetics has replaced first-order cybernetics. From a problem-saturated field we have moved in a direction that is solution-focused; from the intrapsychic to the interpersonal; from linear thinking to circular thinking; from structural frames to more flexible frames; from objectivity to subjectivity. From a noncontextual way of looking at families, we now place great importance upon the context that influences family life. These changes have revolutionized our thinking and have greatly affected the way we work with couples and families. We note that, while many similarities characterize different stages in the field's evolution, vast leaps in thinking have also taken place.

As far back as 1988, Efran, Lukens, and Lukens wrote of the overlap among family therapy theories:

> Techniques such as reframing and positive connotation, which constitute the lifeblood of many family therapy practices, have a decidedly constructivist flavor. Moreover, the many family therapists already accustomed to thinking pragmatically in choosing clinical strategies may, unwittingly, be revealing their constructivist bias.

Even psychoanalytic family therapists who emphasize objectivity and a detailed exploration of the past value the particular meaning given to these events by their clients. Meanwhile, constructivists, rather than focusing upon objectivity and fact-finding, view the family history as the vehicle that gives present events their meaning. In our opinion these two points of view are not incompatible. We believe that as therapists move from linear thinking to a circular perspective, the polarities and dichotomies will be viewed as differences rather than contradictions.

While our own framework is grounded in systemic, Bowenian, and object relations ideas, we are nevertheless strongly influenced by postmodern thinking. We see the assumptions underlying these various models as compatible. Our multidimensional framework has evolved over many years. As you grow and evolve as therapists, you, too, will select aspects of the various theories you encounter to shape your emerging style.

Chapter 2

Connecting What We Think with What We Do

What we do as therapists is inextricably interwoven with who we are. Although each model of therapy emphasizes different aspects of the therapist's role during sessions, the person of the therapist is the most crucial component in the integrity of the therapeutic relationship. A safe holding environment must be created, in which judgments, prejudices, and biases are suspended. The therapist avoids superimposing his or her own value system upon clients. In this nonjudgmental and nonthreatening atmosphere, couples' vulnerabilities may be exposed, experienced, and explored.

Different models of therapy emphasize different roles or skills for clinicians. Our basic treatment format incorporates concepts from several theories, as outlined in Chapter 1. From this theoretical stance the definition of the therapist's role emerges. Let us now bridge this theoretical stance with what the therapist does, connecting what we think with what we do (see Table 2-1).

TABLE **2-1.** *A Synopsis: How We Bridge What We Think with What We Do*

What We Think *Theory, Beliefs, Assumptions*	What We Do *Clinical Skills*
The couple or the family is the client. Circular rather than linear causality. (systems theory)	Join and set boundaries. Notice systemic patterns in present relationship. Explore families of origin. Identify couple's interactions and patterns.

What We Think *Theory, Beliefs, Assumptions*	What We Do *Clinical Skills*
Internalized experiences of past affect present. (object relations theory)	Alternate focus between interpersonal and intrapsychic and between past and present.
Differentiation of self-triangulation relieves anxiety in intense two-person system. (Bowen theory)	Encourage differentiation of self with family of origin. Model detriangulation from family system.
Therapists and families are collaborative partners. Old stories constrain; new stories liberate and expand alternatives. (narrative and collaborative language systems approaches)	Collaborate with clients and guide therapeutic conversation. Encourage rewriting of stories.
The importance of knowing oneself transcends all theories.	Identify countertransference. Contain judgments, values, and biases.

Methods of Intervention

Here we elaborate on some of our methods of intervention as they relate to the theoretical format. You may want to review this for yourself by looking at our step-by-step treatment format outlined in Table 2-2. Further clarification of this outline may be found in the "Guidelines for Assessment and Evaluation of the Couple System" later in the chapter. It is important that students understand that interventions emerge from one's own theoretical stance and underlying assumptions. As you learn didactically and work with couples and families experientially, your own framework, assumptions, and style will emerge.

TABLE 2-2. *Step-by-Step Treatment Format*

This model may be modified for use in any shorter or longer term format.

Session 1 and 2
- Join.
- Set boundaries.
- Establish a safe holding environment.
- Review how each partner perceives situation.

- Notice systemic patterns.
- Explore how couple's present patterns are linked to family of origin.
- Creation of visual picture of couple system (genogram)
- Reframe situation.
- Normalize couple's concerns.
- Elicit brief history of their relationship.
- Focus on couple's strengths and instill hope.
- Review commitment to each other.

Session 3 and 4
- Review responses to earlier sessions.
- Clarify how each partner sees solution to perceived situation.
- Identify the couple's developmental stage.
- Identify couple's interaction.
- Explore couple's expectations regarding change.
- Collaborate and invite partners to consider alternative ways of responding.

Session 5 and 6
- Identify each partner's early survival mechanisms.
- Explore how couple's present patterns are linked to family of origin.
- Explore how patterns and beliefs restrain.
- Educate partners about need for survival skills/defenses developed as children.
- Encourage listening in order to help each understand the other's struggles.
- Reduce blame and defuse anger.

Session 7 and 8
- Review where couple is at this time and how couple is using the therapy.
- Use feedback from couple to refocus direction.
- Identify what is working and punctuate strengths.
- Normalize and prepare for setbacks.
- Empower partners by helping them accept their differences.
- Distinguish between self and other.
- Develop empathy.

Session 9 and 10
- Acknowledge loss and closure of therapy experience.
- Assess the therapeutic work.
- Build upon newly acknowledged competencies.
- Model moving on to the next developmental stage

The therapist engages the couple in a way so that he or she becomes empathically and emotionally connected to each person. Although the relationship is the client, the partners must experience the therapist's support for each of them individually, as well as for them as a couple, in order for a working alliance to be formed. Without adequate and continuous joining, therapy will be blocked and ineffective. Clients must experience the therapist's caring, acceptance, respect, and empathy for joining to occur. This is an ongoing process throughout the course of the therapy.

For the couple and family therapist the job of reframing or relabeling begins with the first telephone contact. What is described as one family member's problem by the caller is redefined as a couple or family dilemma by the therapist. This systemic reframing places behaviors and patterns in a positive perspective and yet challenges the couple's reality, with the intent of bringing forth new responses. Reframing involves what the therapist actually does and says; however, just as important is the attitude of compassion and empathy that underlies the creation of new frames and new contexts.

The therapist asks about, clarifies, and validates each partner's perception of the problem. It is crucial to explore everyone's experience of the problem, until each person's point of view is acknowledged and understood. The therapist conveys acceptance, respect, and understanding for each partner. The problem must then be defined bilaterally so that the spouses can begin to see their circular system. Clearly this is a systemic concept. As the therapist clarifies each individual's perception of the problem, groundwork is being laid for distinguishing self from other. This differentiation-of-self work is the central concept of Bowen family systems theory and is critical to work with couples. Object relations theorists also acknowledge the importance of this concept as they work to help individuals reown formerly projected aspects of self.

By constructing a genogram, the therapist co-creates with the partners a visual picture of the couple system. Typically, the genogram is utilized early on during the assessment process. Have you ever drawn a genogram of your own family? If so, you may have noticed patterns throughout the generations. If not, we suggest that you try it; you may find the process a personally enriching one. In Chapter 6, you can see how the therapist uses a genogram to co-create and clarify with Laura and Michael a visual picture of their family tree.

The therapeutic activity of drawing a family tree is a tangible way to punctuate systemic patterns, reframe and normalize situations, and explore how present issues are connected to a broader generational context. In our clinical experience, creation of a visual picture of the couple system in its larger family context enables both clients and therapist to view the situation from multiple perspectives. When family issues and patterns are seen over generations, problems are reframed, detoxified, and normalized (McGoldrick & Gerson, 1985). Joining with couples and families is enhanced as understanding is deepened. Clients begin to move from a one-dimensional, linear view of situations to a wider systemic one. This process builds hope and enables clients to generate new meanings and alternative solutions. The theoretical underpinning of the genogram is the family systems theory of Murray Bowen.

Normalizing occurs when the therapist validates and acknowledges clients' feelings and circumstances. It is a way of letting the client know that he or she is not crazy and, in fact, that other people in these circumstances behave similarly. Normalizing is conveyed not only by the therapists' words but also by his or her accepting, nonjudgmental attitude. Most couple and family therapists use this type of intervention often, regardless of their theoretical orientation.

All therapeutic interventions have meaning, purpose, and intention. A therapeutic conversation is different from a social conversation. Although the couple or family members are the experts on their situations, the therapist is the expert on the process of guiding the conversation. In order to accomplish this, the clinician must be aware and knowledgeable of the intent of interventions. In other words, what we think always underlies what we do. Karl Tomm (1988a) has written about the intent and assumptions that underpin all questions asked by therapists. We specifically address this subject in Chapter 8, when we discuss the guidelines for crafting questions that generate change.

Just as developmental stages are important in the family life cycle, they are isomorphically relevant in the therapeutic life cycle. There is a beginning, middle, and end stage to each therapeutic experience. Each individual session is also characterized by these three stages. At all levels of any therapy system, a parallel process is occurring. Table 2-3 illustrates our therapeutic life cycle.

TABLE 2-3. *The Therapeutic Life Cycle and Accompanying Tasks*

Therapeutic Tasks in Beginning Stage of Couple Therapy

1. Join and engage the couple system.
2. Create holding environment.
3. Set the frame and boundaries of therapy.
4. Clarify and validate each partner's perception of problem.
5. Elicit history of relationship.
6. Focus on developmental stage and tasks to be accomplished.

7. Instill hope.
8. Clarify here-and-now interaction while attending to intrapsychic dimensions of the couple system.

Therapeutic Tasks in Middle Stage of Couple Therapy
1. Identify couple's patterns of interactions.
2. Explore how these patterns are linked to families of origin.
3. Acknowledge how patterns and beliefs restrain.
4. Collaborate with partners to consider alternative ways of interacting.
5. Empower partners by helping them accept their differences and distinguish between self and other.
6. Explore transferential and countertransferential responses.
7. Elicit partners' responses to therapy, and use this feedback to guide and refocus the work.

Therapeutic Tasks in Terminating Stage of Therapy
1. Acknowledge closure and loss of therapeutic relationship.
2. Explore earlier reactions and patterns of grief and loss.
3. Review what the individual and couple have learned and gained from therapy experience. What strengths and resources have been recognized by clients during the course of the work? What have the partners learned about their patterns and interactions as a couple and as individuals?
4. Assess and facilitate further self-work. Encourage partners to use and build upon newly acquired competencies and skills. Incorporate new rituals into relationship.
5. Experience a model of an ending that is mutual and caring.
6. Model moving on to the next developmental stage. How will couple's changes affect them in their larger context? For example, how will their changes affect them as individuals and as a couple with their parents, their children, and in the wider community?

Guidelines for Assessment and Evaluation of the Couple System

Initial Telephone Contact

WHAT WE DO
The following are some of the questions we ask during the first telephone contact:
1. Who referred you to me?
2. Can you give me a brief description of what is happening?

3. Are there other family members living with you?
4. Does your partner know you are calling me?
5. Would your partner be willing to join us for the first session?
6. What are some possible times that you both may be available?

WHAT WE THINK
Since our basic premise is that the couple is the client, we want to see both partners together. Although we are in charge of the therapeutic boundaries, a collaborative attitude is always maintained with our clients.

First Session

WHAT WE DO
We wait to start the session until both partners are present. In the first session we join with each partner individually as well as with the couple system. We greet the partners warmly and engage them as we make contact.

The following are some of the questions we ask during the first session. These will stimulate your thinking as you develop additional questions of your own.

1. Can you tell me how each of you views your present situation?
2. What is the history of your relationship? How did the two of you meet?
3. What attracted you to each other?
4. How does each of you experience the other's commitment to the relationship today?
5. How does your relationship compare to each of your parents' relationships?
6. Do you think that what you are going through today might be similar to your parents' experiences?

WHAT WE THINK
In an attempt to instill hope and connect the couple with their strengths, we go back in time to the early history of their relationship. We immediately observe systemic patterns and notice interactional sequences. Does one partner defer to the other? Does one pursue while the other distances? Who manages the closeness and who regulates the distance? This is often seen in the couple's seating arrangement. By using circular questions, we can link today's issues to family-of-origin issues and thus perceive transgenerational and contextual patterns.

Subsequent Sessions in Beginning Stage of Treatment

WHAT WE DO

In our effort to bring forth themes, beliefs, and patterns, we continue to ask circular questions. As details of people's stories emerge, intense emotions surface. David Treadway (1989) states, and we agree, that without understanding, awareness, and experience of some of the intense affects from the past, partners will remain stuck in repeating old patterns and roles learned in childhood.

The following are some of the circular questions we ask as treatment continues:

1. Who is your partner most like in your family of origin?
2. How does your parents' relationship compare to your own relationship?
3. How did your parents deal with the kinds of issues you are facing now?
4. How did your family handle differences when you were a child?
5. How did your mother's relationship with your father (partner, boyfriend, lover) affect you? What did you learn about relationships from experiencing their interaction?
6. How did your father's relationship with your mother (partner, girlfriend, lover) affect you? What did you learn about relationships from experiencing their interaction?
7. Which beliefs and roles that you learned in your family are still valuable today? Which are no longer valuable?

WHAT WE THINK

In our ongoing task of noticing systemic patterns, we continually search for connections that link the past to the present. We also explore beliefs and roles in order to understand their impact on today's relationship. In this way we give present behaviors a historical context.

Other Therapeutic Tasks in the Beginning Stage of Treatment

WHAT WE DO

As we gather a couple's history, we use a genogram to augment our exploration. Generally, it is helpful for couples to see their family tree visually and graphically. As the sessions continue, new information is added to the genogram. During this process the couple begins to define their boundaries and their transgenerational family system. Thus the genogram is used as an assessment device.

As we elicit the couple's history, we pay particular attention to how partners hear one another. We help them develop empathy for each other as well as improve their listening skills. Another component of history-gathering involves clarification of the couple's developmental stage. This enables us to normalize their struggles as they navigate difficult transition periods.

What We Think

It is healing for couples to tell their life stories. The process of revealing struggles verbally and then viewing them pictorially is powerful. We are thus readily able to connect the past with the present.

Therapeutic Tasks in the Middle Stage of Treatment

What We Do

As history unfolds, we identify each partner's early survival mechanisms. By helping partners connect their present situation to earlier beliefs and to how they survived and protected themselves as children, we enable them to begin to learn that they no longer need these old defenses. Letting go of old survival mechanisms is difficult, and clients' pacing must be respected. During this process the partners develop compassion for themselves and each other. They begin to honor and accept each other's differences. What we do in this middle stage is the core process of couple therapy.

What We Think

At this stage, the commitment to therapy often parallels the commitment to the relationship. Partners are willing and motivated to do deeper work. By identifying early roles and survival mechanisms, partners learn to correlate present behaviors with past learning. They become aware of how they are restrained by these early beliefs and how these old patterns affect their partnership today. As this early material is explored, it becomes easier to distinguish self from other and to accept each other's differences.

Therapeutic Tasks in the Later Stages of Therapy

What We Do

We continually collaborate and review with the partners how they are responding to treatment. A refocusing of direction is sometimes indicated. Their feedback lets us know how to proceed. At this time the couple may want to include other family members in some sessions. Clarification of their own relationship often leads to a desire to complete unfinished business with parents, children, or other family members. When various members of the family are included, the therapist must direct special attention and sensitivity to the entire family system.

WHAT WE THINK

Because we value collaborating and staying with the client, we remain flexible and sensitive to the couple's feedback. Changing the therapeutic direction to include other family members necessitates a reworking of the therapeutic contract. This change must be acknowledged as a new format is considered. Ethical considerations are taken into account when changing the therapeutic format (see Chapter 3).

Therapeutic Tasks in the Terminating Stage of Therapy

WHAT WE DO

We begin to verbally acknowledge closure of the therapy as dictated by clients' needs. In brief work, closure starts early on in the process. In long-term work the therapist has the luxury of more sessions. In either case, the loss and grief of ending therapy stimulate the expression of earlier losses. The therapist must allow space for this process to unfold. The entire therapeutic experience is reviewed at this time. The following questions are useful:

1. How has each of you experienced separations and loss in the past? How was loss dealt with in your family of origin?
2. Are your reactions to handling loss today similar to or different from lessons learned in your family of origin?
3. What changes have each of you made as individuals and as a couple?
4. How will the changes you've made affect your other relationships? For example, how will these changes affect you as individuals and as a couple with your parents, your children, and in the wider community?
5. What strengths have you acknowledged during the course of therapy? (Review strengths of each partner individually as well as strengths of the relationship.)
6. Which parts of this process worked well for you and which parts did not work so well?
7. Are there any questions you have regarding my perception of our work together?

WHAT WE THINK

We attempt to provide an opportunity for a collaborative closure and a corrective and healing experience for clients. To this end we must pay particular attention to our own personal reactions to loss and grief. A profound parallel process takes place.

Countertransference: Identifying the Therapist's Own Emotional Responses

Experiencing and understanding one's countertransference form the foundation for self-understanding and continued growth as a therapist. Such self-exploration is necessary for doing in-depth clinical work. The therapist who is willing to be continually aware of countertransferential reactions and to examine, explore, and monitor his or her own emotional responses will develop greater empathy for self and for clients. Scharff and Scharff (1992) write, and we agree, that if the therapist is open to his or her internal encounter, then a deeper understanding may be achieved, and the power to transform relationships within couples and families will be enhanced.

Our students commonly ask about containment of their own emotions during sessions. When a couple's intensity and reactivity escalate, novice (and sometimes experienced) therapists become overwhelmed with their own reactivity and anxiety. At this point everyone in the room feels powerless and helpless. The first step in this common clinical dilemma is for the therapist to become aware of his or her own relationship to the intensity of emotions. What we are really talking about here is the notion of countertransference. Some circular questions we ask ourselves as therapists in these situations are:

- How was intensity of emotion handled in our families of origin?
- What did we do when Mom and Dad fought?
- Did expression of emotion unite or divide family members?
- How do these early family interactions affect our personal relationships today?
- How do these early family interactions affect our role as therapists?

What we must understand is how we as human beings manage and contain the very primitive emotions of rage, terror, helplessness, and annihilation. From time to time, these feelings will emerge for even the most experienced therapist. For instance, during a session with a volatile couple, the husband abruptly stood up and started shaking a raised fist at his cowering wife. With that, their therapist, Toby, also began to cower and tremble internally. Unconsciously, she raised her hands to protect her face. The wife immediately reacted by shouting, "You see, she feels just the way I do when you are in a rage and threaten me like that!" Toby had unconsciously become triangled into the couple's tightly knit emotional system. The incident had become a reenactment of her own early family-of-origin drama. She felt as if she were six years old once again. As children often do, she had adopted the role of family protector. This served to keep her parents' marital system in balance. It was Toby's eventual awareness that empowered and enabled her to distinguish her old family role from her present role as therapist. Her personal involvement had a powerful and beneficial effect upon the therapy. As she processed her responses, she was able to step back and understand the system more clearly.

Internal family relationships are alive inside each of us. These images or models of relationships are a rich source of information that inform us about our internal reactions and our responses to the clients we see. The more consciously connected we are to these internal images and their associated emotions, beliefs, values, and attitudes, the better equipped we are to separate our own emotional worlds from our clients'. For example, the early role of caretaker must be identified and made conscious, so the therapist does not confuse this old family role with today's professional role of therapist. If the therapist's own family struggles are not conscious, he or she may unconsciously deflect intensity in a session or overidentify with one partner. The therapist must be able to tolerate and track the full range and intensity of affects that will naturally arise in couples therapy. This is achieved by the therapist's willingness to face the intensity of his or her own reactions through intensive personal therapy, clinical supervision of cases, or consultation with colleagues. We access and identify "internal family relationships" and then connect these internal voices to our clinical work with couples. In this way we connect what we think with what we do.

Identifying and Managing Intense Reactivity of Clients

All of us experience intense emotions—love, anger, rage, jealousy, envy, shame, and fear. Emotions are neither good nor bad. They can be expressed openly and verbally or indirectly and unconsciously. Our work as therapists with couples is to enable them to bring these feelings to consciousness and to express them verbally. Some of us have been taught as children that certain emotions are "good" and others are "bad." Intimate attachments bring out the deepest emotions in all of us. The intensity is often overwhelming and frightening. Generally, couples are at a loss for ways to handle these primitive feelings.

Managing intense emotions is a skill that must be developed by couples therapists both clinically and personally. To effectively address intensity of emotions in the therapeutic encounter, therapists are advised to:

1. Facilitate verbal expression of emotion from each partner.
2. Encourage listening on the part of each partner.
3. Request that each partner speak with him or her rather than to each other.
4. Validate each partner's perception of reality by repeating and/or paraphrasing what has been heard.
5. Connect present emotional intensity with past sources.

By creating a safe holding environment, the therapist encourages freedom of expression. As trust in the therapeutic alliance is developed, the partners become increasingly more willing to share vulnerabilities. When there is a high intensity of emotion, we find it particularly helpful to have all communication directed to the therapist. This process cools the system down so that the partners can hear each other. As the therapist links up the present emotionality to past sources, the spouses begin to experience greater understanding and empathy.

Chapter 3

Ethical and Therapeutic Dilemmas

Therapeutic Responsibility: Some Ethical and Legal Considerations

We have spent many years learning our craft didactically and experientially. Our time as therapists, supervisors, and teachers has made us well aware of the powerful effects of psychotherapy upon individuals, couples, and families. Along with the privilege of serving our clients comes the enormous responsibility of using our power as psychotherapists in an ethical, honest, and accountable manner. Since psychotherapy is more of an art than an exact science, ethical guidelines are often inherently ambiguous. When seeing two or more clients at the same time, as in couple and family work, matters are further complicated and new kinds of ethical dilemmas present themselves.

One of the most important decisions facing a clinician is whether an individual, couple, or family intervention is appropriate. This decision demands great competency upon the part of the therapist, and without specialized training in couple and family work, the therapist may overlook the most helpful therapeutic intervention. If a clinician is trained only to work with individual clients, he or she will be less likely to recommend couple or family work.

If and when couple work is the intervention of choice, the therapist's commitment must be to the relationship. Therapeutic responsibility then extends to considering the impact of the therapy upon the couple as a system. Therapist and couple must collaborate upon the goal of therapy.

What constitutes an improved relationship for one partner may be different for the other. Unbalancing a stuck couple system is precarious work, and our systemic interventions must be sensitively executed. At times this necessitates involvement of other family members in treatment. These decisions must be well thought out and made on a case-by-case basis. As you read the vignettes throughout our book, you will become aware of the multiple and complex choices available to clinicians. Often the most ethical forms of behavior involve consultation with knowledgeable and respected colleagues.

One of the issues to be addressed early in therapy is how to handle the confidentiality of the couple system. Our stance is to encourage the disclosure of any and all information during conjoint sessions. Since individual contact can seldom be avoided (telephone, waiting room), we routinely announce during the first session our policy concerning confidentiality and secrets. We might state it this way: "In order to best serve the needs of your relationship, it is important that whatever is discussed be shared and reviewed by the three of us. At times the need for individual contact may arise. When this occurs, we must be clear that any issues talked about individually will be brought back into the conjoint sessions. How does this sound to both of you?" To reiterate our point, therapists must establish clear boundaries pertaining to the issue of confidentiality when working with couples.

In addition to therapist competency, boundary-setting, and confidentiality, the impact of sex-role issues upon the therapeutic work must be carefully considered. The roles, values, and needs of both sexes should be assessed and addressed. In order to accomplish this, the therapist needs to be aware of his or her own gender biases and values.

The Ethical Standards for Marriage and Family Therapists Part I and Part II, published by the California Association of Marriage and Family Therapists, were revised and became effective on June 7, 1997. It is mandatory that all couple and family therapists read and become familiar with this document. Although all of the ethical standards are extremely important regarding "responsibility to patients," the one that is most pertinent for therapists working with couples and families is the following:

> Marriage and family therapists, when treating a family unit(s), shall carefully consider the potential conflict that may arise between the family unit(s) and each individual. Marriage and family therapists clarify at the commencement of therapy which person or persons are clients and the nature of the relationship(s) the therapist will have with each person involved in the treatment.

Under the section on "confidentiality," the following principle is particularly relevant when intervening with a couple or family:

> In circumstances when more than one person in a family is receiving therapy or treatment, and when a third party seeks information related to any aspect of such treatment, each family member receiving therapy or treatment who is legally competent to execute an authorization must sign the authorization before a marriage and family therapist will disclose information received from any family member.

The clinician's therapeutic responsibility changes and broadens in scope when treating the couple system. The special ethical considerations that have been briefly outlined in this chapter must be reviewed periodically by students and seasoned therapists alike.

Our Philosophy Regarding Diagnosis and Labeling

Labeling and diagnosis present a dilemma for family therapists. Many theoreticians conclude that *DSM-IV* and family systems theory are incompatible in many ways. Systems theory requires circular thinking, whereas the medical model involves linear thinking. Family therapists espouse the co-creation of solutions, while diagnostic thinkers focus upon pathology and individuals' symptomatology. The former perspective emphasizes change, while the latter confirms the problematic state. As Nancy Steiny (1988) writes:

> The art of diagnosis can have and has had destructive consequences to clients in general, and to the therapeutic process specifically. It promotes a sick role for the client and often causes clients to identify themselves with a life filled with illness and problems. If someone has been told their diagnosis, they often come to therapy to confirm this label.

Consider the following clinical situation. A young woman and her fiancé, Alise and Sam, worked with a new counselor, Dorothy, as the supervisor and team observed behind the one-way mirror. Alise, appearing disheveled and confused and unable to control the twitching of her facial muscles, talked about her many experiences over the years with hospitals, doctors, and drugs. Sam interjected that she had been recently diagnosed as "schizophrenic." Her bizarre behavior and the voices she heard frightened him, and he was now certain that the doctors' diagnoses were correct.

He thought that perhaps hospitalization would help. As the counselor listened to the couple respectfully and validated their concerns, the anxiety in the room diminished appreciably. At this time the focus of conversation shifted from Alise's medical diagnosis to the couple's relationship issues. After listening to the session for a while, the supervisor called the counselor in for a consultation. She felt that complexities and layers of this case must be addressed by the team.

Although the counselor, Dorothy, seemed calm during the therapy session, she revealed to the supervisory team her anxiety about working with a couple in which one partner was a schizophrenic. She had never before worked with someone so disturbed. The supervisor then asked, "How would any of you work with this couple if Alise had not been diagnosed as schizophrenic?" The discussion that ensued reflected the team's concerns, which paralleled Dorothy's anxiety. Dorothy's intense reactivity, in turn, was a reflection of the couple's anxiety. The reverberations rippled throughout the client, counselor, and supervisory systems. This is commonly referred to as an isomorphic process and generally occurs in all supervisory experiences. What is felt by the couple is experienced by the therapist and then transmitted to the team behind the mirror. It is the role of the supervisor to identify and bring this process to the consciousness of the entire group.

The session was a moving and revealing one. It was an extremely valuable learning experience for all. The team was struck by the impact of hearing of the many hospitalizations, multiple medications, and myriad of doctors upon this case. An entire medical culture surrounded this young couple. It was as if the medical world had become Alise's family. The team wondered, as we discussed the case, how much of who Alise is today is the result of the many years of conditioning by our medical model/system and how much was the result of other familial, social, and cultural influences?

This case was a clear example of the damaging effects of labeling and diagnosing. This does not mean that drugs and diagnosis have no value. Rather, drugs must be used thoughtfully, for specific purposes, and with attention to side effects. There is no drug for an unhappy marriage. Diagnosis has no meaning, in our opinion, if it is not connected to one's family functioning and stage of development in the life cycle. Alise got lost in the system. The team discussion led to a brainstorming session. We asked, What can we as therapists do to stop the perpetuation of such cases? What an overwhelming question! We don't have any pat answers, but the question certainly heightened our awareness. We must be aware of whose anxiety is being quieted or soothed when we suggest drug treatment or respond too quickly to our client's request for drug evaluation. While we certainly understand and appreciate the value and role of medication, we are convinced that equal weight must be given to the influence of family interaction in the assessment process.

Indications and Contraindications for Couple Therapy

As previously stated, an important assumption underlying work with couples is that the relationship is the client. With Laura and Michael, the couple in Part II, the focus is on the complex interaction between them rather than on individual issues. When specific family-of-origin work is the focus, the therapeutic intent involves bringing this past influence into the context of the present relationship. In other words, we always work under a systemic umbrella. These influences guide us when we are assessing whether or not couple therapy is indicated. The road to couple work often follows a circuitous path. When the "identified patient" is a child, we begin work with the entire family. Generally the presenting problem with the child is soon resolved, and this leads to couple work.

Some couples need preparation to tolerate the intensity of conjoint therapy. Until both partners are willing to risk addressing the painful issues that exist between them, couple work is contraindicated. In some instances, individual work will be helpful in preparing partners for couple therapy. For example, Mary and Joe were having problems in their relationship, and each chose to see different therapists. They thought their separate issues were responsible for what was happening in their relationship. It became clear after several months that couple work was necessary to facilitate further progress. Although working together filled them with apprehension, their separate therapies empowered them to take the step of examining their coupleship.

In other cases, individual work may be destructive and disruptive to a couple system. For example, Susan sought therapy due to her anxiety over her husband's drinking. Arthur refused to acknowledge he had a problem. Her migraines and depression were the focus of intensive individual psychoanalytic work. Arthur's drinking and the marital system were left unexamined. In contrast, our approach weaves the intrapsychic with the interpersonal, thereby including the total system in treatment. With this particular couple, we strongly believe that couple therapy was indicated. In this way, symptoms (migraines, depression, and alcoholism) would be defined and examined in a circular way rather than the traditional linear way.

Sometimes one of the partners has consciously or unconsciously decided to leave the relationship even prior to entering therapy. When this occurs, couple therapy is usually short-lived. Often one or both partners begin individual psychotherapy. The clinician must decide whether to refer one or both partners to a colleague or to continue treating one or both individually. It is preferable, although not always possible, for the clinician and the clients to collaborate in this decision.

When the couple's transference or the therapist's countertransference precludes successful work, couple therapy is contraindicated. Please refer to Table 3-1 for a summary of these indications and contraindications.

TABLE 3-1. *Indications and Contraindications for Couple Therapy*

Indications for Couple Therapy
1. When presenting problem involves the marital relationship.
2. When one partner is symptomatic and viewed as the "identified patient," we recommend treatment for the family or couple system.
3. When one or both partners' individual therapy leads to couple therapy.
4. When the couple has decided to end the relationship and chooses to resolve issues with the help of a therapist.
5. When identified patient is a child, we work with the entire family. Often, this leads to couple work.

Contraindications to Couple Therapy
1. Domestic violence is present in relationship at this time.
2. One partner is actively psychotic, severely emotionally disturbed, dissociated from reality, or in an actively addicted state.
3. When individual work is needed before partners become willing to work together.
4. When the fit of therapist and couple is not conducive to a working relationship.
5. Therapist's countertransference or couple's transference impedes a good working alliance.
6. Therapist's training is inadequate for doing couple work.

Family systems therapists have been criticized for utilizing conjoint therapy as a modality in treating domestic violence. Serious questions have been raised about the different approaches of treatment with this population. These questions and the contraindications to couple therapy when domestic violence is present are discussed in Chapter 18.

The value of therapy is severely limited when one of the partners is actively psychotic or in an altered state of consciousness due to drug or alcohol abuse. While couple therapy is contraindicated in this situation, the clinician may decide to work with the couple in order to facilitate individual treatment for the symptomatic partner. In accordance with the systemic view, we help the partners see how their interactions perpetuate the problem. We then collaborate in developing a plan that includes appropriate treatment for symptom alleviation.

Above all, a responsible clinician must be aware of his or her competencies and limitations. We hope this discussion has begun to raise your consciousness of the myriad of ethical and therapeutic dilemmas that therapists face on a daily basis. Our real strength comes from knowing our limitations.

Part II

The Case Study
of Laura and Michael

Chapter 4

The Initial Contact —
The Couple as a System

JENNIFER REED: Hello, Laura. This is Jennifer Reed, returning your call.

LAURA: I'm glad you called back so quickly. I really hope you can help me. I just found out that my husband, Michael, is having an affair. (*Softly crying*) I'm so upset—I can't sleep at all. I've been up all night. I could hardly get out of bed this morning to get my kids ready for school. I can't even think straight.

JENNIFER: Sounds like things are really rough right now. Who referred you to me?

LAURA: I called my family doctor, Ron Jones, for sleeping pills because I haven't slept for the last three nights, and he suggested that I make an appointment to see you right away.

JENNIFER: Have you discussed this call with your husband?

LAURA: No, he has no idea. I can barely look at him, let alone discuss something like this.

JENNIFER: You and your husband are in a serious crisis at this time. I'd like to see both of you together for the first appointment.

LAURA: You've got to be kidding! I couldn't sit in the same room with that bastard.

JENNIFER: I understand you are furious at him. However, since this situation is a relational one, I need to see you as a couple.

LAURA: Are you saying you won't see me alone?

JENNIFER: In order for me to be as helpful as possible, it is important that I see you both together.

LAURA: I'm afraid I won't be able to keep myself together. I'm a mess. I don't want Michael to see how much I'm hurting. Also, he's a real good talker, and I don't want you to side with him. I'm not even sure he would be comfortable with a female therapist.

JENNIFER: I'm here to help you both understand what's going on and to get his responses to what is happening. I would suggest a three-way telephone conversation this evening, and we can proceed from there.

LAURA: I don't know *(anxious tone, seemingly frustrated and uneasy);* can I think about it and call you back?

JENNIFER: I can understand your hesitation. Give it some thought and let me know how I can help.

The First Telephone Call

Therapy begins with the first telephone contact. From this first contact, Jennifer Reed begins to set the boundaries, structure, and format of treatment. These initial negotiations involve discussions and decisions around the questions of who is the client and who is in charge. Carl Whitaker (Napier & Whitaker, 1978, p. 10) called this initial process the "battle for structure." Calmly setting the structure conveys to the family that the therapist is in charge of the process and can handle whatever issues clients bring to the therapeutic encounter.

The first telephone contact is also a source of information about the dynamics of the couple system. The assumption that guides the therapist in this beginning phase of assessment is that the relationship is the client. The therapist briefly educates the couple by explaining that therapy involves both partners and that problems reside in the interaction of the relationship rather than each individual.

Reframing

Reframing begins with this first telephone contact. The issue of Michael's infidelity is viewed as a relational one rather than an individual one ("You and your husband are in a serious crisis at this time"). By framing the situation in this way, the therapist has already begun to help the couple redefine the problem (Michael's affair) in the context of the couple relationship. The affair symbolizes the pain that exists in the marital system and, indeed, in the entire family. Jennifer Reed reframes or redefines the behavior, thus beginning the process of helping the spouses expand their view from the content of the affair to the relationship (Bobes & Rothman, 1996). Laura and Michael eventually understand that all issues are shared jointly. No one individual takes responsibility for what happens in a couple's relationship. The therapist must be aware that the couple's anxiety is at an all-time high during this time of crisis. It is important to view the problem systemically and help both spouses feel understood. By suggesting the three-way telephone conversation, the therapist conveys to Laura that this is a relationship issue. The therapist is "thinking systemically"; that is, Laura's problem is contextual and exists in an intimate, relational system rather than only within her own psyche (Scarf, 1987).

Many of the couples we see are discouraged about the direction their relationships have taken, feel hopeless about changing, and blame and accuse each other for where they are. This creates increased defensiveness on the part of each partner. David Treadway (1989, pp. 34, 35) talks about interrupting "the endless cycle of recriminations" with reframing techniques. He continues that, "The heart of reframing involves the therapist expressing the view that the actions and motivations of each spouse can be understood from a positive and often protective perspective." Thus the situation can be viewed differently, facilitating new responses.

Individual or Couple Work

Although we much prefer starting with both partners, we have, on occasion, successfully commenced couple work following one meeting with the individual. There are situations in which the caller is so understandably ambivalent and frightened that he or she insists on an individual meeting. After seeing the client, we evaluate whether to continue with individual work and/or refer the couple to another therapist for the conjoint meetings. In order to avoid triangulation, we state clearly that any material discussed during the individual session will be brought into the conjoint sessions. In this way, we do not collude with family secrets. Often the caller will consent to bring the partner in following one individual meeting. In the telephone vignette, the caller, Laura, was ambivalent about bringing her husband in for a session. Along with her own concerns about working as a couple, she stated that Michael might not be comfortable working with a female therapist. During a second telephone call, Laura stated that she had thought it over and would be willing to be part of a three-way conversation that evening.

(Three-way telephone conversation between Michael, Laura, and Jennifer Reed.)

LAURA: Hi, this is Laura, and my husband, Michael, is on the other line. I tried to tell him some of what you said to me earlier today, but I'm so upset I'm not sure I was very clear in my explanation. Can you say again why you need to see both of us together?

JENNIFER: Hi, Michael and Laura. I appreciate that both of you were willing to make this call. I'm sure that with the tension so high at home it wasn't an easy task.

MICHAEL: No, it wasn't, and I'm still pretty uncomfortable about it. I'm not sure I understand Laura's version of why you need to see us both, but Laura and I don't seem to speak the same language these days. Perhaps you can explain more clearly.

JENNIFER: What I said to Laura on the phone earlier today, Michael, was that your issue is a relational one, and, in order to be helpful, I need to see you both together rather than individually. What has occurred symbolizes the pain that exists in your marital system, and this system has to be the focus of our work together.

MICHAEL: That's pretty interesting, because in my own clumsy way I've been trying to say that to Laura, but she gets so furious that I've stopped saying anything to her.

JENNIFER: Let's set up a time so that we can begin to sort out some of these issues together. I have some time open this week on Thursday at 6:00 P.M., if the two of you can come in then.

MICHAEL: I'm game. Things couldn't be worse in your office than they are at home.

LAURA: We'll try a session. I doubt that it will help, but I'll get a babysitter and we'll see you on Thursday at 6:00 P.M.

Each caller who initiates a telephone contact brings his or her own unique perspective. However, as this example illustrates, it is only when both members of the couple are seen together that the system may be fully evaluated. Regardless of what the caller wishes to express at this time, it is the therapist's responsibility to gather the answers to the following questions:

- Who made the referral?
- What is a brief description of the presenting problem?
- Who are the family members living in the home? Do any family members know about the caller's wish to contact a therapist?
- How willing is the partner to attend therapy sessions?
- What is the availability of time?

From this brief first telephone encounter the therapist must convey a conviction about the importance and value of couples therapy. He or she instills hope by maintaining a respectful, empathic attitude. While not promising a quick fix, the therapist lets the client know that the journey toward healing has started with this first telephone call.

Jennifer Reed's first telephone contact with Laura and Michael is clearly based upon the beliefs and assumptions of systems theory. Although Jennifer is respectful of each individual, she is persistent about seeing the couple together. The relationship is the client. Jennifer articulates this systemic view when she tells them both that the marital system will be the focus of their work together.

Chapter 5

The First Session: The Affair Revealed

Jennifer greeted Laura and Michael in the waiting room. As she walked with them into her office, she wondered if their seating preference would reflect their obvious inner tensions and their distance from one another. Laura sat on the large chair and Michael chose the couch across from her. Both looked down. Before they had even settled into their seats, Laura hurled the first accusation, and the attack was on.

LAURA: What did I ever do to you that you would cheat on me, humiliate me, and have an affair with one of our friends? You're such a coward. I had to find the love letter from Susan in the back of your drawer underneath your socks and underwear. It's almost as if you wanted me to find out.

MICHAEL: *(As Michael listened, he sat shamefaced and contrite. Then, suddenly, his face reddened, as he angrily raised his voice.)* You have had a goddamned affair with the kids, the house, your demanding sisters, your father and everything that excluded me! I was never a priority with you. Marriage was just a word. I was your meal ticket and the bill payer.

(Laura is visibly shaken by his words and angry voice. She sinks down into her chair and begins to sob, uncontrollably.)

JENNIFER: Both of you are understandably ashamed, hurt, and angry. But, despite the obvious intensity of your feelings, you had the courage to come together and look at what's happening. In this session, we'll explore with greater depth what's going on between you and what led to this crisis.

Jennifer's words seemed to reduce the tension in the room, and she was then able to begin to elicit Laura and Michael's personal histories. With the recent birth of a son, this couple was developmentally in the chaotic stage of a family with young children. They were particularly vulnerable to crisis at this time and were not prepared for the enormity of stress that followed the birth of their third child. Laura quickly bonded with the baby to the exclusion of Michael. Her time was also taken up with two other young children. Feeling neglected by his wife, Michael turned to other sources of comfort, which eventually led to the present crisis.

Because of their somewhat tumultuous relationship before the arrival of the new baby, they had great difficulty adjusting to the additional demand of a third child. Instead of working as a team, each lapsed into the rigid gender roles they had learned in their families of origin. Laura became the all-nurturing mother, and Michael became the successful wage-earning father.

A couple is a developing relationship that goes through a series of transitions and stages. As the relationship moves through its life cycle, specific tasks must be addressed and negotiated at each stage. As the couple moves through these stages, each partner is also involved in his or her own unique process of growth and change. The therapist learned in this first session that Laura and Michael had not yet negotiated or addressed the tasks of the first stage of marriage. Although they had moved geographically from their families of origin, they had not moved away emotionally in a healthy way. Laura still worried about her dad all the time and spoke to her sisters almost every day. Michael spoke to his parents once a week but was emotionally cut off from them. Both still had not differentiated themselves from their respective families of origin. Murray Bowen states that we choose mates with a level of differentiation similar to our own. Laura and Michael were recreating in their own relationship the difficulties they experienced in their families of origin.

Couples often come for treatment when their usual patterns and ways of coping are no longer working. A crisis develops when the steady state of the system is disrupted by some external situation, such as a family move or loss of a job, or at a transitional time in the life cycle of the couple such as the birth of a child. We have found in-depth knowledge and understanding of stages and tasks to be valuable, especially in discussing and validating the couple's sense of panic or chaos as they face disruptions in the system.

The Power of Family-of-Origin Influences

The couples we see are often restrained by their particular patterns, stories, and beliefs. Partners tell stories about their past and present experiences, and change happens as these stories become conscious. The partners then begin to understand that their present relationship crisis is connected to their families of origin. Reframing the present situation in this way normalizes the couple's concerns and underscores the developmental context of the relationship. Many narrative therapists espouse this way of thinking (e.g., Zimmerman & Dickerson, 1993). Vulnerability generally begins to surface during this kind of exploration. David Treadway (1989) states that without the understanding, awareness, and experience of some of the intense affects from the past, partners will remain stuck in repeating old patterns and roles learned in childhood.

Jennifer Reed begins an in-depth exploration of Laura's and Michael's families of origin. Laura, age 32, the oldest of five girls from a working-class Irish Catholic family, learned early on to nurture and take care of her younger siblings. When her mother died during Laura's second year of college, she returned home to take charge of the household. Questions about the mother's death were unanswered, and each of the sisters had her own version of how Mom had died. Sacrificing her college education, Laura became "wife" to her father and "mother" to her four sisters. The grief-stricken family turned to her for guidance and direction. With hardly a thought of herself, she took over the role of the self-sacrificing woman. When she met and quickly married Michael four years later, she was well-trained to sacrifice her needs and become his caretaker and nurturer. Her birth position as oldest child prepared her well for this role.

As an only child of professional and achieving Jewish parents, Michael, age 34, sought someone who would attend to his overwhelming emotional needs. Michael was sent to boarding school at 12 years of age because of his parents' increasingly demanding schedules and conflictual marital relationship. Michael's mother often confided her worry to Michael about his father's "drinking problem." During his junior year at school his parents divorced. Since they chose not to tell him directly, the headmaster notified Michael of this devastating news. The loneliness of his earlier years intensified at this time. With few friends and no available family to turn to, Michael retreated into his studies. Drinking seemed to help him alleviate the pain. By the time he met Laura, he had just entered an MBA program at Harvard. Although he had developed an aloof intellectual veneer, which appeared to be working fairly well, the inner wounds of his childhood were still unresolved, leaving him raw and vulnerable. Jennifer first takes a generational history from Laura and Michael and then pays particular attention to the historical development of their relationship.

The Couple's Attraction

JENNIFER: So, how did the two of you meet?

LAURA: A friend of mine was in the MBA program with Michael at Harvard, and he arranged for us to meet. For me it was love at first sight.

MICHAEL: I'm not so sure about that. You were still seeing that guy you had dated in high school. Remember?

LAURA: We were just friends by then. As soon as I met you, I knew you were it.

JENNIFER: What attracted you to Michael?

LAURA: It's hard to remember. *(As Laura becomes reflective, her expression relaxes and she smiles.)* Well, he certainly was the most intelligent man I'd ever met. His breadth of knowledge fascinated me. He even made me feel more intelligent, and his reserved manner calmed me down. He was so very different from my family. I found his shyness very appealing. Somehow, I felt safe with him.

JENNIFER: Michael, what was your response to Laura when you first met?

(Michael's facial expression has relaxed as he has listened to Laura's words. The tension in his body is visibly reduced.)

MICHAEL: I was drawn to her warmth and her genuine caring for other people. Everybody liked her. All of a sudden I started to have some fun in my life. Laura seemed to laugh so easily, and people were drawn to us as a couple. That all changed drastically after the children came. Laura seemed to become very moody and difficult. She wanted to stay at home all the time. She hardly ever wanted to go out with our friends.

JENNIFER: Michael, we'll get to the difficult areas a bit later. Right now I'd like to continue with exploring what attracted you to one another. It sounds like Laura brought something special into your life.

MICHAEL: Yes, she did. Without her, I probably would have spent my years at Harvard in the library. Instead, it was a special period in my life. We had great times and I felt really cared for—something I had not known before. My father had recently remarried, and my mother had a live-in boyfriend. It made me think about how my own life could be with Laura.

JENNIFER: Were you aware of Michael's fantasies and strong feelings about you, Laura?

LAURA: *(Tears have welled up while Michael has been speaking.)* Although

Michael didn't often tell me how much he loved me, I know he did. When I think all of this is gone now, it devastates me.

JENNIFER: Michael, do you feel that it's all gone?

MICHAEL: I'm not sure. I guess I hope we can get some of our old relationship back.

LAURA: It certainly feels like it's so far from where we are right now. I don't know if I have the energy to figure it all out.

JENNIFER: It sounds like you appreciated what Michael brought to the relationship. I know you are both struggling with your marriage at this time. Are you willing to commit to four sessions so that we can sort out these issues together? At the end of these four sessions, we'll evaluate where we are and whether you want to continue therapy at that time.

LAURA: I'm certainly willing to. Are you, Michael?

MICHAEL: *(Hesitantly)* Well, if we can learn to communicate with each other, I think we should.

Focus on Strengths and Instilling Hope

In this vignette the therapist vividly captures what originally attracted Laura and Michael to one another. By moving back to an earlier time in the history of their relationship, she is attempting to help Laura and Michael recall their strengths and attractions. Often clients will experience discomfort with the unfamiliar task of stating positives in the relationship. However, this couple's usual habits of complaining were interrupted as the therapist encouraged them to evoke and reexperience earlier memories. This intervention opened a window to their vulnerability.

Through dialogue with each partner, Jennifer punctuates the positive and instills hope. While having them recall their original attraction, she gathers information that will later be used to link up their presenting problems to early history. A historical and developmental context for the therapeutic work is created. The therapist creates a holding environment, a safe place for the spouses to reveal their vulnerabilities and pain.

JENNIFER: Since we all come from our own points of view, I'd like each of you to say what your perception is of what is going on in your relationship at this time.

MICHAEL: I'm not sure what's happened to us. I just know I went from being appreciated to becoming a meal ticket.

LAURA: *(Angrily interrupting Michael)* I hate it when you say that! You're just using that as an excuse for what you did.

JENNIFER: I see that you have a strong reaction and your own point of view.

I wonder if you could allow yourselves, as well as each other, the time to tell your own story. In that way I'll be able to capture each of your experiences. Michael, please go on.

MICHAEL: Things seemed to change drastically after Jonathan was born. He was a demanding baby and Laura's whole life began to center around him. She kept him all to herself. She wouldn't even let me do any of the night feedings.

LAURA: *(Starting to cry)* I was so scared something terrible would happen to Jonathan if I made a wrong move, or if I let anyone else hold him. I just had to keep him close to me. Somehow raising a son felt unfamiliar. I knew about daughters from raising my sisters.

MICHAEL: I'm his father, Laura. And you treated him as if he belonged to you and I was the outsider. Now things are totally out of hand! It was one thing to have Jonathan sleeping with us, but now the girls seem to feel left out so they wander in and out all night long. Most of the time I wind up on the living room couch. There's no room for me in our bed. It's too crowded.

LAURA: I know it shouldn't be this way. It doesn't seem normal. But I can't help myself. I get nervous when I have to say "no" to them.

MICHAEL: You treat the children as if they're your property. And yet, you're always so nervous and anxious with them.

JENNIFER: What do you think your fear is all about, Laura?

LAURA: At first I thought it was my job as a mom to always feed the baby especially since I was nursing. Michael had his job, and I assumed this was mine. It surprises me now to hear that Michael wanted to be more of a help. He was so angry that at times I didn't think he wanted this baby in the first place.

MICHAEL: I did want the baby, but I wanted us to feel like a family. Instead, I felt—and still feel—like the odd man out.

JENNIFER: I wonder if we could get back to what your fear was all about.

LAURA: Well, I was scared something bad would happen to Jonathan if he wasn't always with me. I took care of my siblings, so I thought that being a mom would come to me naturally and very easily. Instead, I felt completely overwhelmed and was scared that Michael would see that and think I wasn't a good mother.

JENNIFER: It seems as if neither one of you knew what the other was thinking. You, Michael, were feeling shut out and disappointed, and you, Laura, were feeling fearful and overwhelmed.

LAURA: *(Speaking slowly and apparently confused)* How can two people who live together and supposedly love each other not know what the other is thinking?

MICHAEL: With all the chaos, we never had a chance to talk.

JENNIFER: That's an important point you both have raised. What we will be doing here is not only learning to talk but also learning to listen to each other. I'm wondering where each of you learned to relate in the way you just described?

MICHAEL: Well, in my family, no one talked or listened, and I was always feeling isolated. No one ever seemed to want to know what I was thinking. So I withdrew and spent a lot of time alone.

LAURA: Everyone in my family talked all the time. But I was always the listener tending to everyone's needs. I guess I began to tend to the baby's needs in much the same way that I cared for my siblings when Mom died. Even though I was scared then, my own fears and needs didn't matter at all. I was always helping and pleasing others.

JENNIFER: So neither one of you was listened to in your families. As children, you learned to keep your needs to yourselves and expected very little from others. These early beliefs are very present in your marriage. It is understandable that these old ways of relating affect your relationship today.

Join the Couple System

Jennifer engages the couple and becomes empathically and emotionally connected to each person. The partners must experience the therapist's empathy and support for each of them individually and as a couple if a working alliance is to be established. To this end, a holding environment and a blame-free context for the therapeutic work must be established. An atmosphere of safety must prevail so that the partners will be free to take risks and explore their vulnerabilities.

Joining with the couple involves collaborating with them. By doing this, the therapist personally experiences the pressures and anxieties of the couple system. The therapist must be an active participant, willing to structure and guide the work while at the same time conveying to clients the belief that they possess the power, strength, and resources to facilitate change. Without adequate and continuous joining, therapy will be blocked and ineffective. Joining is the glue that holds the couple and therapist together.

In this beginning stage of treatment, the therapist's role is to accomplish specific tasks in the assessment process. As Jennifer elicits history from Laura and Michael, focuses on their strengths as a couple, and reframes and clarifies individual perceptions, she instills hope and lays the groundwork for the therapy. While she structures and guides the work in a focused way, she continues to maintain a spirit of collaboration. The next two chapters further describe specific aspects of the assessment process as Jennifer builds a working relationship with Laura and Michael.

Clarify Each Partner's Perception of Problem

The therapist must clearly understand each partner's point of view. In this way the emotional connection between couple and therapist is reinforced. As the therapist clarifies each individual's perception of the problem, groundwork is being laid for distinguishing self from other. This differentiation-of-self work is a central concept of Murray Bowen's family systems theory and is critical to work with couples. Object relations theorists also declare the importance of this concept as they work to help individuals reown aspects of self formerly projected onto the other. As each tells his or her story, the listening partner is advised to contain his or her responses and become more aware of the other's thoughts and feelings. In Laura and Michael's case, it seemed as if this were the first time they were hearing each other. Spouses often assume they know what the other is thinking, and it is illuminating and relieving when the inaccuracies are clarified.

At the beginning of therapy, we prefer to keep ourselves very central to reduce reactivity. Rather than having the partners talk to each other, we gather historical data from each one. This process has the immediate effect of modeling a new way of talking and listening for the couple. The structure of the conversation prevents the usual arguing and interruptions between the partners. The listener is exercising the skill of containment as he or she absorbs and tolerates the range of affects in the session (Scharff & Scharff, 1992). David Treadway encourages each partner to speak without interruption from the other. Treadway (1989, p. 96) underscores this point when he states, "As each individual opens up, I emphasize the spouse's vital role as listener and nurturer." We have learned through clinical experience that it is often extremely difficult and painful for the listening partner to focus on his or her own reactions. However, as partners learn to listen and contain their responses, they soon increase their understanding of each other and empathy is developed.

Connect Presenting Problem to Family-of-Origin

Throughout the therapeutic work, we interweave the presenting problem with the partners' families of origin. This continuing process helps the couple look at their relationship through a developmental lens. Early history-taking lays the groundwork for connecting the presenting problem to the family of origin. In the next chapter, we see Jennifer constructing with Laura and Michael a family genogram, in which patterns throughout the generations are clearly identified. This generational tree is the diagram of a family's relationship system. Including three or four generations enables therapists and clients together to trace recurring familial behavior patterns. This family-of-origin work is based on Murray Bowen's family systems theory and underlies the therapist's thinking as she or he focuses upon systemic patterns and themes.

By the end of this first session Jennifer Reed has joined well with Laura and Michael. In spite of explosive emotions and accusations, a holding environment has been established in which the couple's anxieties have been contained. This ambience of safety develops when the therapist connects with clients in an empathic, respectful, and collaborative way. Only then can couples reveal their deep pain and vulnerabilities. The bumpy journey of therapy has begun.

Set the Frame and Boundaries of Therapy

Beginning with the first telephone contact, the therapist sets the frame and boundaries of therapy. The frame of therapy refers to the ground rules that form the working agreement between the therapist and couple. David and Jill Scharff (1991, p. 105) write about setting the frame as a specific task of couple therapy. They state that the frame is set "by being clear about the arrangements and by staying with the agreed upon treatment format." During the initial telephone contacts it was established with Laura and Michael that the relationship was the client. By the end of the first session, the issues of confidentiality, fees, billing practices, cancellation policy, frequency and length of session, and insurance had been addressed.

The tasks that we have already begun to focus upon are listed in Table 5-1. As you will see during our journey with Laura and Michael, these tasks are ongoing and do not follow a set order.

TABLE 5-1. *Therapeutic Tasks in Beginning Stage of Couple Therapy*

1. Join and engage the couple system.
2. Create holding environment.
3. Set the frame and boundaries of therapy.
4. Clarify and validate each partner's perception of problem.
5. Elicit history of relationship.
6. Focus on developmental stage and tasks to be accomplished.
7. Instill hope.
8. Clarify here-and-now interaction while attending to intrapsychic dimensions of the couple system.

Chapter 6

Family Secrets Exposed

All families have secrets among its members. Sometimes these secrets are a sign of health, but more often they are not. In her book, *The Dance of Deception*, Harriet Lerner (1993, p. 136) states that "Secrets between parents and children often reflect healthy boundaries, allowing each generation to have its separate sphere. Other secrets that adults keep from children, and vice versa, are deeply problematic."

During a subsequent session with Laura and Michael, Jennifer introduced the concept of the genogram, explaining that it was a way of drawing their family tree. By tracing four generations of their family, they would learn their family patterns and history. Some clients know little of their family history, and so this exercise encourages them to seek out more information. Constructing the genogram is part of the joining process of therapist and family; it is also a way of clearly noticing systemic patterns. As the presenting problem is explored, genogram information naturally grows out of this exploration, and a wider family context emerges. Laura and Michael constructed their genogram, and family secrets that had previously been concealed became exposed in a painful session. (See the genogram in Figure 6-1.)

Although Michael was more verbal and forthcoming with his family information, he was shocked by the prevalence of alcoholism throughout the generations. He had never connected his grandfather's death of cirrhosis of the liver to alcoholism. As he talked, he became thoughtful and visibly concerned that he and his father handled stress by drinking. The therapist noticed that he often stole glances at Laura, looking for her response to these disclosures. Was he expecting the same disapproval his mother had shown his father? Did he want to avoid Laura's disapproval? Also noted by the therapist was Michael's lack of affect as he described his maternal grandparents as Holocaust survivors. How had the pain of this profound experience been handled in the family?

As Laura listened to Michael's family history, she expressed concern about the genetic roots of his drinking. She privately wondered how much Michael's drinking precipitated his having an affair. If he continued drinking, would he betray her again in the future? She outwardly wondered how his drinking might affect their children. Michael echoed her concern and then dramatically shifted the focus to the emphasis in his mother's family on academic achievement. This was a deflection away from the pain and concerns about the alcoholism in his family. Michael was protecting himself in the way he had learned to cope with issues that produced personal distress. His strong defenses of withdrawal and avoidance were reinforced in early interactions with his parents and helped him through difficult family situations. Whereas these defenses had protected him well in the past, they now served only to distance him from Laura. At this point, Jennifer chose to contain her thoughts as she observed the process. She could have explored the origin of Michael's beliefs and defenses but decided to postpone this important piece of work until a later time. Because of the volume of material that is revealed as the couple constructs their family tree, issues that have the greatest intensity are talked about first. Other issues are held in abeyance until they unfold in the couple's life story.

Laura now began her family story. When the therapist questioned how her mother had died, Laura hesitated and then burst into tears. She sobbed as she related her family's big secret, to which only she and her father were privy. Michael was astounded as he learned that his mother-in-law had committed suicide. As Laura disclosed this well-kept secret, it was obvious that she felt disloyal to her father and to other family members. In order to allay her anxiety about this "betrayal," she pleaded with Michael to keep this secret, unconsciously perpetuating more secrets. Michael was stunned, realizing for the first time how little he knew about his wife and her family. Privately, he wondered how she could have carried this burden alone all these years. No wonder she was so close to her father. They shared this big secret together. Was he so unavailable that she could not trust him with her deepest anguish? As he tried to answer these questions for himself, Michael became introspective. The more reflective Michael became, the more Laura's anxiety increased. Here was clearly one of this couple's systemic patterns.

LAURA: *(Accusingly)* You're thinking that my family is crazy, aren't you Michael? What are you thinking about me, Michael?

MICHAEL: I'm just hurt that you didn't trust me enough to tell me about your mother's suicide sooner. Didn't you think I'd understand?

LAURA: *(Angrily)* How could you understand? I never have!

MICHAEL: I feel like I've never really known you. I'm surprised that you've held this from me. All you ever talked about was the alcoholism in my family, as if your family were without problems.

JENNIFER: You are both understandably pained and stunned with this new information. We need to work together to examine the meaning of these revelations to both of you.

Clarification of the Visual Picture of Laura and Michael's Genogram

So much information had been revealed in such a short period of time. At this point in the session, Jennifer deliberately focused on clarification of the content by reviewing the genogram. As Laura and Michael became overwhelmed with the emotionality of the material, Jennifer tracked the couple's responses as they moved from content to affect. Noticing that the two areas that provoked the greatest responses were alcoholism and suicidality, Jennifer commented on this observation.

As Laura and Michael looked at each other, they briefly abandoned their anger and shared a poignant moment. The shame that had divided and restrained them for so long now seemed to unite them. A window of vulnerability was slowly beginning to open. Laura and Michael stirred uncomfortably as silence fell over the room.

MICHAEL: *(Breaking the silence)* I guess I'm still pretty confused about why you kept all of this from me.

LAURA: I'm frightened and yet relieved that you finally know. I was terrified that you wouldn't want to be with me if you knew I came from such a crazy family.

MICHAEL: *(Laughing to break the tension)* It seems like we both come from pretty crazy families.

(After sitting for a while and allowing the intensity to build, the therapist frames, normalizes, and consolidates this important piece of work.)

JENNIFER: You were both children who carried and repressed incredibly confusing feelings about the taboo subjects in your families. When this occurs, children become very anxious and quickly get the message that certain issues cannot be talked about. This information is then dealt with on an unconscious level by the entire family.

MICHAEL: In our family, I was afraid to question my grandparents about their experiences during the Holocaust. Somehow I got this message from my parents who never talked about it. Is that what you just meant?
JENNIFER: Yes, exactly, Michael.
LAURA: I guess we did the same in my family. We never talked about my mom's death either.

In the above dialogue, the conversation shifts from the issues of family secrets to what occurs beneath the surface. On a process level, the therapist begins to address the interior of the couple's world and to notice their systemic patterns. The focus is now on the subjective elements that comprise this interior world. Jennifer has moved from the couple's content to a focus upon process. The underlying secrets and taboos generationally concealed in both families have erupted traumatically in Laura and Michael's marriage. The emotionality contained over three generations finally takes its toll. The symptom of the affair precipitated a crisis in this young couple's life. This led to an examination of the intricacies of their families' emotional fields. Jennifer now links the present situation to earlier family-of-origin patterns. The therapist's lenses have been widened to focus upon the multiple dimensions of the intrapsychic as well as the interpersonal. David Schnarch (1991, p. 182) states that, "A therapeutic intervention that is appropriate to the intrapsychic issues of both partners, the systemic patterns between them, and the broader family system is more likely to succeed in treatment than one that addresses a single dimension." Our treatment format incorporates a multidimensional framework that addresses the totality of these systems.

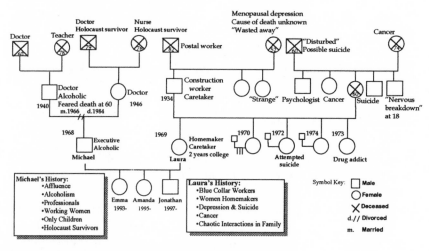

FIGURE 6-1: *Genogram for Michael and Laura*

An issue that has long been ignored in couple and family therapy is the power differential in relationships. One of the rich sources for understanding gender and power differences in a relationship is the information that is elicited as a genogram is co-constructed by client and therapist. As Carmen Knudson-Martin (1997) writes, "Just as one cannot not communicate, one also cannot not do gender." What is needed is a therapist who is aware of the importance of identifying and articulating gender issues. To ignore the power differential is to maintain the homeostasis of an unbalanced system rather than to challenge it.

As the genogram is being constructed, important circular questions for the therapist to ask are:

- How were differences handled in your family?
- When Mom and Dad fought, who generally won?
- How are differences handled between you? What happens when you don't agree?
- How are decisions made between you?
- Which one of you is "boss"?
- What messages did you learn during childhood about being a woman? A man?
- How are these messages influencing you today?

All of these circular questions relating to the gender and power differential are referred to as "gendercentric" questions by Carmen Knudson-Martin. Asking these often unasked questions brings the silenced voices of the past and the present to the fore. Internalized-other interviewing is another excellent tool that uses questioning to immediately get to the heart of the power differential in a relationship. In Chapter 8 this method of questioning is fully explored with Laura and Michael.

Chapter 7

The Crowded Marital Bed

As Laura and Michael walked in to the session, Jennifer noticed obvious tension between them.

LAURA: It doesn't feel like therapy is working for us. Michael is angry all the time and seems to be coming home less and less.

MICHAEL: That's because the house is so chaotic that I can't spend time there. It's more peaceful in my office.

LAURA: *(Speaking with a blaming tone)* A house with little children is not peaceful, Michael. I thought we had come to a new understanding about that. You seem to hear me in this office, yet after we leave you go back to your old ways.

JENNIFER: You both sound angry, and I wonder if you're angry at me for not making this journey an easier one.

LAURA: I guess I am angry at you. I thought therapy would be more helpful.

MICHAEL: I'm discouraged, too.

JENNIFER: I can understand that. Often you take a few steps forward and then slip back into old ways. This is sometimes discouraging and makes you feel like you've made no progress at all.

MICHAEL: This was an unusually demanding work week. Laura takes everything personally and goes back to treating me as if I'm an outsider in the family. It seems as though things will never really change. She's never going to trust me.

LAURA: *(Angrily crying)* How can I trust you when you betrayed me? You say you're at the office, and now I don't believe you. Half the time when

I call you're not there.

MICHAEL: You call so much that after a while I let voicemail pick up. The calls interrupt me and I can't finish my work, so then I get home even later.

JENNIFER: You've both been through such a traumatic experience. You'll need time to rebuild trust.

LAURA: How do we do that?

JENNIFER: It takes time. And it takes the willingness to be open and reveal your vulnerabilities to each other. That certainly happened during the first few sessions.

LAURA: Michael, we only committed to four sessions here. I certainly don't feel ready to stop. Do you?

MICHAEL: No. I think we probably need a lot more work.

JENNIFER: Well, Laura, you mentioned your insurance will allow sixteen more sessions. We should be able to move through the crisis and do good work in that amount of time. How does that sound?

MICHAEL: Sounds like a good idea.

(Laura *nods her agreement.*)

Planning the Next Steps of Therapy

In the above dialogue, Laura gives voice to what many clients feel when she says, "It doesn't feel like therapy is working for us." The disappointment is great when progress is followed by a return to old behaviors. At this time Jennifer acknowledges their discouragement and normalizes what has occurred. Her empathy and understanding reinforce the working alliance as she now sets the groundwork for further therapy. Jennifer reiterates that the relationship is the client. She tells Laura and Michael that all sessions will continue to include the two of them together. Any changes in this format will be discussed among the three of them. Details regarding paperwork for insurance and the boundaries of therapy are explained more fully. Although Jennifer is the authority who is in charge of the process of therapy, she works flexibly and may modify the therapeutic frame when appropriate. Laura and Michael are the authority about their coupleship. The three of them must collaborate to find workable solutions for this young family.

Boundaries and the Couple System

Boundaries must be clear for healthy couple functioning. The partners need protection from external intrusions in order to safeguard the integrity of their relationship. With parents, in-laws, and children, the task of defining clear boundaries has to be addressed and negotiated.

In every system boundaries mark the separation among the different parts of the whole. In terms of family systems theory, the boundary is the line that marks off a particular subsystem (individual, couple, children) from the larger family and/or community system. There are boundaries within the self, between self and other, as well as between the couple or family and the outside world (Scarf, 1995; Solomon, 1989). Figure 7-1 illustrates the interconnections among the various subsystems involving Laura and Michael. Frequent violations of the boundary by children, Laura's sisters, and, most recently, Michael's affair, have eroded this couple's sense of functioning together as a separate unit.

Boundaries Between Self and Other

Boundary issues arise from the moment of birth. The process of differentiating self from other is one of the first developmental tasks of the newborn infant. Daniel Stern (1985, p. 70) writes ". . . the infant's first order of business, in creating an interpersonal world, is to form the sense of a core self and core others. The evidence supports the notion that this task is largely accomplished during the period between two and seven months." Yet, as children develop, they constantly struggle with the individuation process. Simultaneously, parents are grappling with similar issues, depending upon their own differentiation process from their families of origin. If the parents have individuated successfully, they will contain their own anxieties and allow their child to move toward autonomy and independence. If, however, they have not accomplished this task for themselves, they will impede their child's natural tendency toward a solid sense of self. For example, if a child is constantly infantilized by an overprotective mother, or rejected by an unreachable parent, the boundary around the self as a separate entity will be fuzzy and unclear. Consequently, one's capacity to distinguish self from other will be sharply reduced. Then, in later relationships, this individual will unconsciously choose someone with whom the early interaction between self and mother will be recreated and reexperienced. In fact, all relationships will be influenced by this inability to distinguish self and others clearly. This entire process is what we are referring to when we speak of object relations theory. It is as if one has a clouded, blurred pair of lenses with which to view the world.

Object Relations Theory

As we said earlier, object relations theory focuses on a person's early inter-actions with primary caretakers and upon how these early interactions shape the child's internal world and affect present adult behaviors and relationships. A basic premise of object relations theory is that all of us have internalized models of relationships and that these internal experiences, formed in childhood, provide the framework for perceiving objective reality in adulthood.

Our inner models (i.e., our inner father, mother, child) are alive inside each of us and are based upon our original direct experiences with parents and other significant people. These internal family relations are powerful forces that shape our perceptions and interactions in all relationships. They are subject to continual modification as we evolve and develop throughout the life cycle. It is understandable that these images affect us so profoundly that we inevitably confuse them with our actual intimate partners. It is crucial that Jennifer understand Laura and Michael's interior worlds, so that she will then be able to assist them in perceiving and ana-lyzing how their internal family relations affect their relationship and con-tribute to their present interpersonal situations.

It is axiomatic that partners will project early internalized images onto one another. When these projections occur, the communication becomes confused and emotional reactivity is usually high. We often see examples of this confusion in Laura and Michael's communication. The partners have stopped hearing each other. For example, Laura experienced and internalized her relationship with her depressed mother, who was distant and unavailable. She therefore developed a belief that led her to perceive closeness with people as hurtful and rejecting. It is no wonder, then, that she experienced her husband, Michael, as emotionally distant, withdrawn, and rejecting. She confused her "inner mother" with her actual partner. Michael also experienced his hardworking parents as remote and unavail-able. When he was at boarding school and they divorced, he felt totally abandoned and betrayed. The themes of abandonment and deception resurfaced in his relationship with Laura. Maggie Scarf (1987, pp. 188-189) writes:

> Difficulties and confusions arise, however, when such mental images affect our perceptions so profoundly that it becomes difficult to discern the differences between the inner object from the past and the real attributes of the intimate partner in a relationship in the present—that is, to disconnect an old fantasy from an actual person out there, now.

In every couple, each partner's system of internalized family relationships influences, interacts, and overlaps with his or her actual intimate other. This lack of distinction between self and other may result in projections between partners that erode self-esteem and produce painful wounds. It is important that the couples therapist be aware of such patterns, so that they may be made conscious, examined, and understood. With this awareness, the partners may then be empowered to make decisions regarding change.

The following exchange with Laura and Michael clearly shows the interaction of intrapsychic and interpersonal dimensions:

MICHAEL: I'm glad we decided that we need more sessions because I think we really do. Sometimes it feels like our relationship just won't work.

LAURA: Well, it never will if you don't get more involved with the family. You're just like your father!

MICHAEL: What's that supposed to mean? You always have to throw my parents into the discussion.

JENNIFER: I'm going to stop both of you now. This kind of argument is what gets you into trouble at home. Let's explore how you can slow down the intensity so you can hear and understand one another. Michael, would you be willing to talk about your strong reactions?

MICHAEL: How can't they be strong when Laura becomes so accusatory?

JENNIFER: It's important that we look beyond the words and understand how you fuel each other's intensity. All couples have their own unique way of dancing with each other. We must learn the pattern that goes on between the two of you in the here and now and also look at what goes on beneath the surface.

MICHAEL: I'm not sure I understand what you mean. If Laura treated me better, I'd behave differently.

JENNIFER: How was anger handled in your family, Michael?

MICHAEL: Well, nothing was ever resolved. It always felt like the same fight with different words. It kept escalating until my dad left the house in a rage and my mom went to their room and slammed the door. I could hear her crying.

JENNIFER: That must have been a very painful time for you as a young boy. What did you do when Dad left and you heard Mom crying?

MICHAEL: I went to my room and tried to bury myself in my homework. I felt helpless and always wondered if my dad would come back. I didn't know what to do. *(Michael appeared sad as he spoke.)*

LAURA: *(Slowly)* That's interesting to hear—because you always pull away when I'm upset and crying. And I always wonder if you're coming back.

JENNIFER: I guess what worked for Michael in the past is no longer working.

MICHAEL: What do you mean?

JENNIFER: Well, Michael, withdrawing from the intensity and chaos in your family was the way you protected yourself as a child. It enabled you to survive. However, as an adult, that defense mechanism gets in the way in your marriage. It no longer works for you.

MICHAEL: *(Sounding frightened and confused)* So what do I do now? I don't know any other way to act.

LAURA: It would be better for me if you asked why I am upset. Your leaving feels like you don't want to be with me. It's as if you don't care at all. It makes me crazy!

MICHAEL: *(Throwing his arms up in despair)* There's just too much coming at me right now. I can't even think.

JENNIFER: What each of you just acknowledged is key to our work together. The ways you learned to survive as children saved you at that time. Today those old ways don't work anymore. In fact, these old behaviors have led to distance between you. Our work is to create new behavior that will enable you to hear and understand each other better.

Projective Identification: An Intrapsychic and Interpersonal Concept of Object Relations Theory

Though the concept of projective identification is a difficult one to understand, it provides a framework of thinking within which the therapist can defuse very intense couple interactions (Siegel, 1992). Projective identification is both an intrapsychic and interpersonal process. Jennifer alternates her focus between the intrapsychic and interpersonal dimensions while working with Laura and Michael. By clarifying and validating each partner's responses, and by empathically exploring the internal subjectivity of each partner, the therapist may move towards an exploration of the personal meaning of the experience for each individual (Siegel, 1992). For example, in exploring Michael's responses to the intensity and chaos he experienced in reaction to his parents' fighting episodes, Jennifer pointed out how withdrawal to his room was a way he survived as a child. It became clear to this couple how Michael's early struggles affect his marriage today. Laura and Michael softened visibly as they listened to each other in a different way.

Keeping in mind the unconscious nature of the interaction, the therapist must proceed slowly and gently. It is often a shaming experience for a person to recognize a formerly unconscious part of himself. Since disclosures and acknowledgments can be very painful and exposing, it is important for the therapist to track the responses of the listening partner. This process was evident as Laura and Michael slowly began to reveal their pain and vulnerability to each other. Empathy may be experienced as each hears the other's struggles. In summary, the role of the couples therapist is to help each partner take responsibility for his or her own projected conflicts and to understand the individual dynamics in the context of the couple's relationship.

The essence of all therapy is to have each partner relate to the other as the other rather than as an extension of the self. This concept of distinguishing self from other is pivotal to understanding projective identification and object relations theory. In this session, Laura and Michael gained clarity, as each began to understand his or her own internal boundaries, as well as the necessary boundary around their couple system. In reference to our framework, this session illustrates the bridging of object relations theory and systems thinking.

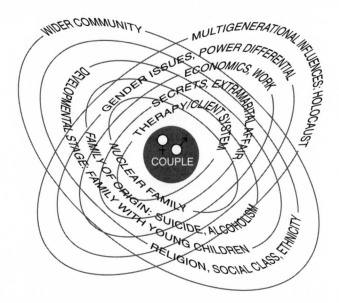

FIGURE 7-1: *Contextual Influences That Crowd Laura and Michael's "Marital Bed"*

Chapter 8

The Couple's Dance

As Jennifer greeted Laura and Michael in the waiting room, they were laughing. This mood continued as they entered her office.

MICHAEL: We're not really sure what happened here last week, but things at home certainly seem better.

LAURA: It is as if a black cloud has lifted.

MICHAEL: We're both still afraid to be too optimistic in case that black cloud returns. I guess you can say we are proceeding cautiously.

JENNIFER: Can you tell me what was different that made this week better?

LAURA: Well, Michael worked less and was home much more. We felt like a real family. Even going with all three kids to McDonald's was fun.

MICHAEL: Laura was different with me so I wanted to come home more.

JENNIFER: Do you know what Michael means, Laura, when he says "different"?

LAURA: Somehow I didn't feel as uptight with Michael or the kids, and I guess he could sense that. The house was still chaotic, but we handled it more easily.

MICHAEL: When things work better with the two of us, we become better parents.

JENNIFER: When the two of you collaborate and work as a team, the kids know who is in charge, and they calm down because they feel safer.

MICHAEL: We even started to talk to Amanda and Emma about sleeping in their own room again. Laura brought it up and said she didn't realize how unfair it was to me that I sometimes slept on the sofa.

JENNIFER: So, Laura, you became aware of the impact this had on Michael.

LAURA: I guess the biggest impact on me now is seeing how thoughtless I've been. I feel so guilty about so many things.

JENNIFER: You both seem to be seeing things very differently this week. Our collaborative efforts in therapy parallel your renewed commitment to the relationship. Your strength as parents has filtered down to the children. They feel this effect and benefit from your changes.

Punctuate Strengths of Couple

Jennifer punctuated Laura and Michael's strengths as a couple and as parents by complimenting them on their teamwork. The power of complimenting clients on what is working cannot be emphasized enough. Offering support and encouragement promotes self-esteem and builds confidence as the couple ventures out to take further risks. Laura and Michael are fortifying the boundaries around their couple system and, as they do so, changing their pattern of involving "a third party" (in this case the children) to reduce the intensity between them.

Triangular Patterns

In Murray Bowen's theory, one of the key concepts is triangulation. By this he referred to the process whereby any two-party relationship that is experiencing great intensity will naturally involve a third party to reduce anxiety. This third party can be a person, issue, substance, or any entity that takes the focus off the relationship and thereby reduces the tension (Bowen 1978; Kerr & Bowen, 1988). In Laura and Michael's situation, at different times, they triangled in parents, Laura's siblings, Michael's affair, the children, and/or alcohol.

Although Laura and Michael had a few weeks of relative tranquility, they sometimes lapsed back into old, familiar patterns. In the following dialogue, we will see the triangulation that occurs when their emotional intensity escalates beyond what they can tolerate. The journey of therapy never proceeds in a straight, predictable path. There are many bumps and setbacks along the way.

MICHAEL: Out of the blue, Laura is back to her old behavior.

LAURA: What's that supposed to mean?!

MICHAEL: Just when I thought we were making great strides, you go and ruin it all.

LAURA: I've had a really hard week, and you were totally insensitive to me.

MICHAEL: I didn't even know you were having a hard week. Why didn't you tell me? You must think I can read your mind.

LAURA: It's just too hard to talk to you about.

JENNIFER: I'm in the dark, too. What is going on?

LAURA: I was just starting to trust Michael again. And this week I got a bunch of hangups on the phone. I'm sure that woman is calling again.

MICHAEL: *(Raising his voice angrily)* I'm so damned fed up with your unfair accusations, Laura! I told you the affair was over, and it is. I'm sick and tired of your not believing me. Can't you stop her vicious attacks, Jennifer? She's just wearing me down and taking the life out of our marriage. I feel like I am trying so hard and getting absolutely nowhere.

LAURA: Your response, Michael, is exactly why I was afraid to tell you this at home. *(Turning to Jennifer)* You understand that, don't you?

JENNIFER: Each of you wants me to stop the pain of your struggle. And I can't do that for you. I wonder if you'd be willing to try something different here. I'd like each of you to imagine for a moment that you, Michael, are Laura as I ask you a few questions. Then, Laura, I'll have you be Michael and do the same. This is a little exercise that may help you to tune in to what the other is experiencing.

The pace of the session markedly changes as Michael and Laura look expectantly at each other. Their blaming tones have been interrupted by a request that they become reflective as an alternative dialogue is suggested. Jennifer avoids being triangled in to the couple's dilemma. She creates a context for moving from impasse to dialogue.

Jennifer's request has the paradoxical effect of joining Laura and Michael as a team as they resist her suggestion in the dialogue that follows. It is more familiar for them to protect themselves and each other from change. The following demonstrates how their former locked-in positions against each other shift as they unite against the therapist.

MICHAEL: That exercise sounds too tough for me. I have a hard enough time answering questions for myself. Answering them as Laura would be impossible.

LAURA: I agree with Michael. If I knew what was going on in his mind and he knew what was going on in mine, we probably wouldn't have needed therapy in the first place.

JENNIFER: I certainly understand your hesitancy. Anything new involves risk-taking and is scary. However, you've both been so courageous and taken so many risks with each other since you started coming here that

I was hoping you'd be willing to try another one.

LAURA: *(Hesitantly)* Well, do you really think it will help us? If so, I guess I might possibly try it. But maybe you'll go first, Michael, cause you always catch on to things faster than I do.

MICHAEL: Why do I feel coerced by that compliment? Okay, so how do I do this—do I have to put on Laura's clothes first?

JENNIFER: *(Smiling)* That's certainly one way of getting into this exercise. But I'm going to try to make it a little easier than that. So, Michael, I'd like you to simply be Laura and answer some questions as you think Laura might answer them. Is that OK with you?

MICHAEL: Sure. I'll try. If I get confused at times, I guess you'll pull me back on track?

JENNIFER: Of course I will.

(Interview begins with Michael responding as internalized Laura.)

JENNIFER: I want to start off by asking a couple of questions about your relationship with your husband and a few about yourself. I'd like you to tell me what some of the strengths in your marriage are.

MICHAEL: *(As internalized Laura)* Well, at times we have a lot of fun together. Michael makes me laugh and not take myself so seriously. When we're getting along, we do a good job of parenting. And we love our kids a lot. I just wish Michael would spend more time at home. And then I know things would be better.

JENNIFER: You guys have a lot going for you. Fun, laughter, and good parenting are certainly important strengths in your marriage. Now, Laura, perhaps you can tell me a bit about your experience in therapy. How was it for you to come to today's session?

MICHAEL: *(As internalized Laura)* I was pretty nervous. I knew I wanted to say some hard things to Michael that I couldn't say at home.

Jennifer: How come you could say them here and not at home?

MICHAEL: *(As internalized Laura)* Because I knew if I mentioned "that woman" again, the whole week would be ruined. When I become nervous and feel threatened, Michael pays the price.

LAURA: Wow! I couldn't have answered better for myself. Michael, I'm really surprised that you knew all of this was going on for me.

JENNIFER: This seems like a good place to discuss this exchange I just had with Michael. Laura, I, too, was struck by how tuned in Michael is to you. Michael, how was this experience for you?

MICHAEL: I'm surprised at how easily I became Laura's voice and how tuned in to her I am. I'm glad she noticed this.

LAURA: Now I'm really afraid to have my turn because I don't think I know Michael as well as he knows me.

JENNIFER: Michael, what's it like for you when Laura puts you up on that pedestal?

MICHAEL: I always have a mixed response. No one has ever put me on a pedestal before. So some of it makes me feel good. And, yet, it also makes me feel burdened, like somehow I always have to be the strong and bright one.

JENNIFER: Something really profound just took place. The interaction the two of you had is a perfect example of your dance together. You, Laura, put Michael on a pedestal. And you, Michael, accept that role. And then, instead of feeling like equal partners, your way of relating becomes unequal, almost like a parent/child relationship.

LAURA: Do you mean I'm causing this problem?

JENNIFER REED: No, not at all, Laura. It's a pattern you've both gotten into. It's totally irrelevant how it started. It's the loop that you are in together. The more one of you overfunctions, the more the other will under-function.

This dialogue clearly illustrates the gender and power differences that often impact the interactions of a couple system. Laura defers to Michael and assumes the less powerful position in their relationship. Men and women in our culture assume that the man has more power than the woman (Low, 1990). The extreme consequences of relationships that are based on power, control, and male domination are discussed in Chapter 18. For further reading on the subject of gender and power differences, we suggest Natalie Low's article and Carol Gilligan's work, which are listed in the bibliography.

Loops, Patterns, and Circularity

We must understand relationship patterns in order to move to new levels of understanding and change. In the above dialogue, it became clear how Laura and Michael got stuck in a repetitive pattern that perpetuated their painful dilemma. Michael's overfunctioning and Laura's underfunctioning is a loop of behavior that was clarified by Jennifer in this session. Partners develop reciprocal positions or roles that are complementary to each other. Other examples may be a pursuer and a distancer, or a strong individual who often rescues a "sick" or helpless mate. Couples become organized in these ways of relating. Each invites the same habitual responses in the other. These reciprocal behaviors often serve the couple and enable them to function in a fairly predictable way. However, these responses sometimes result in an escalating cycle of interaction (Papp, 1990). This is what had occurred in Laura and Michael's situation. The issue of Michael's affair had polarized them even further. The differences that had once attracted and united them were now sharply dividing them. In Jennifer's efforts to create a context for moving from impasse to dialogue, she creatively utilized Karl Tomm's method of internalized-other interviewing. (David Epston [1993] devised a similar practice in 1985. He referred to his method as cross-referential questioning.) This experiential mode of questioning elicits greater empathy and understanding of the partner as each moves into the other's experience. Laura and Michael's surprise at how deeply Michael knew Laura was evidence of this. At the next session, Laura, though anxious, wanted to take her turn at being "the internalized Michael." Since Laura was not often a risk-taker, her eagerness to work was a new strength that was noted by Michael as well as Jennifer.

(Internalized other interview begins with Laura responding as internalized Michael.)

JENNIFER: So, Michael, let's hear how you view your relationship with Laura.

LAURA: *(As internalized Michael)* Not so good at this time. It seems as if all the things that originally attracted us are not working now. Having kids put a huge strain on the marriage. I never feel special or appreciated anymore. So I seem to want to come home less and less.

JENNIFER: Well, Michael, you sound clear about what is not working. Can you comment on some of the things that are working?

LAURA: *(As internalized Michael)* I'll have to admit some things are better since we started coming here. I'm not relegated to sleeping on the couch anymore since it's not so crowded in our bed. We're even having sex once in a while.

JENNIFER: So some things are starting to work better. Michael, do you think you and Laura have a strong enough foundation for working things out between you?

LAURA: *(As internalized Michael)* I used to think we did. But now I'm not so sure.

MICHAEL: *(Breaking in)* I'm confused. Are you answering for me or for you?

JENNIFER: We'll get to your question in a moment, Michael. First I'd like to ask Laura about her experience. What was it like for you to answer as Michael?

LAURA: I was a bit confused at times because I didn't know whether I was answering for Michael or for me.

JENNIFER: That's one of the values of this exercise. We get to clarify the confusions between ourselves and our partners. And that leads me to my next question. How accurate do you think you were with your answers?

LAURA: I think I was pretty accurate. What do you think, Michael?

MICHAEL: Some of it sounded more like your way of thinking than mine.

LAURA: What do you mean?

MICHAEL: Well, at the beginning. When you talked about me wanting to come home less and less, that's changed a lot recently.

LAURA: I guess I still feel pretty insecure with you. And your affair always makes me think you have one foot out the door.

JENNIFER: The deep wounds in your marriage will take time to heal for both of you. You have definitely begun that journey, but you will need more time. These old betrayals leave scars that will resurface from time to time. You'll learn new ways to deal with the old hurts.

MICHAEL: I guess this journey at times feels overwhelming for both of us. It has taken us seven years to bottom out. I hope it won't take another seven years to be happy and romantic again.

JENNIFER: I know it is difficult for you both to be immersed in this struggle. Hanging in there and struggling is what gets you to the other side.

LAURA: Would you repeat that so I can write it down and look at it again when I feel discouraged?

MICHAEL: I guess I need to remember it, too.

JENNIFER: Your enthusiasm and responsiveness really touch me. Maybe now would be a good time to return to your reactions about the exercise. Michael, any other areas that felt inaccurate for you?

MICHAEL: I guess overall in Laura's answers she sees me as less hopeful and committed than I actually am. I think that comes from her pessimistic nature. She always sees the glass as half-empty.

LAURA: Well, you certainly give me reason to be pessimistic when you ignore our problems. Then I worry and expect the worst. And the worst certainly happened.

JENNIFER: Here's another variation of your dance. You, Laura, do all the worrying for both of you. And you, Michael, are then free from any worry. Together, you form two parts of a whole.

MICHAEL: You mean to say if I was the worrier, Laura would be more optimistic?

LAURA: I'm sure I would. But I think I never remember not worrying. Is it possible for me to change now?

JENNIFER: Change is always possible. The roots of your roles and patterns today go back to your families of origin. Since our time is up now, I think it's important that we continue to explore this next week.

Internalized-Other Interviewing: Creating a Pathway for Change

By doing this important work together, Laura and Michael experienced another dimension of understanding in their relationship. They now knew how to differentiate their internalized partner from their actual partner. As we mentioned in Chapter 7, we internalize our experiences of others from the moment of birth. Therefore, we have a model of relationships inside of us as we enter adult life. Jennifer's task with Laura and Michael was to help them develop a consciousness of the impact of these internalized experiences upon their relationship today.

Internalized-other interviewing enabled change in the couple by correcting misperceptions and enhancing empathy. Each partner came to realize how one experienced the other differently than he or she originally thought. In other words, the interview enhanced the ability of both Laura and Michael to take the perspective of the other. This brought forth new thinking. The conversation opened a pathway from impasse to dialogue.

While internalized-other questioning increases one's capacity for empathy, understanding, and acceptance, there are some limitations. For example, this type of questioning is sometimes awkward for clients and may even produce confusion. However, we find that most clients are intrigued by the exercise. We believe that clients' receptivity has to do with their level of comfort with the therapist. Some people may benefit from a very brief interview, while others actively enjoy the process and invite further questioning from the therapist. We have also found that the experience increases one's curiosity regarding the actual experiences of others.

Externalizing Conversations: Creating More Pathways for Change

When we first learned about externalization several years ago, we realized we had already had some experience with the concept and its application in a psychodrama training group for therapists in the mid-'80s. Our training included the practice of interviewing the multiple voices, parts, or aspects of people. The intent of this work was to enable individuals to identify and become familiar with formerly unknown parts of themselves. We found that these externalizing conversations could also be modified and incorporated into our clinical work with individuals, couples, and families. This training for us as therapists provided a nice fit with our systems orientation. As we continued to read and learn, we were introduced to the more sophisticated concept of "externalizing conversations" through the writings and workshops of Michael White, David Epston, Karl Tomm, Sallyann Roth, and Bill O'Hanlon.

The process of interviewing these various parts of people encouraged them to actually develop a relationship with "the problem." According to David Epston and Sallyann Roth (1994, p. 1), by externalizing "the problem" in this way, a context is established in which "people experience themselves as separate from the problem. That is, separate from problem-saturated descriptions that have encompassed or have become their identities. It changes persons' relationship to problems, and shifts the conversation to a focus on the relationship between the person and the problem instead of a focus on a problem-person."

Some examples of externalizing questions for Laura and Michael are:

- How can "the affair" as a dominant influence upon your relationship be reduced?
- How has alcohol influenced the regulation of closeness and distance in your relationship?
- As your "crowded bed" empties out, how do you imagine your relationship will be different?

The concept became clearer to us as we made the distinction between problem-internalizing questions and problem-externalizing questions (Roth & Epston, 1996). The former are linear and inherently judgmental, whereas the latter are circular, respectful, and challenge people to give up long-held negative beliefs. For example, the question, "Why are you depressed?" presumes that depression is the problem and that it resides within the personality of the individual. The implication is that something is wrong and that someone's very being or identity must be changed. In contrast, the couples therapist might ask the partners, "If depression were no longer a dominant force in your lives, how do you imagine your relationship would be different?" This type of question presupposes that change is possible and also has the potential for increasing motivation and for stimulating ideas for new possibilities. Externalizing questions and conversations are thus very liberating for people who have identified their core beings with illness, depression, or problems. Bill O'Hanlon (1994) writes that we may be freed from the insidious effects of negative beliefs and thoughts if we can become conscious that these beliefs are, in fact, separate from our personal identities. Externalization is not just a technique. It is a way of thinking and working that is used in the context of narrative work and typically generates hope and optimism for clients and therapists alike (O'Hanlon, 1994).

The Art of Questioning

The attitude and personal qualities of the therapist are of central importance in determining the effectiveness of what happens in therapy. It is our strong conviction that the therapist's qualities of empathy, respect, and acceptance of the client are the cornerstone of good therapy. The effectiveness of the process depends upon the quality of the therapeutic relationship, the presence of the therapist's respect for and acceptance of the client, and the ability to join, collaborate, and instill hope (Bobes & Rothman, 1996). All of these factors provide the necessary environment within which change may occur.

We have found that a close examination of the effects of questioning deepens one's understanding of the circular components in a couple system. What kinds of questions create new pathways for change, loosen constraints, and open space for new thinking? What kinds of questions reinforce existing constraints and close space for new ideas? What are the elements required for an effective therapeutic conversation? Harlene Anderson (1997, pp.150-151) sums up the key points of questioning when she notes, "Any question can be asked, any comment can be made, anything can be talked about. What is important, however, is the stance from which it comes—the manner, the tone, and the timing." The art of questioning and the attitude of the therapist together create pathways for change.

Circular Questioning

JENNIFER: We left off last week connecting today's roles and patterns to your families of origin.

LAURA: Most of the time we don't think much about our patterns and where they come from. But I sure see where Michael's behavior comes from when his parents visit us.

MICHAEL: What, for example?

JENNIFER: *(Interrupting)* Michael, we'll get to your question in a moment. Laura, let's focus for a moment on your family, and then we'll have Michael focus on his. So, Laura, how might your parents have managed the kinds of issues you and Michael are grappling with today?

LAURA: My mom probably would have taken to her bed. And my dad would have ignored the problems and gone on with business as usual.

JENNIFER: I wonder how these responses might be affecting you today?

LAURA: Well, I'm not sure. As I think about it now, I guess I kind of took to my bed too after learning about Michael's affair.

JENNIFER: Michael, how did your parents handle conflict and differences in their marriage?

MICHAEL: As I said earlier, my dad would leave the house, and my mom would go to her room and cry.

JENNIFER REED: Actually, both sets of parents handled conflict and differences in a similar way. Each of you had moms who retreated in despair and dads who ignored and withdrew. You reacted with each other in the way that you learned at home.

There was a stillness in the room as Laura and Michael reflected upon what they had just heard.

The dialogue above illustrates circular questioning. This manner of questioning is exploratory and stimulates clients to consider new meanings to their life experiences. As questions are asked, clients move from content to process, from intrapsychic to interpersonal, from linear thinking to circular thinking. This shift enables them to experience their relationship in a more expansive way thus providing new options and choices. For example, by asking Laura and Michael how their parents handled differences and conflict in their relationship, Jennifer Reed's intention was to stimulate them to look at patterns from a generational perspective. Once the couple becomes aware of these repetitive behaviors as part of a larger family context, they will then become empowered to make decisions based upon greater awareness. (For further examples of circular questions you may find it useful to review the "Guidelines for Assessment and Evaluation of the Couple System" in Chapter 2.)

Reflexive Questions

JENNIFER: Michael, I wonder what Laura would do if, instead of withdrawing or leaving when the intensity at home reaches a difficult level, you stayed with her and the two of you simply sat together and talked?

MICHAEL: I don't know if I could do that. I don't know if Laura could either.

JENNIFER: Laura, if you thought that Michael's reasons for leaving were because he was protecting himself from experiencing his vulnerability, how do you imagine you might respond if he developed the courage to remain at home despite his discomfort?

LAURA: That would probably be hard for me because we've never done it before.

JENNIFER: What do you think would happen if you both made an agreement to stay together during moments of intensity even if it were for a limited time?

(Michael and Laura exchanged glances and shifted uncomfortably in their seats. They shrugged their shoulders. A working silence filled the room. After a couple of moments Jennifer Reed asked another question.)

JENNIFER: Which of you would be most optimistic that such an agreement would have a favorable outcome?

As you may surmise in reading these samples of reflexive questioning, the variety and possibilities for stimulating new responses and generating change are enormous. Reflexive questions are designed to enable change in couples and individuals by stimulating them to give new meaning to their actions, perceptions, and behaviors. Since people interpret their worlds in a particular way and attribute certain premises and beliefs to the problems they have, it is helpful to invite them to consider alternative responses (Tomm, 1987, 1988a, b). Karl Tomm (1987, p. 172) writes:

> Reflexive questions are questions asked with the intent to facilitate self-healing in an individual or family by activating the reflexivity among meanings within pre-existing belief systems that enable family members to generate or generalize constructive patterns of cognition and behavior on their own.

Guidelines for Crafting Questions That Generate Change

The act of questioning and the act of changing may occur simultaneously. If the questions asked invite the people being interviewed to consider new meanings to their behaviors and patterns, then a new way of thinking may be generated. This is the crux of the postmodern view as well as of systemic thinking. Thus, pathways for change may be created as new ideas are brought forth by the questioning. The following guidelines[1] are essential for therapists to consider as they craft questions that will enable change.

- Questions should be short and simple enough to be easily understood.

---

[1] These guidelines are abbreviated from a handout developed by David Epston and Sallyann Roth in May, 1996, Ann Arbor, Michigan. The handout is entitled "Working with Plot and Alternative Plot." Copyright © David Epston and Sallyann Roth.

- Questions should invite the person being interviewed to notice small steps to take in the direction he or she wants to go.
- Questions should stay close to the interviewee's experience, dreams, hopes, desires, and intentions.
- Questions should incorporate active rather than passive language.
- Questions should show respect for the difficulties of people while simultaneously helping them access their strengths.
- All questions must come from a place of compassion.

In formulating questions, the therapist should be clear about his or her intentions. Is the therapist gathering information in order to understand the client better? Is the intention to stimulate the client to generate new ideas and consider alternative ways of responding? Is the therapist attempting to uncover family-of-origin patterns that may relate to the current presenting issues? Developing a conscious awareness of one's intentions for any therapeutic activity is of paramount importance in guiding a therapeutic conversation. Karl Tomm's articles on questioning (1987, 1988a, b) are rich resources for those wanting to explore further the various types of questions available to therapists. His conceptual postures incorporate the intents and effects of linear, strategic, circular, and reflexive questions and are helpful to anyone learning to differentiate the various types of questions. Tomm presents in diagram form the conceptual postures or guidelines that distinguish four major groups of questions (Tomm, 1988a; see Figure 8-1). In this diagram he points out the "predominant intent and probable effects of differing questions." Every question embodies some

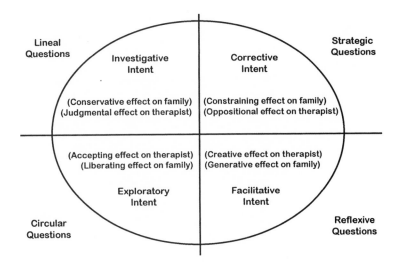

FIGURE 8-1. *Karl Tomm's Conceptual Postures*
Reprinted with permission from Tomm, 1988a.

intention, and our therapeutic work will be enhanced by our becoming conscious of those intentions. In our experience, the identification of intentions that underlie what we say and do as therapists enhances our consciousness and sensitivity to clients. This experience and awareness inform and guide our decision-making and choices in the therapeutic conversation.

One's impact as a therapist may be enhanced by careful differentiation and intentional selection of specific questions that enable a couple or family to attain self-healing capacity (Tomm, 1987). While linear questions facilitated Jennifer's joining with Laura and Michael, the intent of these questions was mainly to gather information. As therapy progressed, Jennifer utilized a wide range of questions in order to explore the couple's patterns. She extensively utilized circular questions when she interviewed the internalized other in both Laura and Michael. And, finally, Jennifer asked reflexive questions that generated further reflection and invited the couple to consider new meanings to their long-standing behavior and patterns.

Chapter 9

Unconscious Agendas

Jennifer Reed's bed is crowded, too. Just as Laura and Michael look at the various people, voices, and intrusions that crowd their bed, so does Jennifer. Clients' and therapists' issues are tightly interwoven. Privately, Jennifer had become increasingly concerned about Michael's alcoholism. Although he and Laura initially acknowledged his family's alcoholic history, in subsequent sessions the topic seemed to be avoided. It was as if Laura and Michael had mutually agreed to leave this can of worms unopened.

Laura and Michael entered this session barely looking at each other. Laura was visibly agitated while Michael appeared contrite.

JENNIFER: *(Experiencing their distance)* What's going on? The room feels pretty heavy with tension.

LAURA: I can't handle this relationship anymore! I think I want Michael to move out. Last night he stayed out until 4:00 in the morning and came home stumbling and reeking of alcohol. I've had it with him!

MICHAEL: I told you I was sorry. Do we have to dredge all this up again?

LAURA: I'm sick and tired of all your "sorrys." You're always sorry and nothing changes. You're sorry when you're with another woman, you're sorry when you go on a binge, you're sorry when you stay late at the office, you're sorry when you break the kids' toys in a rage. I'm fed up with it all!

(Jennifer Reed's body reacted to the intense affect in the room. Internally she felt herself tightening up as she became caught up in the couple's system.)

JENNIFER: What happened this week to precipitate this crisis?

LAURA: I have no idea. Michael uses any excuse to spoil things. He just can't seem to tolerate things being good at home. He's hell bent on destroying our family. I hate him!

JENNIFER: You've been quiet, Michael. How do you see the situation?

MICHAEL: It's pretty dismal. I don't even know where I'll be sleeping tonight.

LAURA: You can go back to wherever you were last night.

JENNIFER: I know the situation seems grim to both of you. A number of new issues have come up today that are upsetting.

LAURA: It's not just last night. These blow-ups don't happen all the time, but when they do they're always terrifying. There's usually a calm after the storm, but I don't want to be part of this anymore. I want Michael to leave.

MICHAEL: Maybe that's not a bad idea. Things are going from bad to worse. It may surprise you to know I have no idea where I was last night. I don't even remember coming home.

JENNIFER: Things have escalated and your situation is a serious one. I can understand how you both need some distance to calm things down. Let's take some time to explore what a separation would mean to each of you.

Jennifer Reed's Crowded Bed

From the very first contact with Laura and Michael, Jennifer experienced echoes from her past. The therapeutic triangle recreated for her the old triangle with her parents, particularly when conflict escalated about Michael's drinking. This produced within her a chaotic, helpless child feeling that mirrored Laura and Michael's helplessness and chaos. Since her overfunctioning father and underfunctioning mother danced a similar dance as this couple, she knew she had to separate her early role as caretaker from her role as therapist today. Jennifer Reed found herself walking a narrow line between her old role as "fixer" in the triangle with her parents and her role with Laura and Michael as their therapist. In her effort to distinguish her internal responses from her external relationship with the couple, she repeatedly asked herself, "Whose needs are being served by my responses—my clients' or my own?"

Couples therapy will arouse intense emotions for clients and therapists alike. The therapist and couple together form a mini-group in which the therapeutic triangle symbolically represents the original parent-child relationship for all involved. Augustus Napier (Napier & Whitaker, 1978, p. 129) clearly describes this process: "the family is so 'powerful' and so involving that it sets off reverberations that go deep into the therapist's own life. The family you are treating suddenly becomes a version of the family you grew up in, and you become a 'patient,' struggling with your own feelings."

Belief Systems of Jennifer Reed

Just as Jennifer helped Laura and Michael explore their family-of-origin issues and belief systems, it was also necessary for her to be aware of her own family-of-origin issues and belief systems. Her father was an excessive drinker and often very explosive. Her mother was passive and expended a lot of energy attempting to calm her husband's volatility. The children never knew what they would find at home. Life in the Reed household was unpredictable. In her role as family caretaker, she learned that intensity of emotion was not acceptable. Consequently, she worked hard to mediate her parents' fights when Mother was unable to calm Dad down. It was not uncommon for her to go from one parent to the other in a desperate attempt to create peace in the household. She often did the same with her two younger siblings. As oldest child and caretaker, she saw herself as the family peacemaker.

In her own private therapy and in her training as a therapist, Jennifer Reed had become well-acquainted with her family role. As a young therapist she continued to explore her belief systems so that she could distinguish her own personal issues from those of her clients. For a long time, she avoided doing couple work, unconsciously protecting herself from recreating her early pain as family peacemaker. However, in her evolution as a professional she slowly began work with families and couples while continuing to address her own internal struggles. Couple work is difficult for most of us because it stirs up images and primitive emotions of this early first triangle. For the therapist, as well as the couple, it is, indeed, a crowded bed from the very beginning!

Containment Versus Disclosure

We are well trained by societal forces to talk, to reveal, to say, to tell, sometimes without thinking. On the other hand, we have little training in listening, reflecting, and containing our reactions to what has been said or done. Communication is enhanced by both examining and understanding the forces of containment and disclosure.

Jennifer was well aware of her choice to contain her responses as she experienced and listened to Laura and Michael's escalation of conflict. Her years of experience coupled with her sensitivity to her own subjective reactions enabled her to keep the therapy on track. Her ability to accept and tolerate the full range of affects in the room validated the couple's intense feelings and provided a safe holding environment for them. Her therapeutic interventions were aimed at calming the system down and working realistically on the crisis at hand.

(Continuation of previous dialogue)

LAURA: I think at this point a separation is what I need. I'd be able to focus on myself and the children without constantly worrying about where Michael is.

MICHAEL: What are you worrying about now? You make it sound like I'm the only one with problems. What about you?

JENNIFER: *(Speaking in an irritated tone, voice raised)* Maybe Laura does need some time away from you. It sounds as if your drinking is out of control and may be dangerous for your family. I think it's time for you to start going to Alcoholics Anonymous.

MICHAEL: *(Enraged)* I'm not going to any fucking AA meetings! How do you know my drinking is out of control? The last thing I need is two nagging women on my case.

JENNIFER: *(Speaking in a moralistic tone)* I certainly didn't mean to sound nagging. I'm just very concerned for Laura and the children.

As Jennifer spoke, she became aware of how completely she had identified with Laura. A brief look at Michael confirmed how betrayed he felt by her reprimand. Realizing her mistake, she felt bewildered. She took a moment to collect her thoughts. Knowing her reaction was out of proportion to the exchange in the room, Jennifer realized her countertransference had interfered in the session. Her awareness of her internal state was the key to getting back on track. Due to her immersion in her own emotions, Jennifer had temporarily abandoned the couple work. She knew she must address her insensitivity and failure of empathy. The rupture in the work had to be acknowledged.

JENNIFER: I want to acknowledge that I just got off track as your therapist. I can see from your reactions that you feel something is amiss also.

LAURA: I was surprised when you talked to Michael differently than you usually do. At first I was glad you sided with me. Then I felt bad for Michael.

MICHAEL: I sure felt ganged up on. Hearing you both now makes me feel my reaction wasn't crazy.

JENNIFER: No, Michael, you certainly weren't overreacting. If anything, I was. And, Laura, my overidentification with you got us off track. And it was important that you, Michael, called me on it. And, Laura, by your response to my taking your side, you showed how sensitive you were to what was going on. Now let's see what more we can learn from what just happened. I think that part of my overreaction was a response to the seriousness of what you are both going through. The element of danger in your family is affecting me in a profound way.

LAURA: I guess I think it's dangerous, too, if I've asked Michael to move out. When he starts to throw things at home, he frightens the kids, and I don't feel safe.

JENNIFER: Michael, how is it for you when Laura says this?

MICHAEL: I never think I'm going to wind up throwing things, but some-how my rage takes over.

JENNIFER: How do you both manage conflict when alcohol is not involved?

LAURA: Michael's more reasonable. He doesn't scream or throw things when he is not drinking.

MICHAEL: I'm more reasonable, Laura, because you treat me differently. When I have a few drinks, you stay away from me like I have the plague.

LAURA: I stay away because I'm afraid of you.

JENNIFER: You guys have created a strong loop together. Your distancing behavior, Laura, triggers Michael's rage. And your rage, Michael, encourages more distance. On the one hand, each of you protects the other with your respective behaviors. And at the same time you incite each other. This is how I view your interaction. How are you under-standing my view of your relating?

Impact of Countertransference Disclosure

Experiencing and understanding one's countertransference is the core and foundation for the therapist's continued growth and self-under-standing. It is a necessary requirement for doing clinical work. This inter-nal exploration is also the source of new learning and, most importantly, a fertile field for transformation and healing. Since personal responses are interwoven throughout the treatment process, the therapist will continually struggle with identification of countertransference. When the therapist is open to immersion into his or her internal world during treatment, then the powers of empathy and healing are greatly en-hanced.

Conscious and unconscious aspects of the therapist's internal world will inevitably surface in clinical work. In the above dialogue, we saw how old wounds and vulnerabilities were activated in Jennifer. Long before the seriousness of the substance abuse was acknowledged by Laura and Michael, Jennifer was internally feeling its impact. In this last session, as she learned of the angry outbursts that accompanied Michael's drinking, and of Laura's fears for her safety, her own chaotic family of origin loomed large before her. She momentarily abandoned Laura and Michael as she became unable to distinguish her old role as a child from her present role as therapist.

While Jennifer's internal chaos was stirring up the therapeutic work, the reverberations were also felt within the couple relationship. A parallel process was occurring in the therapist/couple system. The intensity was escalating for everyone in the room. In therapeutic terms, Jennifer's internal reactions demonstrate her countertransference. Similarly, Laura and Michael's responses reflect their transference to Jennifer. In the previous dialogue, Michael's strong reaction to what he perceives as Jennifer's "nagging" is an example of this transference. Laura joined with him when she expressed her surprise as well as her empathy for Michael at this time.

Gender Influences

Working with couples is very complex due to the many systems operating together. Each of the following is an interacting element of the whole: Laura's individual issues, Michael's individual issues, Laura and Michael's interpersonal relationship, Jennifer's subjective self, the interacting system of the couple and therapist. Contextual issues are another important dimension affecting all of these systems. Let us take this opportunity to look at the influences of gender, ethnicity, and religion.

In many ways, Laura's and Michael's behaviors represent centuries of ingrained stereotypical thinking. Since the beginning of mankind, men and women have learned different messages about their respective places in the world. Cultural and societal influences interact with family dynamics to perpetuate rigid gender roles, attitudes, and beliefs. Typically, the man's traditional role as wage-earner and family provider carries with it the belief that he has greater power than the woman. The woman's role is caretaker and nurturer, and she assumes the less powerful position. In our society, there is an inequality between men and women in relation to the issues of power and authority. This lack of total equality is a crucial relational aspect of all couple and family interactions.

Throughout our case study of Laura and Michael, you have seen the effects of the influences of the gender and power differential upon their couple system. Laura is more emotional, while Michael is rational. Laura is the caretaker of the children at home, and Michael is the wage-earner out in the world. When Laura underfunctions, Michael overfunctions. We refer to this description of polarities as the "see-saw syndrome." Like children on a see-saw in a playground, when one is up, the other is down. Rarely is there a good balance when intense situations exist. Laura's and Michael's gender roles and positions, reinforced from early childhood, are now very evident in their marriage. As Jennifer continues her work with this couple, we will see how the complementarity of their gender and power differences are challenged.

Jennifer's gender also influenced the therapy. At times she overidentified with Laura, while at other times she was overly protective and concerned about Michael. In addition to the strong cultural and societal gender influences, Jennifer's family background impacted her therapeutic work. Since she was raised in an alcoholic family with a volatile, dominant father and subordinate mother, she learned early on not to confront male power. Her challenge as a professional woman, therefore, was to assert her authority without reverting to the old placating role in her family. Michele Bograd (1990, p. 55) states, "The binds male and female therapists may find themselves in with opposite-sex clients often have more to do with the way gender roles structure intimate relationships than with individual countertransference or family-of-origin issues." Jennifer often found it more difficult to confront Michael due to the belief that men are unable to express feelings and that women must protect them. Women are not only taught to protect men but also to avoid their expressions of anger. Women often believe, in fact, that they are responsible for the man's anger. Jennifer's challenge was to address her own gender beliefs and biases in order to view the clinical work more clearly.

Ethnicity and Religious Influences

Equally important as gender are the ethnic and religious influences that affect a couple's interaction and functioning. In Laura and Michael's case, their different backgrounds often brought a richness to their marriage. At other times, their differences divided them. It was difficult for Laura to understand the enormous unspoken impact of the Holocaust experience upon Michael's family, while the closeness and blurred boundaries of Laura's family were hard for Michael to handle.

Since the cultural influences were not talked about in their families of origin, Jennifer's task was to help Laura and Michael uncover these subtle and powerful elements within their couple system.

JENNIFER: Laura, you've mentioned that you are very frightened when Michael drinks. Have you had other experiences before in which you've felt frightened by someone's drinking?

LAURA: Yes, I think I've always been that way around drinking. I remember my grandfather drinking and how frightened I was that something bad would happen. Once when he was babysitting all of us, he fell down the steps. And I ran to get help.

JENNIFER: Laura, what were your parents' attitudes about alcohol?

LAURA: Alcohol was not even allowed in our house because of my dad's experience with his father. This was confusing because, being Irish, the families I knew drank a lot. (Angrily) I had hoped that the man I would marry would not be a drinker. I was so disappointed when I saw the extent of Michael's drinking problem.

MICHAEL: I'm different from your family. Can't you respect that? In fact, when I was a boy, I always drank wine as part of Jewish holiday rituals. You can't even understand my Jewish heritage.

LAURA: I guess I don't understand you at times. Our backgrounds are so different.

JENNIFER: What we're addressing here are the ethnic and religious differences between you. We can understand from your stories how beliefs and judgments learned as a child impact you both today.

MICHAEL: She's just furious at me because I drank and had the affair. I had hoped we were past that.

In Laura and Michael's dialogue we clearly see the multiple levels of complexity affecting the couple and therapist system: the present marital crisis; gender, ethnic, and religious issues; the escalating rage; underlying fears and vulnerabilities concerning the survival of the relationship; and hidden family-of-origin influences. Still, the issue of alcoholism had not been directly addressed. All of these factors affect not only the couple's relationship but also Jennifer's interaction with them. Since Jennifer's religious and ethnic background was different from Laura's and Michael's, she brought her own learned prejudices into the room.

Internal Processing and Musings of Jennifer Reed

The last session with Laura and Michael left Jennifer feeling that something was amiss. In spite of the fact that many important issues had been brought to the surface, she knew that unless the drinking were directly addressed, the deeper work that lay ahead would not be accomplished.

Her countertransference issues with her own alcoholic background had delayed this realization.

JENNIFER: It feels as if our work together is moving to a deeper level. Your willingness to struggle and your courage to expose your vulnerabilities has led us to this place. At this point it seems important that we address the effect of problem drinking upon your couple system.

MICHAEL: I don't know if I'm ready for this now. I've tried to deal with it on my own before.

JENNIFER: What gave you the strength to do that?

LAURA: Soon after we met, I remember you went to a few AA meetings and then you stopped going.

MICHAEL: At first I tried to do it to please you. But you weren't very supportive. I don't think you even understood how hard it was for me.

LAURA: I didn't realize what a big problem it had already been for you.

JENNIFER: Alcohol has certainly played a major role in your relationship and now is an issue for you as a family. It deeply affects your relationship today and is also a transgenerational legacy.

MICHAEL: My father only drank heavily when he was under stress and when my mom ragged on him. I guess I do the same. (Michael turned and looked directly at Laura as he said this.)

LAURA: So now you're blaming me for your drinking?

JENNIFER: Growing up in your families has played a big part in how you each deal with the drinking today. Equally important to addressing the alcoholic behavior is understanding the patterns of your interaction that support it.

Because of the situation at home, with Laura no longer willing to tolerate the effects of Michael's drinking episodes and the negative impact upon the children, a crisis had been reached. The organization of Laura and Michael's system was no longer working. Laura was not willing to protect Michael in the way she had in the past, when her willingness to carry all the anxiety in their couple system had enabled and perpetuated his alcoholic behavior.

A change was stimulated when Laura stated that she would not continue to live with Michael unless he stopped drinking. Realizing that this was not an idle threat, Michael became alarmed. Even though some acknowledgment had been made about his father's and grandfather's excessive drinking, Michael was still in denial about the degree to which alcohol affected his life today. The drastic change in Laura's position finally prompted Michael's decision to take responsibility for his drinking.

Over the next two months, many changes took place. Michael began to attend AA meetings, and Laura joined Al-Anon. Slowly their system began to reorganize. What had once been an inflexible and blaming system became less rigid and more tentative as they experimented with new ways of being with themselves and each other. The therapist now redirected her focus to Laura and Michael as individuals, with an emphasis upon differentiation of self in each partner's family of origin. This redirection helped to alleviate the pressure in the marital system. In this phase of treatment, Jennifer collaborated with Laura and Michael as they worked toward stabilizing the family system during early sobriety.

As we have seen in this chapter, intense emotions are aroused in the therapist as well as in the couple. Transferential and countertransferential reactions occur simultaneously. Although both these concepts are specifically described and included in object relations literature, they are crucial components in all therapeutic relationships. Early primitive emotions emerge in the therapeutic triangle. In order for therapy to be successful, these processes must be addressed by therapists and couples alike.

At this time the therapeutic process has significantly deepened. The middle stage of couple therapy is well underway. Let us review the tasks that need to be accomplished during this stage (Table 8-1).

Table 8-1. Therapeutic Tasks in Middle Stage of Couple Therapy

1. Identify couple's patterns of interactions.
2. Explore how these patterns are linked to families of origin.
3. Acknowledge how patterns and beliefs restrain.
4. Collaborate with partners to consider alternative ways of interacting.
5. Empower partners by helping them accept their differences and distinguish between self and other.
6. Explore transferential and countertransferential responses.
7. Elicit partners' responses to therapy, and use this feedback to guide and refocus the work.

Chapter 10

The Untouchable Wound

Secrets abound in families. When they are perpetuated from one generation to the next, they become deep wounds. A festering sore that is neglected over time becomes infected. Similarly, secrets that pass from generation to generation become untouchable wounds. In Laura's family, the issues of depression and suicidality were unspoken. The fact of her mother's suicide was kept from the rest of the family by Laura and her father. As she grew up, she often hid her own depression by becoming overly positive and outgoing in nature. This way of relating served her well with other people. However, internally she often felt the emptiness and despondency of her childhood.

On Michael's side, the horror of his grandparents' experience in the Holocaust left its indelible mark upon the entire Greenberg family. When the topic of the Holocaust came up in elementary school, Michael's questions to his parents and grandparents went unanswered. As he grew up, nondisclosure became second nature to him. Relationships with parents and others suffered because of his internal isolation and despair. He became a container for the family's unexpressed emotion and bleak sense of the world.

JENNIFER: You left the last session with a lot of intensity. I'm curious how you both dealt with it.

MICHAEL: *(Looking at Laura)* Our week was pretty good. I'm not sure what we even talked about last week.

LAURA: I don't remember what we talked about. But I do remember feeling misunderstood.

MICHAEL: You said some pretty nasty things to me. I remember how angry you were.

LAURA: I felt so misunderstood. You didn't try to understand me.

MICHAEL: I felt like I was being stabbed when you said you were disappointed that you married a drinker.

LAURA: When you say it, it does sound awful. But don't I have a right to be furious that you stayed out all night? That felt like you were stabbing me.

JENNIFER: You're both enraged at one another. I wonder if we can look at this painful and vulnerable time as an opportunity to learn what these deep wounds are all about. Michael, perhaps we can try to talk about your grandparents' Holocaust experience and how it affects you today.

MICHAEL: I'm nervous about that topic because I don't know where it will take me. My heart began to pound and my hands started to sweat as soon as you brought up the subject.

LAURA: I guess I'm feeling nervous, too.

MICHAEL: I'm remembering now that the nervousness and sadness are the same feelings I had when I stayed overnight at my grandparents' house when I was a child. Even though I loved them both, sometimes I didn't want to go there because it always felt dark and dreary. There was one room no one ever went into. When I looked from the doorway, I could see a bureau that was covered with photographs framed in black. And the mirror above it was covered with a black cloth. There was a burning candle on the bureau.

(As Michael spoke, tears filled his eyes. All three of them became witnesses to the grandparents' pain-filled house. Silently, they became immersed in Michael's grief.)

JENNIFER: *(Softly)* How old were you, Michael, when you experienced this?

MICHAEL: I was probably about six or seven years old. I didn't learn what the photographs, covered mirror, and candle were all about until I was in my teens. Even then, when I asked, my mother had difficulty responding.

JENNIFER: What did you finally learn?

MICHAEL: I learned that the room was a shrine to all of my grandparents' relatives who were murdered in the camps. The candle was the memorial (yahrzeit) candle in memory of the dead, and the mirror was covered in their memory. When Jews are in mourning they often cover all the mirrors in the house. My mom also said she was afraid to go near that room or ask questions about it.

JENNIFER: Michael, your family's story is very moving. Laura, what's going on with you?

LAURA: I am so connected to Michael's sadness and pain that I can't tell whether it's his or mine. Somehow I've never felt closer to him.

JENNIFER: I wonder if that's because you understand him better now.

LAURA: I think so. It's the first time I've pictured him as a small vulnerable child.

MICHAEL: Sometimes today I still feel as lost and as lonely as I did then. I guess I just try to hide it better. There's one more thing I'm remembering. I was about eight when I asked my mom about the black numbers on my grandparents' arms. She said that when they were locked in a terrible concentration camp some bad men had put them on them. When my parents talked about sending me to camp when I was 11 or 12 I became terrified, had nightmares and refused to go. I kept thinking that if those numbers were put on my grandparents by bad people at camp why did my parents want to send me to a place like that?

Opening Windows of Vulnerability

One of our assumptions in doing couple work is that unresolved family-of-origin issues will crowd a couple's bed and become a barrier to intimacy. In the above dialogue, it became clear that an untouchable wound deeply affected Laura and Michael's present relationship. The strong emotions contained for years in the Greenberg family finally take their toll in the present generation.

Formerly, the alcoholic system had anesthetized this couple. However, now old wounds resurfaced and were addressed in the session as Jennifer worked individually with Laura and Michael. When Laura learned of Michael's early terror and pain, she was able to empathize and express her compassion. No longer did Michael feel so alone. Through this empathic connection, partners are able to begin the healing process with each other. While working with one individual, the therapist must also pay close attention to the listening and observing partner. Jennifer alternates her focus from the intrapsychic work with Michael to the interpersonal relationship of the couple.

Afterward, as Jennifer thought about the session, she felt remiss. In her attempt to focus the entire session upon Michael's pain, she had not attended to Laura's vulnerability. As Laura and Michael walked into the next session it was apparent that Laura's first words corroborated Jennifer Reed's thoughts.

LAURA: Our last session stayed with me all week. Michael spent more time with the family, and I felt much closer to him. We talked about the stuff we covered here last week. It amazed me that we've been together for so long, and I never really knew how painful Michael's childhood was.

MICHAEL: I never really faced it either. I thought our family just had a deep dark secret, and I had to keep it to myself.

JENNIFER: And what a burden that was for such a young child to carry. Laura, what burdens and worries did you carry as a child?

LAURA: I think I was born worrying. I never remember being a carefree child. My mom always seemed fragile. I know she had a miscarriage after I was born. And then it seemed she was always pregnant, nursing, and not feeling well. My dad always worried about her.

JENNIFER: What do you know about the miscarriage?

LAURA: Very little. We didn't talk about it much but my dad told me that my mom never got over it. My sisters and I always wondered if it was a boy.

JENNIFER: You and Michael both were confused little children. This often happens when families are secretive.

LAURA: I guess my dad was just trying to protect me. He probably thought I was too young to understand. All it really did was confuse me. Even when my grandparents died, no one talked about their deaths. It was as if it didn't happen.

JENNIFER: So grief and loss were not dealt with openly in your family-of-origin either.

LAURA: That's probably why we never talked about my mom's suicide. It was a taboo topic. I thought it was because my dad was so ashamed that my mom left him like she did. But now I'm wondering if the silence was because death was never talked about in our family.

MICHAEL: Boy, shame and death were taboo topics in both of our families. We were taught to keep secrets. No wonder we have trouble being open with each other.

JENNIFER: You've both done very important and powerful work in the last two sessions. It already has and will continue to impact your lives together. Your courage here bodes well for continuing to build good will and commitment in your relationship.

The Impact of Stories, Secrets, and Myths

Families give meaning to their lives through the stories they tell. These stories influence our perceptions and often determine how we interpret life events. In fact, while telling stories, people are actively shaping their lives and relationships (White & Epston, 1990). Sometimes family members avoid talking about particular issues. The unspoken word may become very powerful indeed, and the silence that prevails often results in a very confusing situation, particularly for children. In *The Dance of Deception* (p.142), Harriet Lerner writes about the negative power of secrets: "When children sense a disturbance in the field, but do not feel free to ask questions, they flounder in unconscious fantasies that cannot be put to rest."

Certainly for Michael and Laura, the family stories and secrets about loss and death had a profound impact upon their later lives. As we have seen in the dialogue in this chapter, they both learned that death and suicide were taboo topics. Thus they learned to silence their voices in these areas. Imagine the energy it takes for an individual to carry an internal vigilance in order to keep the secret. These constraints took their toll on this couple. However, the couple therapy became an arena in which the family myths and secrets were examined and understood, and thus served as a valuable channel for new communication.

Grief, Loss, and Healing

By acknowledging the enormity of their losses, Laura and Michael had begun the process of grieving together. The unresolved grief and loss that had been passed down from generation to generation was now being addressed in couple therapy. Until these important issues are brought to the surface, the family grief will continue to affect the couple system in subtle ways. The mourning process provides the opportunity to do the work that will free them from the powerful constraints of the past. As they witness each other's childhood anguish, healing occurs, and a new intimacy becomes possible.

Secrecy and Shame

In the preceding dialogue, Laura and Michael were both enveloped by the shame and secrecy in their families. Shame is an important dynamic that generally operates out of consciousness in the couple system. It is of paramount importance that therapists clearly understand how shame emerges in the couple system. Balcom, Lee, and Tager (1995, p. 56) write that "Systemic shame occurs when one member of the couple feels shame (triggered by either an internal or external event) and expresses it verbally or nonverbally in a manner that intentionally or unintentionally induces shame in the partner." In a shame-based couple system there is constant fighting, with issues never resolved, incessant blaming, and little or no good will toward one another.

Secrets in a family often reinforce shame and erode the self-esteem of the entire system. In Laura and Michael's case, the secrets of the Holocaust, suicidality, and alcoholism all led to a shame-based relationship. The presenting problem of Michael's affair was the culmination of the underlying secrecy and shame in the couple system.

How does the therapist learn to recognize and become attuned to the various manifestations of shame? Most importantly, we must understand the presence of shame in our own lives. Because of the primitive nature of shame, this acknowledgment is difficult for therapists as well as for clients. Once the therapist has become self-aware, the next step is to listen to the language of shame. This is expressed verbally and nonverbally by our clients. Verbal expressions include: "I'm ashamed." "I'm humiliated." "I feel worthless." "I always feel angry!" "I'm depressed." In Laura's first telephone conversation with Jennifer, her words, "I'm a mess . . . I'm hurting," alerted Jennifer to the underlying shame. Laura and Michael's verbal exchange during their very first session is an excellent example of a shame-based couple interaction:

LAURA: What did I ever do to you that you would cheat on me, humiliate me, and have an affair with one of our friends? You're such a coward. I had to find the love letter from Susan in the back of your drawer underneath your socks and underwear. It's almost as if you wanted me to find out.

MICHAEL: *(As Michael listened, he sat shamefaced and contrite. Then, suddenly, his face reddened, as he angrily raised his voice.)* You have had a goddamned affair with the kids, the house, your demanding sister, your father and everything that excluded me! I was never a priority with you. Marriage was just a word. I was your meal ticket and the bill payer.

Nonverbal expressions of shame can often be detected in the experience of the session. Flushes of embarrassment, avoidance of eye contact, physical withdrawal, and extended silences are all evidence of the presence of shame.

Exploring the Nonverbal Realm

Jennifer takes this opportunity to punctuate the process and consolidate the gains made thus far. She utilizes a nonverbal exercise with Laura and Michael to accomplish this. It is often useful to pause in therapy to look at the big picture. This enables the couple to refocus their goals and explore the question—where do we go from here? Let us now turn to a discussion of the interplay of verbal and nonverbal communication and then proceed with dialogue that illustrates the use of both.

As we have seen from these sessions, therapy involves more than the spoken word. An axiom of communication is that *one cannot **not** communicate* (Watzlawick, Beavin, & Jackson, 1967). Gestures, glances, body postures, and silences are all ways of communicating nonverbally. This metacommunication often accompanies a verbal message and sometimes alters its meaning. When mixed messages arise in the therapy session, it is important that the therapist be aware of the metacommunication. We must distinguish between messages sent and messages received. What are the choices for intervention when this situation arises? One very useful technique in our experience is the talking and listening exercise. Skilled as we both think we are as "communicators," we personally sometimes find that the message that we intend is not the message received. This can occur with each other, a colleague, a friend, a mate, a child. And so, of course, it will occur often in the therapeutic encounter.

For example, consider this situation: Don compliments Sarah's appearance as they prepare to go out for the evening but then gives her a disapproving look when she is fully dressed. This mixed message totally confuses her. Did he really mean that he likes her appearance? Was he just trying to placate her? What does the disapproving glance mean?

In order to help this couple communicate more clearly, the therapist asks Sarah to verbalize her confusion and state the message that she heard from Don. The therapist then checks with him whether this was the message he intended. If not, Don restates the message he intended. We keep going back and forth until an understanding is reached and the message intended is the one received. This exercise does not always work with very embattled couples; nevertheless, the process of asking the questions plants the seeds for other ways of thinking, responding, and reflecting, and so reactivity is reduced.

Other verbal methods we have discussed thus far in the book are internalized-other interviewing and various types of questioning. Sometimes, however, words alone are not adequate to describe a situation. Words at times are limiting, and therapists need other modes of expression, such as psychodrama, dance therapy, sculpting, art therapy, journal writing, visualization, and guided imagery.

A Psychodramatic Journey with Laura and Michael

We will now turn our attention to the use of a modified form of psychodrama in our work with Laura and Michael. A psychodramatic enactment of their crowded bed will be a powerful nonverbal experience for this couple.

JENNIFER: Our last two sessions together have been very moving. I've been thinking about the many powerful forces from the past that influence your relationship today. I wonder if you both would consider looking at these issues in a nonverbal way.
MICHAEL: What's the point of it? I'm already so drained from talking about my past and our problems.
JENNIFER: I'm sure you are, Michael. It has been a painful journey. I thought the exercise I have in mind might be a way to consolidate the hard work the two of you have done here and punctuate it in a meaningful way.
LAURA: I like the idea of pulling our work here together. We've talked about so many different things, and I feel so overwhelmed by it all at times. Michael seems to be able to put it together more easily than I do.
MICHAEL: I'm not so sure about that. Sometimes none of it makes sense to me. So even though I'm reluctant, maybe this will help me too.
JENNIFER: I appreciate your willingness to try something new. What I'd like you to do today is to look at your crowded bed in a nonverbal way. I'd like you first to imagine that the couch you are sitting upon is the bed you sleep in at home. Then I'd like you to use the pillows around this room to represent each of the issues, family members, images, and memories that fill your bed.
LAURA: I'm not sure there are enough pillows here.
JENNIFER: If you run out of them, feel free to use any other objects in this room. What are your reactions so far to this different kind of session?
MICHAEL: It feels a little weird but I'll try it.
LAURA: I like the idea of something different.
JENNIFER: As you each take your turn, I'll guide you. Which one of you would like to go first?
LAURA: I guess I'm feeling gutsy enough to finally go first *(all three of them laugh as Laura says this)*.
JENNIFER: Let's begin, Laura, with you imagining that this couch is your bed at home. Start to think about those times when your bed feels comfortable for just the two of you. Reflect upon this silently and notice how you are experiencing these thoughts and memories. I notice you are closing your eyes as you respond. Continue to immerse yourself in this experience.

(Note that Jennifer Reed respectfully follows Laura's pace and pauses before moving on. At the same time she tracks Michael's reactions as she observes his body language.)

JENNIFER: Laura, now I'd like you to think about the times when your marital bed does not feel so comfortable. Allow yourself a moment to reflect about this place. When you're there, I'd like you to open your eyes. Use the pillows in this room to represent the various things that crowd your bed at home and place them on the couch in this office. Continue to do this silently.

Laura slowly and thoughtfully places two pillows on each end of the couch. She then puts five other pillows at various spots between them, glancing at Michael from time to time as she does this. After a few moments she steps back to survey the "bed."

JENNIFER: Laura, as you observe what you have done, I wonder if you can tell us about it.

LAURA: The pillow that represented my mom was the hardest for me to put in the bed. Since it is the anniversary of her death this week, I've been thinking more about her. One of the pillows represents the children, one my dad, one my sisters, and the other my in-laws. The first two that I placed at either end of the bed were for Michael and me.

JENNIFER: So, how do you think all of these family members affect your relationship with Michael?

LAURA: As I look at the bed, I'm surprised that there's so much separating us. No wonder we needed therapy.

MICHAEL: I think there are even more things that we take to our bed with us.

JENNIFER: Do you want to take your turn now and add them?

MICHAEL solemnly gets up and picks up two more pillows and adds them to the bed. He places one next to the pillow representing Laura and the other next to the pillow representing himself. He then takes the two remaining pillows in the office and arbitrarily tosses them in the bed. After stepping back and surveying his work, he returns to the bed, retrieves the pillow representing himself, and places it on the floor a few feet away. Sadly he returns to his original chair in Jennifer Reed's office.

LAURA: *(Looking surprised and startled)* Michael, what made you remove yourself from our bed?

MICHAEL: I surprised myself also. As I started adding more things to our bed, I realized that I still feel crowded out at times. Although I'm no longer relegated to the couch and the children are not physically in bed with us, there is a lot that still gets between us and interferes in our lives. I'm no longer blaming you for that, Laura. A lot of it is mine.

JENNIFER: Do you know what he is referring to, Laura?

LAURA: No, I don't. Michael, can you tell me what the pillows represent that you added to our bed?

MICHAEL: Well, the first pillow that I placed next to you represents your fears about mental illness that I know are connected to your mom's suicide. The pillow that I placed next to me stands for my grandparents' experience in the Holocaust and how that affects our lives today. The other two pillows I added each represent my work and Alcoholics Anonymous, two big influences in our lives. When I stepped back and looked at how filled up our bed was, I became overwhelmed so I removed my pillow. It was almost as if there was no room for me in it.

LAURA: I become overwhelmed with all of it, too. But I don't withdraw like you, Michael, when I feel this way.

JENNIFER: I wonder what would happen, Michael, if, instead of withdrawing when you become overwhelmed, you stayed with Laura and talked?

MICHAEL: I'm not sure I could do that. I'm not even sure Laura could either.

JENNIFER: Laura, how do you imagine you might respond if Michael developed the courage to sit with you despite his discomfort with the intensity?

LAURA: We've talked about this in our sessions before. I think it's hard for both of us.

JENNIFER: Yes, we are revisiting an issue we discussed previously. Managing intensity is a subject for all couples to grapple with. What do you think would happen if you both made an agreement to stay together during moments of intensity even if it were for a limited time?

(Laura and Michael look expectantly at each other. The tension and discomfort they both feel are reflected in their body language.)

LAURA: I guess we could try it.

JENNIFER: I can understand your hesitation. The decision to try a new behavior is certainly a risk. I have already observed your ability and willingness to sit with difficult moments in our therapy sessions. So I think we are really talking about solidifying your gains in this area.

Jennifer used the reenactment of a previously acknowledged pattern to punctuate gains already made by the couple. She also used several reflexive questions as the session moved toward closure. The nonverbal exercise became a stimulus for discussion about Laura and Michael's reactions to managing intensity. This dialogue demonstrates the interplay of the usual verbal dialogue with the nonverbal exercise.

Exploring the nonverbal realm in therapy may deepen the experience for clients and therapists. Of course, the therapist's consciousness of the whole range of subjective responses is fundamental to effective clinical work. Spontaneous emotional responses may occur in our clients at any time, and we must be open to these expressive responses. The therapist may choose to explore the nonverbal realm with highly verbal clients in order to access deeper layers of consciousness than might ordinarily be available. The following methods have proven useful in tapping into our clients' unconscious processes: guided imagery, visualization, art therapy, mapping, genogram construction, aspects of psychodrama, internalized-other interviewing, and family sculpting. Since all of these methods are vehicles to the unconscious, the therapist must carefully track clients' responses as they shift to another way of working. As people tap into deeper levels of consciousness, formerly unknown perceptions, thoughts, and feelings may be experienced. The therapist must be aware of these possibilities and pay attention to the interactional processes of the couple or family as the work unfolds. Examples of this attention to process and content were evident as Jennifer explored the nonverbal realm with Laura and Michael. They have begun to understand how the family stories, secrets, losses, and shame inside each of them affect their relationship. Understanding their subjective worlds in greater depth not only benefits their couple relationship but also produces reverberations throughout the entire family. In the next chapter we will see how this ripple effect of change impacts the family system.

Chapter 11

The Ripple Effect of Change

As Jennifer thought about her work with Laura and Michael, she realized they were approaching the fifteenth session. With only six sessions remaining of the twenty agreed upon earlier, the termination process must now begin. From Jennifer's perspective, much had been explored as this young couple moved from crisis to deeper therapeutic work in a brief period of time.

Jennifer was aware of her warm feelings and fondness for Laura and Michael as she went to greet them in the waiting room. Before she opened the door, the sound of young children's laughter took her by surprise. When she entered the waiting room, young Jonathan was sitting in Laura's lap, while five-year-old Emma and her younger sister Amanda were giggling and wrestling on the floor. Laura quickly explained that the children's nanny had unexpectedly been called home to be with her ailing mother. Rather than cancel at the last minute, Laura had decided to bring the children with her. Since she had been unable to reach Michael, she wondered aloud what he would think of her decision. Just at this moment, Michael walked in. His expression of surprise mixed with delight answered her question. The girls ran to hug him, and the five of them joined Jennifer in her cozy and inviting office. Drawing paper and crayons immediately occupied the girls, while the cuddly bear in the corner drew Jonathan's attention.

JENNIFER: How wonderful it is to meet the entire Greenberg clan.
LAURA: Michael, I tried to reach you to tell you that Rose had to leave

because of her mother's illness, but you had already left the office. I decided to bring the kids rather than miss the session. I felt it would probably be OK with you. And secretly, I wanted to show them off.

MICHAEL: Well, let's see if we can rise above the noise level here. We often have trouble hearing each other talk at home.

JENNIFER: We can use this session as an opportunity to look at how you are working as a team with the children. After all, you have both made so many changes in your marriage. The children undoubtedly feel the effects of these changes.

At this moment, Emma and Amanda began to argue over the red crayon. Looking at Michael, Laura resisted her urge to mediate. Michael nodded approvingly to Laura as the girls settled their own difference.

LAURA: I guess it's hard for me not to interfere, but I'm learning. And since Michael stopped drinking, he really backs me up with the children. He helps to make me feel more sure of myself.

MICHAEL: I'm glad I'm doing that for you. I don't always do it for myself. When the house is noisy, it feels very shaky and chaotic for me.

JENNIFER: Laura, are you aware of Michael's shakiness?

LAURA: I am. That's why I always tried to stop the kids' fights.

JENNIFER: With drinking no longer part of your relationship, you're both trying to learn new ways to comfort one another.

Apparently picking up the anxiety in her parents' voices, Emma moved away from her drawing during this interchange and approached the three adults.

EMMA: I like it best when Mommy and Daddy are laughing. And I hate it when they fight.

JENNIFER: What do Amanda and Jonathan do when they fight?

EMMA: Jonathan cries, and Amanda covers her ears.

JENNIFER: And what do you do, Emma, when Jonathan cries and Amanda covers her ears?

EMMA: I get scared that Daddy will go away again.

As Emma and Jennifer spoke, Laura and Michael looked worriedly at each other. Their surprised looks indicated they were hearing the fear of abandonment from Emma for the first time.

MICHAEL: Emma, I didn't know that you were scared that I'd leave again. When I was unhappy and confused, I did a lot of things I shouldn't have.

And I'm sorry now. But Mommy and I want you to know that this lady is helping us. I'm not going to leave any of you again.

Emma's smile indicated her relief at hearing this. Amanda, too, had stopped drawing and listened carefully. Jonathan hugged his bear. A calm seemed to come over the room.

LAURA: I'm glad the whole family came in today. Our kids really pick up on everything that is going on. Maybe we better listen to them more.
JENNIFER: Learning to listen to each other has had a ripple effect with your children. Emma's verbal openness is in direct response to your availability, willingness, and capacity to hear.

Effects of Couple Therapy upon the Children

When children accompany parents to family therapy, the sessions are often more chaotic than the above dialogue would suggest. Usually we see an entire family at a time of crisis, when one of the children is viewed as the identified patient. In this particular case, the presenting problem was Michael's affair, and the couple had worked through this crisis. They were now able to function as a strong parenting team and were, indeed, proud of this accomplishment. Emma's openness was evidence of the safety she now felt with her parents. As Laura and Michael redefined their coupleship, the chaotic, alcoholic system was transformed. The boundaries and structure of the family became clearer, and the children knew their parents were in charge. When Laura and Michael started to thrive in this more secure environment, so did the children.

Effects of Couple Therapy upon Family-of-Origin

Following the session with the children, the entire family went back East to visit Michael's parents for the Thanksgiving holiday. Although his parents had been divorced for years, they maintained a friendly relationship. Since neither had remarried, they often spent holidays together. As a matter of fact, their divorce worked out better than their marriage. Since each highly valued the relationship with their only child, there was much enthusiasm around the visits of Michael and his family. During an early session, Michael had spoken about anxiety-filled visits to his parents. More recently, he had expressed a desire to talk with his parents about some of his childhood memories. Michael's newfound openness with his own children had a profound affect upon him. His longing for a deeper connection with his own parents began to emerge.

Jennifer had worked with Laura and Michael to prepare for this visit home. She had taught Michael how to use circular questions as a non-threatening approach to his parents. Instead of directly questioning his mother about her reactions to the Holocaust experience, he asked her about his grandparents' responses. When questioned in this way, she was less defensive. Not only did she talk about her parents, but she also began to relate her own enormous fears as a child. Michael began to have a deeper understanding of his own fears. Since it was not this family's usual pattern of relating, Michael and his mother soon retreated to a more comfortable distance. However, this moment of intensity left an indelible mark. The generational pattern of silence had shifted. Although important questions were answered, many still remained unanswered.

As Michael reported the visit to Jennifer, he was pleased with the results of the efforts he had made. Since he felt less reactive to his parents, his own anxiety was reduced. When anxiety is decreased in one's family of origin, the pressure is reduced in the nuclear family. What had started within Laura and Michael's nuclear family moved up a generation to Michael's work with his parents. The effect of these changes now filtered back down to his children. This is a clear example of the ripple effect of change.

As Laura and Michael entered Jennifer's office, their voices were high-pitched and tinged with anxiety. Before Jennifer could comment upon her observation, Laura started to speak.

LAURA: We both arrived early to meet for lunch at that cute little coffee shop downstairs. We began to get a little scared that we only have a few sessions left. Aside from missing you, we're wondering how we're going to get along on our own.

MICHAEL: What happens if we go back to our old ways together? I'm nervous that we won't remember what we've learned here.

JENNIFER: I, too, will miss you and our work together. I have great respect for your courage and for your willingness to address your struggles. It shows your commitment to your relationship and your family.

LAURA: I didn't know how deep our commitment was or whether our marriage would even stay together when we first came in here.

JENNIFER: Nevertheless, you both took the risk to address very painful family issues. By examining old wounds and learning to talk more meaningfully and differently to one another, you have changed your relationship. It is very different now. As my grandmother used to say, "You can't turn a pickle back into a cucumber!"

MICHAEL: *(Laughing)* I'll remember that. But just in case we run into trouble, I'm glad you'll be here. Won't you?

JENNIFER: *(Reassuringly)* I certainly plan to be here. And I understand your concerns about ending therapy. Any ending activates responses to earlier losses. Perhaps if memories of these losses come up for you during our next few weeks, we can talk about them.

MICHAEL: One of the things I've noticed recently is how much closer Laura and I have become. I was really looking forward to our lunch together today. It felt like a date. Our sex life has improved too *(winking at Laura)*.

LAURA: *(Face reddening)* It has not only improved. It's better than ever. Especially with the kids sleeping in their own rooms.

JENNIFER: Your newfound closeness does sound wonderful. I noticed, however, that our conversation shifted from talk of ending therapy to a more positive note. And, on that note, one of the things I've been thinking about is how to incorporate new rituals into your life that will support the changes you've made. At the moment, we are immersed in the ritual of ending therapy.

MICHAEL: It's hard now to talk about losses and ending therapy. Talking with my parents last week was enough loss for me. I need time to digest that.

(Jennifer Reed was respectful of Michael's obvious reluctance to talk about loss.)

JENNIFER: I can certainly understand what you're saying, Michael. You did important work with your parents. And you'll be digesting that for a long time. Laura, you probably will too. I'll respect your pacing as we wind down these last few weeks.

MICHAEL: Thanks, I really appreciate that. You've always been so respectful of both of us. I'll miss our sessions together.

LAURA: Me, too. I'm feeling sad about saying goodbye. I've never been good with goodbyes.

During this session the termination process was specifically addressed. Clients' responses to ending therapy vary. It is important that the therapist acknowledge the closure of therapy. In the following chapter, Laura, Michael, and Jennifer continue to process closure. Along with this acknowledgment, Jennifer has planted the seed for the idea of rituals to further continue the discussion to support the changes Laura and Michael have made.

Rituals Relating to the Life Cycle

During our assessment process, we pay particular attention to the family's rituals and keep them in mind as we facilitate conversations. Many rituals are not conscious. That is, the family members are not aware that they are ongoing interactive patterns. For example, with a newly married couple one of us recently saw in therapy, we learned of the young bride's pattern of speaking with her mother every evening. This long-established ritual interfered with the couple's time together and produced tension between them. What was once a bonding ritual between mother and daughter must now be reassessed as this young couple makes the transition into a new life-cycle stage.

All cultures have rituals that mark beginnings, endings, and transitions throughout the life cycle. They may mark major events or be as simple as sharing breakfast together. In Laura and Michael's nuclear family, reading stories to their children at bedtime was a simple and important ritual. However, transgenerationally, the process of attending to loss was virtually absent. The survival of Michael's grandparents in the Holocaust, the divorce of his parents, and the suicide of Laura's mother were traumatic events that were not clearly marked or ritualized. In therapy, Laura and Michael acquired ways to identify, deepen their understanding of, and give meaning to these events. Examples of these recently developed rituals are visits to Laura's mother's grave as well as a cemetery visit to Michael's grandparents. In this way they were able to develop ways to mark the losses and thus facilitate the expression of grief. Evan Imber-Black (1991, p. 207) writes that rituals "mark the loss of a member, affirm the life lived by the person who has died, facilitate the expression of grief." She also points out that rituals allow for expression of pain while at the same time encouraging connectedness among family members. This is certainly congruent with our personal and clinical experiences.

The theme of loss has appeared repeatedly throughout this book. We have expressed our belief that unresolved grief is a barrier to intimacy and have presented ways to address this life dilemma in relationships. Jennifer has guided her clients toward conversations that have been healing and that have stimulated the expression of unresolved grief. These therapeutic conversations have also moved Laura and Michael into dialogues about new ways to enrich life events, handle conflict, and deal with loss. During the termination phase of therapy, we have the opportunity to actively model a ritual of ending and saying goodbye. We presume that clients learn through the therapy process a new way to address loss that they may use in other life stages. Newly formed rituals enhance change in these areas.

Chapter 12

Endings and New Beginnings

With every loss and ending, space opens up for a new beginning. Even with clients who find it difficult to say goodbye, the termination process is a model for moving on to the next developmental stage. This process evokes memories of earlier experiences of loss and endings. Old wounds can now be healed in the context of the present relationship. The therapeutic encounter becomes a paradigm for a different and corrective experience.

During their therapeutic journey, Laura and Michael had learned how to address and negotiate the various stages and accompanying tasks of their marriage. They now had the necessary tools to handle the developmental challenges that inevitably face every couple and family. Although still immersed in reshaping and redefining their relationship, Laura and Michael would leave therapy with a greater sense of clarity and hope for their future together.

During the next few sessions, Jennifer focused upon the tasks of the last stage of therapy. These tasks and some accompanying questions are listed in Table 12-1. We have listed and numbered these tasks in a sequential fashion. However, they are circular and overlapping. Managed care has compelled us to view the termination process in a more focused way. Because of the brevity of the work, thoughts of termination begin with the first session. No longer do we have the luxury of open-ended work. Our philosophy now incorporates the idea that "less is more." Our experience has been that longer-term work does not necessarily yield a better outcome. Our couples leave therapy with the knowledge that work on their relationship is a lifelong process. They have acquired the skills that will enable them to build upon newly acquired competencies. Knowledge of their individual patterns expands to their interpersonal relationship, and each partner takes responsibility for his or her contribution to the matter at hand. Since Laura and Michael have learned to shift from linear to circular thinking, they are now able to experience their coupleship in a more expansive way.

TABLE 12-1. *Tasks in Terminating Stage of Therapy*

1. Acknowledge closure and loss of therapeutic relationship.
2. Explore earlier reactions and patterns of grief and loss. How have the individual and couple experienced separations and loss in the past? How was loss dealt with in family of origin? Are partners' reactions to handling loss today similar to or different from lessons learned in family of origin?
3. Review what the individual and couple have learned and gained from therapy experience. What strengths and resources have been recognized by clients during the course of the work? What have the partners learned about their patterns and interactions as a couple and as individuals?
4. Assess and facilitate further self-work. Encourage partners to use and build upon newly acquired competencies and skills. Incorporate new rituals into relationship.
5. Experience a model of an ending that is mutual and caring.
6. Model moving on to the next developmental stage. How will couple's changes affect them in their larger context? For example, how will their changes affect them as individuals and as a couple with their parents, their children, and in the wider community?

Although the warmth of the last session still permeated the therapeutic system, tension and sadness were evident as Laura and Michael entered the office.

JENNIFER: *(Silently aware of her own sadness as the end of therapy approached)* It feels a bit heavy in here today. I'm aware that our work together is coming to a close.

LAURA: I had a bad dream last night and woke up feeling scared.

JENNIFER: Tell us about it.

LAURA: I dreamed about my mother's death. I knew she had died because my dad, my sisters, and I were all home together. Something terrible had happened, and no one was saying anything about it. And when I woke up, I had an empty feeling in the pit of my stomach. I was so upset that I talked to Michael about the dream.

(Jennifer glanced at Michael as Laura spoke. He, too, felt the intensity and was relieved that Laura had the opportunity to talk about the dream further in therapy.)

LAURA: After my mom died, I had similar dreams very often, but I haven't had them for many years. I feel like I am reliving her death, and I still have that pit in my stomach now. It's like she died all over again.

JENNIFER: As we talked about last session, any significant ending activates responses to earlier losses. It sounds as if your dream is a clear example of this process. Your loss at the time of your mom's death was overwhelming. Not only did you lose your mom, but there were additional losses that occurred for you because of her death. You gave up your college experience, and you lost your sibling position when you had to fill Mom's role.

LAURA: *(Crying)* I guess I lost myself too at that time. I was starting to have so much fun at college, and that was suddenly taken away from me. At times I was angry about it all, but I felt guilty having those feelings.

MICHAEL: That's the first time you've ever mentioned being angry about anything relating to your mom's death. It seemed like I was the only one you ever got angry at.

JENNIFER: Apparently a lot of Laura's repressed anger was displaced onto you. Often unresolved grief becomes a barrier to intimacy. This went on in your family, too, Michael. When this grief is finally acknowledged, a closer, more intimate relationship is possible.

LAURA: So are my tears for now or for then?

JENNIFER: For both. The loss of therapy is stirring up all the losses related to your mom's death. You're grieving for both periods of time.

In this session with Laura and Michael, we see how the past and present converge. Earlier losses are reexperienced as the termination process is explored. Although many couples are reluctant to say goodbye, it is important that the therapist attend to the tasks of this last phase of therapy. Of course, the therapist's own attitude toward loss is of paramount importance. If she has not acknowledged and addressed issues of endings in her own life, she will avoid this important stage and collude with couples who are uncomfortable with closure. In this case, however, Jennifer brings a willingness and focus to this last stage. Earlier reactions and patterns of grief and loss emerge and are explored.

As Jennifer thought about the remaining tasks of closure to be accomplished in this last session, she was aware of her own feelings of sadness. Terminations usually brought up her own feelings of grief and loss. Since she had worked through many of these family-of-origin issues for herself, she was now able to fully address this important clinical issue. Even if a therapist is aware of his or her own personal process, the ending of intense therapeutic relationships, whether long-term or brief, is usually emotional and highly charged.

MICHAEL: I have something I want to clear up. You said earlier that Laura's repressed anger was displaced onto me. And you said that this went on in my family, too. It is hard for me to make sense of all that.

JENNIFER: What we talked about was that unresolved grief is a barrier to intimacy. In both of your families the grief process was avoided—in Laura's with the suicide of her mother, and in yours, Michael, with the unspoken legacy of the Holocaust. You then entered your marriage, and this unresolved grief restrained your relationship. When people learn to disown their sadness, anger often becomes an expression of their vulnerability. So in this situation, Laura's formerly repressed anger was displaced onto you.

MICHAEL: OK, now I understand it better.

LAURA: I feel relieved to know that we both understand it because I don't feel like the bad guy. Expressing anger was always hard for me. It was easier for me to express sadness, and I'm feeling real sad now. I don't like endings, and I don't like the thought of not seeing you again *(turning to Jennifer Reed)*.

MICHAEL: It's funny that I didn't want to come here to begin with, and today I don't want to leave.

JENNIFER: The ending of our work together has brought up sad feelings in me, too. It feels as if we've all struggled together, and your relationship has evolved and blossomed. I'll miss seeing you both.

LAURA: All endings are hard for me. My mother died so suddenly that I never had a chance to say goodbye to her. Since then I've always avoided goodbyes. This is the first time I have faced an ending, and I have mixed feelings about it.

JENNIFER: That's understandable. Old patterns are hard to change.

MICHAEL: In my family, death was always alluded to because of the Holocaust, but it was never spoken about directly. This is the first awareness I have had that endings don't necessarily mean death.

JENNIFER: What an important insight that is for you, Michael! Each of you has learned to handle loss and endings in a different way. And you'll be able to use these new skills as your family moves through various life transitions.

MICHAEL: All this talk about loss and endings makes me realize that my parents won't be around forever. It seems important that I continue the conversations with them that began on my last trip home.

LAURA: And I guess I won't have my dad forever either. We both need to plan more family trips. I want our children to really know their grandparents.

JENNIFER: Sounds like you'll be incorporating what you've learned here within each of your families for some time to come. It will be an interesting and exciting journey as family members react to each other in new ways.

MICHAEL: Our journey in this office has certainly taken many twists and turns. We're pretty well-prepared in case the road gets bumpy. And just in case things get too hard for us to handle, can we return for a tune-up?

JENNIFER: Sure. My door is always open for you. And I think we're all having a hard time saying goodbye. I'm noticing our time was up a few minutes ago.

As all three rose from their chairs, there was a moment of silence. Laura embraced Jennifer first, and Michael then put his arms around both of them. The moment was warm and poignant. As Laura and Michael left the office holding hands, Jennifer smiled and felt mixed emotions. On the one hand, she felt proud and gratified; on the other hand, she felt an enormous loss.

Varieties of Endings in Therapy

With this particular couple, the termination process went extremely well. Unfortunately, not all therapeutic encounters end in this way. Some couples terminate prematurely for a variety of reasons: (1) therapist and couple may not have joined well; (2) amelioration of presenting crisis has occurred and couple does not wish to continue further; (3) financial reasons obstruct continuing therapy; (4) hidden and unspoken agendas on the part of one partner interfere with the course of therapy; and (5) couple's transference and therapist's countertransference impede the process. Let us elaborate briefly on each of these scenarios.

1. Therapist and Couple May Not Have Joined Well

Generally, it is the therapist's responsibility to join with each partner as well as with the couple system. However, in certain instances, this task is not accomplished. For example, one of us had great difficulty joining with a couple of a different culture. Although they both spoke some English, the language barrier impeded understanding between therapist and the couple system. Additionally, since personal disclosure of any kind was not acceptable in that culture, joining felt almost impossible. This couple was referred to a colleague who was of their culture and with whom there was a better fit.

2. Amelioration of Presenting Crisis Has Occurred and Couple Does Not Wish To Continue Further

Although a crisis initially propels a couple into therapy, the partners may choose to terminate after a few sessions. A case in point was a couple referred by a gynecologist for pregnancy counseling. Once the decision to terminate the pregnancy was made, the couple also decided to quickly terminate therapy. They chose not to examine any underlying issues at this time. (They did, however, resume therapy at a later date when another crisis occurred.)

3. Financial Reasons Obstruct Continuing Therapy

Sometimes insurance benefits, managed care limitations, and financial reversals impinge upon the therapy. Depending upon the specific situation, the options may include cessation of therapy, renegotiation of fee, or taking a break from therapy until financial circumstances allow resumption of the work. In some instances, referral to a low-fee clinic may be appropriate.

4. Hidden and Unspoken Agendas on the Part of One Partner Interfere with the Course of Therapy

Sometimes unspoken agendas are conscious, but more often they are unconscious. A fairly typical example of a conscious agenda is when one of the partners already knows he or she wants to leave the marriage. This person's intention has not been verbalized. Often the therapist will do individual work with the "abandoned partner." When the agenda is unconscious, the work involves bringing it to consciousness.

5. Couple's Transference and Therapist's Countertransference Impede the Process

One of the couples one of us saw felt they had made a mistake by seeing a female therapist. During the first session, one of the partners verbalized feelings of discomfort and said he thought a male therapist would be more appropriate for them. Upon further exploration it was learned that both of them thought a male would be stronger in handling their rage. They felt they would be inhibited in relating to a female.

Enormous stress and vulnerability in a therapist's own life often lead to countertransferential issues. For example, the death of a parent has affected each of us and has necessitated professional changes. One of us reduced our client load for a period of time. The other took a six-month sabbatical from supervisory and teaching responsibilities.

Termination is a catalyst for change. During this last phase of therapy, there is an opportunity to review the multiple levels and layers of the complexities in a couple's relationship. As Laura and Michael's crowded bed emptied out, they learned to work as a team, took more risks with each other, and found new energy as a couple. By examining the restraints of their past, witnessing each other's deep pain, and healing old wounds, they were able to reach a new level of commitment and understanding.

Part III

Our Step-by-Step Treatment Format with Various Populations

Chapter 13

Becoming a Couple in a Mixed Marriage

We refer to "mixed marriages" as those unions in which the partners bring to the relationship different racial, religious, ethnic, cultural, class, and/ or socioeconomic influences. While coming from different backgrounds brings a richness to these relationships, it also adds many complexities that must be addressed, especially at the early stage of becoming a couple.

TABLE 13-1. *Assumptions Underlying Our Couple Work*

---

1. Universally, the couple is an evolving relationship which goes through a series of developmental stages.
2. At each stage, there are relationship tasks that must be accomplished.
3. The negotiation of these tasks is profoundly influenced by each partner's family culture and by the values, belief systems, rituals, and traditions that are passed down through the generations.
4. We also assume that the more complex the couple's relationship, the wider the therapist's lens must be to accommodate and understand the multiple layers of the system. In turn, the therapeutic work must provide clients with a way to widen their own lenses and to use contextual differences to their advantage.

Basically, all unions are "mixed marriages." Even people who are brought up in similar households view their environments differently. Therefore, all couples must acknowledge, accept, and honor their differences. When the differences are vast, the tasks of negotiation and integration become even

more complex. The following case is an example of a young couple struggling with these issues. The therapist is a young, Hispanic male who was in
a supervision group we co-led at a counseling center. Part of each group
member's training was to work behind the one-way mirror in order to
sharpen and develop clinical skills. A reflecting team was utilized as part
of the process.

Melinda, age 29, and Dario, age 32, entered therapy during their second
year of marriage. Their presenting problem was the strain created by a
recent extended visit by Dario's mother. Tension had escalated between
Melinda and Dario at this time, and each blamed the other for the relationship difficulties. Melinda said that she had felt like an outsider in her
own home. Dario could not understand Melinda's anger and feeling of isolation, especially since he knew Melinda liked his mother.

As the therapist gathered more information, he learned that the couple
had lived together for a year and a half before marrying. Dario had moved
from Italy to the United States to complete his education and was subsequently introduced to Melinda by a mutual friend. They were immediately
drawn to one another, and an extremely passionate relationship ensued.
Within a few months, Dario had moved into Melinda's apartment. Melinda
soon filled Dario's apparent need for closeness and intimacy. In an attempt
to make up for the loss of his own family life in Italy, Melinda's close family became his own. The young couple rarely left each other's side during
this early stage of their relationship. When they decided to marry, this pattern of overdependence continued. The therapist, José Rios,[1] noted to himself a low level of differentiation of self during his assessment. This was
something he would explore later in the therapy as he questioned them
about their families of origin.

When José asked Melinda to elaborate further upon the presenting
problem, he learned that Dario and his mother spoke Italian to one
another during the entire visit. Although Melinda had taken two Italian
courses since meeting Dario, her knowledge was rudimentary. Consequently, most of the time she could not follow their conversation and felt
totally excluded and threatened. She was the outsider in her own home. As
she articulated her story, José empathized with her feelings as an outsider.
Having come to the United States as a school-aged child speaking only
Spanish, he resonated with Melinda's dilemma.

At this point, José turned to Dario, who had appeared angry and rest-
less while his wife spoke. He now related his view of the situation. He
described how torn he was during his mother's entire visit. On the one
hand, he felt an obligation to spend time with his mother, whom he had not

---

[1]Here, and throughout Part III, the therapists' names are pseudonyms.

seen since his wedding. On the other hand, he was aware that something was amiss with Melinda a few days into the visit. When he questioned her, however, she was noncommittal and dismissive. He knew she was angry at him but did not know why.

Melinda's unspoken thought was, "If you really loved me, you would know what is bothering me." Meanwhile Dario wondered, "If you loved me, how come you can't accept my mother and see how difficult you're making things for me?"

José took this opportunity to validate the partners as individuals and as a couple. "Each of you was feeling misunderstood. And yet neither of you was able to express this clearly to the other. I wonder how the two of you negotiated and dealt with earlier experiences of conflict in your relationship?"

As they sat back and reflected upon José's question, Melinda and Dario came to the conclusion that they never thought about negotiation as part of a marriage. Further questioning about family-of-origin influences revealed that rigid roles in Melinda's family had precluded the need to negotiate tasks. Her father was the "patriarch" and breadwinner. Although her mother worked, she was primarily the caretaker of the three children and household.

Since Dario was an only child, and his father had died when he was three years old, he had always lived with his mother and grandmother. While his mother worked, his grandmother took care of him. Although this female team functioned as parents for Dario, there was often underlying tension in their unspoken power struggle. With no other male living at home, there was role confusion as well as divided loyalty. Conflict was dealt with in a covert way, and issues were left unresolved.

José normalized and reframed the couple's dilemma in the following way: "In this early developmental stage of becoming a couple, people are not generally aware of the need to become a separate unit from families of origin and to develop a method to negotiate tasks, differences, and conflict. In your case in particular, your closeness and passion for each other created the sense that everything would always go smoothly. However, conflict inevitably arises in all couples. Therefore, it is necessary to build a strong marital foundation that has the resources the couple can draw upon in times of stress. (*Pause*) This seems to be a good time to call in the reflecting team and hear their thoughts. The three of us will now go into the room on the observing side of the mirror. And a few members of the reflecting team will come into this room."

Let us talk a bit about the purpose and function of the reflecting team before the couple and team exchange rooms. The role of the reflecting team is to help generate ideas and alternatives while maintaining a curious, respectful, nonhierarchical position. It is a practice arena for learning and thinking about human systems (Davidson, Lax, Lussardi, Miller, & Ratheau, 1988). The collaborative attitude of the team members is evident as they discuss their perceptions and ideas about the interview. This experience is an opportunity for counselors-in-training to formulate reflections in a nonjudgmental manner. Reflections may include self-disclosures; for example, "I went through a similar struggle...." It should be noted that the roles of therapist and reflecting team participants are very different, especially regarding the issue of self-disclosure. Clear boundaries must be maintained during actual therapy sessions, whereas the reflecting team introduces greater flexibility. When the reflections are concluded, the therapist and clients discuss the team's conversations. It is important for the therapist to ask clients for reactions.

The team's discussion evolves as new ideas are co-created among participants. Reflections are presented as tentative offerings, not pronouncements, interpretations, or supervisory remarks. Everything said should be speculative, with the intent of generating and inviting new thoughts. Words such as "perhaps," "I wonder," "I'm curious" are used. The importance of language must not be underestimated. In order to prevent client overload, the reflections are generally no more than four or five minutes. At the conclusion of the comments, the family and team again exchange rooms. The therapist reviews with the couple the impact of the experience upon them. Let us now return to our case and the reflecting team.

Barbara and two supervisees went in front of the mirror as reflecting team members. The other supervisor, Toby, remained in the observation room with the other four members of the team and José, Dario, and Melinda. Barbara began the reflecting process.

BARBARA: I am struck by Melinda and Dario's courage to work in front of the mirror in spite of their initial reservations.

JOHN: Although Dario and Melinda came in at a time of crisis and vulnerability, I wonder if they are aware of the underlying strength it took to address the issues so early in their marriage. I experienced in-law problems early in my own marriage and wish that my wife and I had gone for help much sooner than we did.

BECKY: *(Nodding as she picked up on John's comments)* I agree with both of you, and I'm curious if Melinda and Dario see themselves as risk-takers? Not only have they come in to therapy and been willing to be viewed before the one-way mirror, but they have also entered a challenging relationship.

JOHN: Becky, what do you mean when you say, "challenging relationship"?

BECKY: I was basically referring to their very different backgrounds.

JOHN: My own interracial marriage has certainly been challenging also. Like Melinda, I often felt isolated in my wife's white family. As an African-American, at times it felt like we didn't speak the same language either. And, like Dario, I was an only child, and sometimes my responsibilities to my parents felt burdensome. I wonder if Dario also feels burdened.

BARBARA: *(Glancing at the clock)* I wonder how Melinda and Dario are responding to our comments. Maybe this would be a good time to end our reflections and change rooms once again.

As the two groups changed rooms, the eye contact among them indicated that a strong shift had occurred. As they resettled in their chairs, it was apparent that the process had been a profound one. José asked Melinda and Dario how the experience had been for them.

JOSÉ: So, Melinda and Dario, what are your thoughts and reactions?

DARIO: I liked what they said about our courage and risk-taking, because I felt ashamed that we couldn't handle our problems on our own.

MELINDA: *(Slowly and tearfully)* I could hardly believe so many people seemed to care about us and understand us. It doesn't feel as if that happens very much in our lives. At times I wonder if even our parents understand our relationship.

DARIO: I thought the man in there who talked about his own struggle in his marriage was right on. Because we're the same color, people think we are more alike than we are.

MELINDA: We never really gave much thought to how all of these issues would affect us. I guess my mother-in-law's visit stirred up a lot for me. Before that everything between Dario and me was wonderful.

JOSÉ: So, actually, your mother-in-law's visit created an opportunity for you both to address and examine many issues that had never come up before.

DARIO: I guess that's one way to look at it. Before, I blamed myself for not being better able to take care of my wife as well as my mother.

MELINDA: And I blamed myself too for all of these problems.

DARIO: Another thing that guy said also made me think. He wondered if I felt burdened by my mother. That's hard for me even to admit to myself because it makes me feel guilty.

MELINDA: I thought I was the only one who felt at all burdened. It makes me feel less crazy to hear that you relate to that man's comment.

JOSÉ: Well, the reflecting team has certainly added another dimension to our work together. Time's running out, and we have to stop now. I want to thank you for working in front of the mirror and for opening your-selves to this new experience. We'll be continuing to process all of this in future sessions.

In this first session with Dario and Melinda, José, the therapist, basically concentrated on joining with them, reviewing how each partner perceived the situation, and eliciting a brief history of their relationship. The reflect-ing team further deepened the work by reframing the couple's dilemma, normalizing their concerns, focusing on their strengths, and instilling hope.

After saying goodbye to Melinda and Dario, José reentered the super-vision room. Everyone complimented him on his fine work. Toby remarked about the parallel process that was taking place. What had occurred in the therapy room between José and the couple was further reinforced by the reflecting team. Patterns of interaction in the therapy were mirrored as the entire supervisory and therapist systems celebrated the couple's hopefulness. It was as if the process was contagious! In this particular session, the contagion was jubilant. At times, in other cases, when the work feels hopeless, the contagion may be painful and lead to despair. These emotions are experienced at every level of the system.

The Interconnection of Interactions at Different Levels of a System

The isomorphic process in therapy and supervision was illustrated in the case situation just described. Schwartz, Liddle, and Breunlin (1988, p. 185) write about the isomorphic process: "patterns of interaction at one level of the training/therapy system tend to mirror or replicate patterns at other levels." It is our basic belief that the major instruments of change are the therapist-couple or (or therapist-family) relationship and the supervisor-therapist relationship; therefore, it is incumbent upon the clinician to understand how each of these relationships mirrors the other. You may recall that we discussed the interplay and connection of the therapist and client systems as Jennifer Reed worked with Laura and Michael. In Chap-ter 9, in particular, the parallel process between this client-couple and their therapist was described. This was an example of the interplay and inter-connection between two subsystems. Isomorphism refers not only to the interactions between two subsystems but also, on a broader level, to the replication of interactional sequences at the various levels of the total sys-tem.

We have personally experienced the applicability of these principles in our work as both supervisors and therapists. The theoretical assumptions, values, and beliefs about change that guide our daily work are the same regardless of whether we are supervising or conducting therapy. Whatever happens in one subsystem will be reflected in related subsystems (Liddle & Saba, 1985). For example, we believe it is imperative to establish clear boundaries in the beginning stage of supervision. When we attend to this developmental task, it is more likely that the therapist in training will be clearer with clients. The corollary is also true. If we are not clear, this lack of clarity in the supervisory system will have an impact upon the therapist's work with the couple or family. Of course, isomorphic principles may be manifested in any system. If the parental hierarchy has unclear rules, the reverberations of this lack of clarity may be felt in the sibling subsystem. Consider your own family. Are you aware of relationship patterns? If so, have these patterns repeated or replicated themselves at various levels of the family system? We believe these concepts may be best understood when one relates to them on both personal and clinical levels. For further study we recommend that you discuss these ideas in your supervision groups and consult the literature. We found *The Handbook of Family Therapy Training and Supervision,* edited by Liddle, Breunlin, and Schwartz (1988), particularly useful.

Further post-session work on the case of Melinda and Dario focused upon possible directions of the therapy. The group felt that developmental issues were of primary importance and must be addressed at this time. Toby and Barbara concurred and began a discussion of life cycle stages and accompanying tasks. Much has been written in the literature about this subject. Here are the tasks that we developed for this stage of becoming a couple.

1. Prioritize commitment and allegiance to one another.
2. Redefine relationship to family of origin.
3. Set partnership boundaries that distinguish the couple as a system.
4. Negotiate household tasks and defining roles.
5. Define rules of relationship.
6. Integrate and incorporate traditions and rituals from each partner's background.

After presenting this information, we asked the group for feedback and reactions. A discussion followed which focused on the application of this material to clinical work.

Because of the cultural diversity in both the couple and the group, this contextual issue became forefront. An additional important task was now added:

7. Acknowledge, accept, and honor the couple's differences.

José contracted to work with Melinda and Dario for 19 more sessions. The supervision group continued to be a resource for consultation, learning, and support. Toward the end of the couple's therapy, the reflecting team once again worked with them. Seeing how this young couple had evolved was indeed a most gratifying experience.

Chapter 14

A Hispanic Couple with Teenage Children

The Ortega family was referred to John and Mary Saunders, who often do co-therapy with families in their private practices. Since Mary, like the Ortegas, is of Hispanic descent and bilingual, this particular team was a good match for this family. This case was presented by John and Mary in the context of a supervision group. We learned the following background information as John and Mary verbally presented the case to the group.

Terry, 37, and Antonio, 39, are a Mexican-born couple who each moved with their respective families to the United States as young children. Married for the past 18 years, they have four teenagers: Tony, age 17, Carmen, age 16, Susie, age 14, and Daisy, age 12. The presenting problem is Carmen's "disobedience, ditching school, and lack of respect." Terry and Antonio learned of Carmen's recent repeated absences when they received a telephone call from the school counselor. Concerned and bewildered, the Ortegas called a close family friend, who referred them to John and Mary Saunders.

The initial telephone call to the Saunders' office was made by Antonio. When Mary returned his call, he explained their "problem with Carmen" and requested a therapy session for her. After acknowledging Antonio's distress, Mary recommended a session for the entire family. She explained that she and her husband worked as co-therapists with families. Antonio was perplexed and questioned the need for all family members to participate since the problem concerned only Carmen. Mary went on to explain her view that individual problems affect all family members. For this reason, it was important to hear and learn how each person perceived what was going on. Still confused, but willing to try anything to "get to the root of" Carmen's problem, Antonio hesitantly agreed to bring in everyone. Mary suggested he confer with Terry, gave him some available times, and said she would await his call.

The next day Terry called, and the appointment was scheduled for Wednesday at 4:00 P.M. Since each parent had made contact with her, Mary noted the strength of their shared parental responsibility. Often, when both parents become involved early on, it bodes well for the therapy.

John described the first session as follows. As the six members of the Ortega family entered the Saunders' large office, they presented themselves as an anxious, though united group. Tony sat on the couch between his parents, Susie and Daisy sat together on the smaller love seat, and Carmen took a chair near Mary. John and Mary sat in large chairs across from each other, roughly closing the circle. As Carmen removed her black leather jacket and carelessly dropped it on the floor, her father shot her a disapproving look and the tension rose. Smiling at both therapists, Terry retrieved the jacket and held it on her lap. Already the family dynamics were beginning to unfold, as the unspoken power struggle was enacted.

After checking in with each family member to find out his or her understanding of why the session needed to include all of them, Mary explained a bit about the power of family systems. John reiterated the premise that individual issues deeply affect the whole family. John and Mary proceeded to explore the context of the presenting problem.

JOHN: Antonio, after you and Terry learned of Carmen's school absences, who next learned about the situation?

ANTONIO: When I came home from work, Tony already knew, and he was in Carmen's room arguing with her.

MARY: Susie, how do you think Tony learned about this?

SUSIE: Well, probably from Mom, but Daisy and I knew long before everyone else.

TERRY: *(Surprised and angry)* You both knew and you never told Dad or me?!

SUSIE: We don't have to tell you everything! Sometimes even if we wanted to tell you something, you'd be at Grandma's anyway.

CARMEN: Yeah, so what do you care if I'm at school or not?

ANTONIO: Don't be disrespectful to your mom. She has enough to handle right now without you being fresh. Daisy, how come you never told me about what was going on?

DAISY: I don't know. I didn't even think about it.

CARMEN: What's the big deal anyway? We can't all be "goody-goodies" like Tony.

TONY: You're always picking on me. Who will you pick on when I'm gone next year?

JOHN: Terry, from what you said on the telephone, Tony will be leaving for college in a few months. I'm curious—how are losses and leavetakings handled in this family?

TERRY: Well, my Dad's death has been really hard on all of us, especially on my mom. She's so depressed that I seem to spend most of my time with her. I feel as if I'm neglecting the kids. You'd think that Carmen would help me at a time like this rather than acting up.

MARY: Who does Mom usually turn to when things get really tough for her?

DAISY: Tony, because Dad is away at work all the time.

MARY: And if Dad and Tony are not around, who does Mom turn to?

DAISY: Mom always used to talk everything over with Grandpa, but he's gone now. I guess that's why she cries so much these days. She doesn't have someone she can really count on anymore.

JOHN: Daisy, your mom is still in mourning for your grandfather. And now with Tony's anticipated departure for college, the family will be dealing with another big loss.

John paused in his presentation to further clarify with his colleagues how to best proceed. He expressed his and Mary's concern about the heavy issue of loss that had come up in this first session. Often when great intensity surfaces so rapidly, the therapist must slow down the process in order to track each family member's responses. The individual perceptions must then be understood in relation to the larger family system.

Grief, Loss, and the Family Life Cycle

Grief and loss are issues that must be addressed at each stage of the life cycle. Scharff and Scharff (1987, p. 398) state it well when they write: "Loss and mourning are features of the family's passage through each stage of its development and through every life crisis." When a deep loss is not fully acknowledged by the family members, the transition to the next developmental stage is more difficult. John and Mary noted the timing of Carmen's symptoms in relation to the past critical event of her grandfather's death, her mother's emotional unavailability, and her brother's imminent departure for college.

As John and Mary received feedback from the supervision group, issues surrounding the assessment process were discussed, and the following questions were pondered:

- Why is this particular symptom appearing at this particular time?
- What is each family member's understanding of why the entire family has come to therapy?
- How does each family member view the presenting problem?
- In the past, how has the family dealt with crisis situations?
- How is Carmen's symptom serving the family system?
- How are losses dealt with in this family?

Although these questions were brought up in relation to the Ortega family, they are applicable to all the families we see. Therapists must keep these questions in mind during the assessment process and ask them at appropriate times. Let use now look at the specific and general aspects of each of these process questions.

Why is this particular symptom appearing at this particular time? The Ortega family is approaching the developmental stage of "launching children and moving on." Since many teenagers rebel as a way of flexing their muscles, Carmen's behavior in another family might be seen as somewhat age-appropriate. However, Antonio and Terry Ortega viewed their oldest daughter's actions as disrespectful and defiant. As discussed in earlier chapters, people attribute certain beliefs and meanings to behaviors based on their worldview. The Ortegas' outlook has been shaped by their own families of origin, as well as by the influence of the blending of their Hispanic roots with their newer American heritage. Carmen's symptoms may metaphorically represent her family's struggles to negotiate both cultures. When working with families undergoing cultural change, Vincenzo DiNicola (1997, p. 184) calls the work "threshold therapy." The philosophy he embodies certainly applies to the Ortegas. "Threshold people, moving between societies or caught in cultural changes in their own society, experience cultural conflict" (DiNicola, 1997, p. 184).

What is each family member's understanding of why the entire family has come to therapy? In the Ortega case, the parents were not yet clear as to why the Saunders wanted to see the whole family. They had explained to the children that they were going for help to get Carmen to change her behavior. Through the use of circular questions, the therapists' intention was to expand the way the family viewed the presenting problem. This, however, is an ongoing process. Change occurs when circular thinking replaces linear thinking and the focus of treatment shifts from the intrapsychic to the interpersonal.

How does each family member view the presenting problem? As you can see from the vignette of the first session, each family member perceives the situation differently. As these different perceptions are explored, the therapist's curiosity, empathy, and manner of questioning produce a shift in thinking. Artful questioning encourages change.

In the past, how has the family dealt with crisis situations? The purpose of this question is to understand the present crisis in relation to the handling and/or resolution of previous critical events in the Ortega family. A three- or four-generational genogram is particularly useful to illuminate transgenerational patterns.

How is Carmen's symptom serving the family system? We hypothesize that, since the death of the grandfather, Carmen's parents had pulled even further apart. While Terry has been spending less time at home and more time with her depressed mother, Antonio has retreated even more deeply into his work. Carmen, internalizing her grandmother's and mother's despair and desolation, has unconsciously chosen behavior that protects the family from facing the intensity of emotion. It further serves to bring her parents back together as a marital and parental team.

How are losses dealt with in this family? The individual members of the Ortega family have each dealt in their own way with the grandfather's death, the grandmother's depression, the mother's absence from the home, and Tony's impending departure for college. The family has not mourned these losses together, and this issue must be addressed by the therapy team.

During John and Mary's next few sessions with the family, they gathered information for a genogram, discussed the Ortega family's developmental stage and its accompanying tasks, and talked briefly during one session about how culture and ethnicity had affected each family member. While the Saunders noticed that Carmen's behavior was protecting and serving the family system, the Ortegas' expressed goal was to influence Carmen to behave differently and more in keeping with family tradition. Most of the members of the supervision group endorsed the direction of the therapy. Two of the therapists, however, stated that an in-depth exploration of ethnicity and how it impacted the Ortegas must be more fully addressed in subsequent sessions.

Ethnic and Cultural Considerations

Just as an individual is deeply affected by his or her family, the family is affected by the larger social environment. Included in this larger social community are the contextual influences of culture, gender, race, religion, class, age, sexual orientation, and ethnicity. Family therapists must raise their own consciousness and sensitivity and not make assumptions that emanate from the cultural majority when working with clients whose cultural patterns differ from their own. The therapist must pay particular attention to what is unique for each minority family. DiNicola (1997, p. 11) states that we must not "alleviate our anxieties about strangers by searching for universal human qualities but to find ways to embrace differences and to live with diversity."

Let us now focus upon these ethnic and cultural considerations in this particular family. The Ortegas entered the Saunders' office for their sixth family therapy session. The conversation began before they were even seated.

ANTONIO: I'm not sure this therapy is helping at all. Carmen stayed out well past her curfew last night and Terry still practically lives at her mother's house. When I come home from work, I have to do everything. I feel like the mother and father in this family.

(As Antonio expressed his anger, a note of despair and a sense of helplessness crept in.)

MARY: Antonio, it sounds like you're feeling overwhelmed and alone.
TERRY: *(Looking concerned)* I guess I'm neglecting you as well as the kids.
DAISY: Mom, you still need to be at Grandma's to help her out. Besides, we can all take care of ourselves.
MARY: Terry and Antonio, how do you both work as a team in times of stress?
TERRY: I guess not very well. We need to do that better. I'm surprised to hear that Antonio feels that way. He always seems so independent.
TONY: Something's going on with you two. I heard Daisy and Susie talking. They sounded worried about both of you. I'm kind of concerned about going away, especially with you fighting so much about Carmen.
SUSIE: I always thought we were such a happy family, and now everything seems so crazy. My best friend's parents are even getting divorced, and I'm so sad for Jeannie.
JOHN: Are you worried your parents will get divorced too?

CARMEN: Maybe if they did, they'd get off my back and stop blaming me for everything!

TERRY: That's ridiculous! Just because we're having a few problems doesn't mean we are getting divorced. If you would only behave yourself, everything would be a lot better.

JOHN: I'm curious, Terry and Antonio, how would each of your parents have handled the kind of situations you're facing now?

ANTONIO: In my family, we always respected our parents. None of us ever acted as disrespectful as Carmen. We would never even think of speaking back to our parents. Even though they spoke very little English, they worked their fingers to the bone to provide for us. Our kids take everything they have for granted.

TERRY: It was the same in my family. We all respected our parents and grandparents and knew what they had sacrificed for us. They moved away from their families and friends in Mexico to come here and give us a better life. *(Tearfully)* I never even thought about how lonely they must have been and how hard it was for them to try to fit in. Even today, my mother still talks about going back to Mexico. Since Dad died, she wants to return to be with her sisters and brothers.

MARY: I clearly understand what both of you are saying. My parents immigrated from El Salvador when I was very young. And our family became closer than ever as we all tried to adjust to living here. As young kids, we learned English very quickly and soon became our parents' protectors.

TERRY: I never realized that I was actually protecting my parents. But as you talk I can see that I was.

ANTONIO: *(Softly and thoughtfully)* So that's why you're at your parents' house so much. And now that your mom is alone you're protecting her even more. I guess I was always jealous that you paid them more attention than me. I never thought you felt you needed to protect them.

TERRY: Neither did I. Somehow, I just knew I had to be there each day to help them out.

(A quietness descended upon the room as the children listened attentively. As the family's history unfolded for the first time, they joined together in this new experience.)

As Terry and Antonio spoke with each other, Mary's countertransference stirred within her as she thought of herself as a young girl. She recalled the turmoil she felt while trying to fit in with new friends and a new culture and still remain loyal to her parents. Although they had brought her to the United States, they strongly resisted her new behavior, since it was in total opposition to their Hispanic cultural values. They disapproved of her wearing any makeup, dating, or hanging out with her friends. Anytime she tried to talk to her parents about any of this, they thought she was being disrespectful. Trying to live in both worlds at once was a continuous struggle for Mary. As she grew up and continued her personal and professional journey, she began to better understand the world of her childhood and the new world she eventually entered. Moving through this process greatly enhanced Mary's understanding of her parents' difficult journey and enabled her to relate empathically as the Ortegas' story unfolded.

This session with the Ortegas marked a turning point for their family. Although the road continued to be bumpy at times, Antonio and Terry started to work more as a parental team. As their marriage became more solid, the children felt less responsibility and were able to get on with their own lives.

Chapter 15

Crisis Work with a Couple Encountering Multiple Losses at Midlife

Crisis situations present couples and families with an opportunity to examine their usual coping patterns. Many clients are challenged to expand their problem-solving capacities and formulate creative new solutions in the context of therapy. The therapist and family together co-create new alternatives. Thus, the family's problem-solving capacities are expanded, and clients are prepared to use new skills as they face other developmental crises.

Our treatment model is particularly effective with clients whose lives have been temporarily or permanently affected by some transitional or developmental event, such as the one illustrated by Laura and Michael's situation in Part II. With Laura and Michael, Jennifer Reed had the luxury of 20 sessions. The following example of Vicki and Bob illustrates skillful use of our step-by-step model conducted in 10 sessions. See Table 2-2, p. 21, for a review of the model. For this chapter, we use bracketed bold type to identify the salient points of our treatment model.

Vicki and Bob's Story

Vicki, age 46, and Bob, age 50, presented a youthful, attractive appearance that belied their ages as they entered Toby's office for their first appoint-

This chapter is a revised version of the case vignette from the article "Meeting the Challenge: Providing Effective Couple Therapy in the Age of Managed Care" by Toby Bobes and Barbara Rothman, *The California Therapist,* Sept./Oct., 1996.

ment. As they began to relate their story, grief and despair filled the room. Bob had learned the day before, while at his urologist's office, that a biopsy following lab work confirmed the diagnosis of prostate cancer. Vicki was stunned by the news, and they both decided to seek therapy. They were understandably distraught, especially since Bob's father had died six months earlier following a long battle with stomach cancer. As Toby responded to the intensity of emotion in the room, she was aware of her own personal history and experiences with similar issues. Her identification of her countertransference certainly deepened her understanding, facilitated her engagement with the couple, and thus enhanced the process of joining. **[Join.] [Establish a safe holding environment.]**

The partners perceived the situation in very different ways. Vicki's anxiety was palpable in the session, while Bob presented a calm and even manner. As Toby elicited a brief description of their relationship, their interaction and complementarity were evident. Vicki expressed the pain and suffering for both of them, while Bob's seemingly strong exterior was an attempt to keep emotionality in check. Vicki's forthright manner and wish for help, in contrast to Bob's reserve and stoic affect, made it easier for Toby to join with her. Vicki's availability and Bob's withdrawal, especially at times of stress, were individual characteristics that existed long before they met each other. **[Identify couple's interaction.]** A brief exploration of their families of origin confirmed that these roles had been established long ago. **[Explore how couple's present patterns are linked to family of origin.]** As the initial session drew to a close, it was clear that Vicki was hopeful and wanted to return, while Bob questioned the value of continuing therapy. However, they did set another appointment. At this time, Toby explained the boundaries of therapy, which included fee-setting, 50-minute hour, and cancellation policy. **[Set boundaries.]** Despite the gravity of their situation, they felt empowered as a couple because they had established a plan of action.

When Bob and Vicki returned for their second session, their demeanor was more relaxed. They had sought another opinion regarding Bob's medical situation, which reduced their overwhelming anxiety and fears. As Bob's verbal participation and emotional presence increased, Vicki's intense reactivity decreased. **[Notice systemic patterns.]** When Toby reviewed with them how each partner perceived the situation, they acknowledged a greater sense of hopefulness. **[Clarify how each partner perceives situation.]** During the week they had moved from despair to a guarded optimism and seemed more receptive to the possibilities of change in their relationship. Vicki wanted Bob to be closer and not so "far away" emotionally. Bob wanted "more space" and wished Vicki would stop hovering over him. In his words, "She is too emotional." The dance of pursuit and withdrawal became clearer to Vicki and Bob as they clarified the pattern. **[Identify couple's interaction.]**

The effects of their sibling positions were certainly reflected in their marital patterns. Vicki was the oldest of three daughters, and often the caretaker; this was very attractive to Bob. He was nine years younger than his sister and distant from her. With parents who were frequently absent, Bob became a "lost child" who needed caretaking. However, as we observe so often, complementarity does not necessarily result in harmony and intimacy (McGoldrick, 1995).

Vicki and Bob described a brief history of their relationship. **[Elicit brief history of their relationship.]** After a long courtship, they had married during Bob's last year in law school. Both sets of parents contributed to their financial support and continued to help until Bob went to work for a prestigious law firm in another city. Their own financial security as a couple enabled them to start planning to have children. Within the next five years Vicki became a homemaker and mother of two boys and a girl. Their move stimulated them to further differentiate from their respective families of origin. In the years to follow, Bob became a full partner in a law firm. Vicki stayed at home until the last child started college. In many ways they were now starting a new relationship, just the two of them. When they entered therapy, they had just celebrated their 20th wedding anniversary. Developmentally they were at the stage of "launching children and moving on." **[Identify the couple's developmental stage.]** Significant losses were impacting their relationship: (1) the loss of the nuclear family as they had known it, (2) the aging of their parents, (3) the recent loss of Bob's father, and (4) the loss of Bob's good health. The discussion of the impact of these losses upon each of them produced a greater depth of understanding. As Vicki and Bob listened to each other, their faces softened and they moved closer to one another. **[Encourage listening in order to help each understand the other's struggles.]**

In view of this couple's basic goodwill and 20-year history together, Toby suggested that the present situation could become an opportunity for changing long-term patterns that had previously kept them distant, especially in times of crisis. Vicki and Bob felt validated and acknowledged their deep commitment to each other. **[Review commitment to each other.]** They had recently been confronted with their first experience of the "empty nest" and were apprehensive about life without children at home. After discussing it in session, they realized that what lay ahead was the exciting challenge of redefining their relationship. **[Reframe situation.]** The session ended by focusing upon their strengths and instilling hope. **[Focus on couple's strengths and instill hope.]**

As Bob and Vicki entered the room for their third session, their tension and anger were immediately evident. When the urologist initially discussed the treatment choices and informed them that surgery might produce impotence, they were forced to look at the options and implications together. Possible loss of their way of relating sexually was almost too much for them to bear. It was easier for them to lapse into fighting and anger than to experience their pain and vulnerability. This interactional process replicated how they had handled stressful situations previously and in their families of origin. Tolerating intensity of emotion had been avoided in their history as a couple. At this time, Toby took the opportunity to explore with Vicki and Bob how these historical patterns were affecting them today. **[Explore how patterns and beliefs restrain.]** Earlier survival mechanisms of caretaking for Vicki and withdrawal for Bob had enabled them to survive in their families of origin. These patterns of behavior were no longer working for them in their present relationship. The task was to educate the couple about how they once needed these survival skills as children. As adults, however, the development of new skills and new ways of responding to each other would be one of the goals of their work. **[Identify each partner's early survival mechanisms.] [Educate partners about need for survival skills/defenses developed as children.]** After sorting out the pros and cons, Bob finally decided to elect radiation therapy rather than surgery. This decision not only provided an optimistic outlook for long-term survival but was also of great psychological benefit to their relationship.

The medical issue loomed large. The threat of changing aspects of their sexual functioning became an opportunity for Vicki and Bob to explore and handle this situation differently. Collaboration replaced their former pattern of separate decision-making. As they reviewed their process during the past week, they realized that what they had experienced as a setback in the relationship was actually an important turning point. **[Collaborate and invite partners to consider alternative ways of responding.]** They had moved from avoidance of pain and unilateral decision-making to working together.

Over the next five sessions Vicki and Bob continued to explore their patterns and work hard in therapy. They were able to more clearly identify what worked for them individually and in their marriage. **[Assess the therapeutic work.]** As tensions lessened, they began to focus on self issues. **[Distinguish between self and other.]** Each listened to the other in a new and empathic way. As each told of early struggles, a context was created for understanding today's intense reactions. It also enabled them to further accept and appreciate their differences. **[Empower partners by helping them accept their differences.]**

At times during the last few sessions, Vicki and Bob reverted to old reactive ways of relating. The therapist, knowing that change does not proceed in a linear way, wisely tracked their responses and respected their pace. Normalizing the couple's process in this way continued to encourage them and punctuated their strengths. **[Normalize and prepare for setbacks.]**

At the ninth session, closure and termination issues were addressed. Managed care had approved ten sessions. **[Acknowledge closure of therapy experience.]** Vicki and Bob had worked as a team through their medical crisis and now felt they had new tools with which to confront future developmental events. **[Build upon newly acknowledged competencies.]** Although still immersed in redefining their relationship, Vicki and Bob left therapy with a greater sense of clarity and hope for their future.

Our treatment format, with its emphasis upon collaboration and building upon the couple's resources and strengths, is time- and cost-effective without sacrificing the integrity and quality of the therapeutic experience. While maintaining a sharper focus in today's managed-care environment, we must be willing to be patient and respect our clients' pacing. Vicki and Bob needed help in adjusting to the crisis of a physical illness. Multiple losses and long-term issues were identified but not worked through. Perhaps they will choose some future work in therapy. Their readiness to stop at this time indicated their ability and willingness to manage on their own. It was important to validate their confidence in newfound strengths as they put closure to this experience.

Chapter 16

A Blended Marriage

In the case study in this chapter we focus on the life-cycle stage of remarriage and its accompanying tasks. Today probably half to three-quarters of the families we see as therapists live in what might be considered "nontraditional" households. The concepts of the 1950s style nuclear family with married parents and 2.5 children has changed. Today the stepfamily is more the norm. More than half of all marriages end in divorce, and the majority of divorced partners remarry. Most divorced couples have children and, when they remarry, these children become part of a stepfamily. The blending of these families involves an enormous amount of commitment, flexibility, and a willingness to face the challenges inherent in this situation.

Betty Carter and Monica McGoldrick (1989) talk about the need for clinicians to help the family create a new form of family structure after remarriage. This is truly a transition point between endings and new beginnings. The old model of family must be mourned as a newer and more complex family is shaped. The emotionality of the entire system and the individuals within it must be clarified. The assumption underlying our work is that unresolved grief is often a barrier to intimacy and to optimal family functioning at any stage of the life cycle. This is particularly valid in the situation of divorce and remarriage.

Little attention has been paid to the issues of grief and loss that accompany divorce and remarriage. When couples rejoice in the experience of remarriage, they are reluctant to reexamine the earlier pain and loss of the divorce. An opportunity presents itself to address unspoken issues when a remarried family enters therapy. Often, the process of acknowledging and examining these earlier painful issues enables the family to get back on their life cycle track.

In *Stepfamilies in Therapy* (1992, p. xii), Don and Maggie Martin write:

> Uniting individuals who previously belonged to other nuclear families carries the potential for complex family dynamics. New relationships must be formed, new territory must be defined, and new roles have to be assumed. Adding to the complexity is the new extended family, which includes not only current and former blood relatives but also relatives from all previous marriages. Healthy stability is the goal, but the path is often strewn with difficulties that make the intervention of a skilled therapist critical.

The following case study illustrates the multiple levels of complexity that must be addressed. Robert Greene, a child psychologist and colleague of Barbara, called her about the possible referral of a blended family. He had had one session with the parents of Patty, an eight-year-old he had been seeing individually for six months. The parents initially described her symptom as her fear of going to school. As he learned about the complexities of the family, he decided that family therapy would be helpful in augmenting the work he was doing with Patty. After Robert briefly described the family situation, Barbara agreed to accept the referral. The next day, James Wilder phoned for an appointment. Having already spoken to Robert about the need for the entire family to be seen together, James was amenable and was prepared to bring everyone in.

Family Composition at a Glance

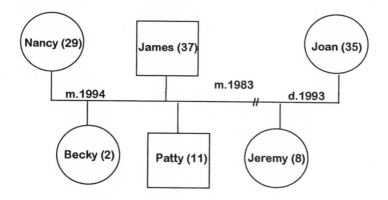

FIGURE 16-1. *Genogram of the Wilder Family*

The Wilder family members arrived punctually for their Monday after-noon family session. James and Nancy sat on one couch with Becky on her mother's lap, while Joan sat on the other couch between Jeremy and Patty. Barbara silently observed the seating arrangement. Nancy and Joan exchanged small talk as they entered the office. James and Jeremy talked about the previous evening's Lakers game. Becky examined the toys in the basket near Barbara's chair. Patty glanced around the room anxiously as if wondering what was about to happen.

BARBARA: I wonder what James told all of you about coming here?

NANCY: James told me he had spoken to Patty's therapist who had suggested that some sessions with the whole family would be helpful.

JEREMY: I don't know why we all need to be here. I think everything is fine.

BARBARA: When Dr. Greene called, he thought some sessions with the entire family would help the work he and Patty were doing together. And he thought the sessions might also benefit the whole family. Often one person is unknowingly chosen to carry the family's pain. By seeing all of you, we can see if that is the case here.

JOAN: That's interesting. Patty is the one who has always been the most sensitive. When James and I used to fight, she had a harder time getting over it than we did.

BARBARA: Patty, do you think your mother is right about that?

PATTY: No, she isn't. I didn't even care when they yelled at each other. *(Sulking)*

JAMES: Patty is definitely the family worrier. No matter how hard I try to reassure her about things, she always worries.

PATTY: Sure, you told me you and Mom would work things out. And then you got divorced. How can I believe you?

BARBARA: *(Noting James's hurt look at his daughter's outburst)* Separation and divorce are very hard on everyone in the family. I wonder how each of you has dealt with the loss and the grief process.

JOAN: Well, we were never a family that communicated easily. We always fought instead of talking things out. Growing up in my family we never talked about things either. After my mom died when I was a teenager, my dad hardly mentioned her again.

JAMES: Yeah, Joan and I were kids when we met. We never knew what a relationship was all about. Nancy and I met when we were adults so things are different for us.

NANCY: Yes, we do get along pretty well. If we argue it's generally about the kids. Since Jeremy and Patty spend one week with us and one week with Joan, things are often hectic and confusing.

JOAN: Things are more relaxed in my house because the kids have always lived here, and they know my rules. In James's house the rules changed after he married Nancy. And there's a third child there, too.

BARBARA: Coordinating two households must be difficult. Let's talk about how the decision for this arrangement was worked out.

In this session and in subsequent ones, the Wilder family discussed their struggles, successes, and feelings of failure in their attempts to blend this new family. James felt torn between accommodating his former wife and pleasing Nancy and his children. Attempts at forming a working parental subsystem for the children were thwarted by Nancy's and Joan's jealousies toward one another. Each tried to be the better mother. The children were confused by the parental struggles and by their own divided loyalties. One of our working hypotheses was that Patty's school phobia was a symptom that served the family. By staying home, Patty was a companion for her "abandoned" mother. She also kept the family from focusing upon issues of grief and loss.

Creation of a safe holding environment involves great skill and sensitivity on the part of the therapist. Because of the complexity of the entire system, the therapist must learn from the family how the parental subsystem is functioning. By parental subsystem we are referring to the biological parents and the stepparents. The following questions enable us to gather important information about the blended family.

- Do the children spend equal or unequal time in each household?
- How did the two families work out this living arrangement?
- Which aspects of the arrangement work and which aspects do not work?
- Are the rules similar or different in the households?
- Who sets the rules?
- What is the interaction like between the biological parents?
- Are they the rule-setters or are the stepparents also involved?
- How are other boundaries addressed?
- In the past, how did the family deal with loss and grief? Was this issue talked about in relation to the divorce?

As the therapist assesses and evaluates the family, she gathers information that will assist her in formulating a working systems hypothesis. During these early sessions in the Wilder case, the therapist has done a simple genogram as well as a map of the family's triangular patterns (Figure 16-2). The dialogue conveys how each member perceives the family. Developmental tasks unique to blended families are assessed and reviewed in the ongoing work of this case. As Barbara explores the parental subsystem, Joan, Nancy, and James eventually become a more powerful working team. Although many divorced parents and stepparents will never resolve certain issues, the parental boundaries must be clarified for the blended family to function in a healthy way.

The Ruptured Bond

The loss involved in marital separation and divorce is profound. A particular way of life for the family is over. All of the former rituals of everyday family living change. The long-established patterns and rhythms are gone. The familiarity of a two-parent system is lost. In spite of the fact that the parents may not have worked as a team, their behaviors were known. All of this familiarity is replaced by the unknown—for the parents as well as for the children. Robert Garfield (1982, p. 4) states:

> Perhaps the most painful aspect of marital separation is the rupture of attachment bonds that exist between the spouses. . . . When these bonds are undone, spouses often feel overtaken by a terrible sense of loneliness, a sense that they are no longer at home or secure in their world.

For most people this emotional tearing apart replicates earlier separation disruptions in the mother-child relationship. Because of the widespread prevalence of divorce today, there is a tendency to minimize the pain and agony of the emotional process of divorcing families. Before wounds are healed and families can move on, attention must be paid to the enormous loss. What has occurred is the death of a family. And in our culture all forms of death are denied. No wonder the issue of loss in divorcing families gets so little attention.

Froma Walsh and Monica McGoldrick (1991) write about the failure of the family therapy literature to adequately address the impact of loss upon the family. We, too, have noted this inattention to the taboo subject of death and loss; accordingly, we have returned to the theme of loss several times. In this chapter we relate it to the death of the marriage.

Continuation of Therapy with the Wilder Family

Because of the complexity of the many issues involved with remarried families, the work with the Wilder family spanned 20 sessions over a period of one year. Following the first "civilized" session, the next few meetings became volatile and angry, as the system expressed itself more openly and fully. The focus shifted from Patty as the identified patient to the underlying rivalries and shifting triangles among the members of the parental sub-system. McGoldrick and Gerson (1985) discuss the importance of triangles in the remarried family, where the structure of the family, rather than the personality of the participants, defines the situation. Joan and Nancy became rivals as they fought for the position of "favored mom" with the children.

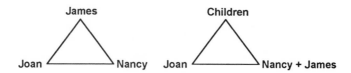

FIGURE 16-2. *Shifting Triangular Patterns*

James shifted in his role as peacemaker, sometimes placating Joan and at other times pleasing Nancy.

After hard work on the part of Barbara and the Wilder family, the system calmed down considerably. As Joan was able to talk about the loss of her marriage and became less depressed, Patty was no longer needed at home to take care of her. The symptom of school phobia disappeared. The parental team became more solid as James felt less guilty about the divorce, as Joan moved on in her own life, and as Nancy and James redefined their new coupleship. Just as the system had stabilized, a frantic call from Joan indicated that the family was again in a crisis mode. An emergency session was scheduled for Saturday morning.

As the Wilder family entered Barbara's office it was apparent that tensions were high. Everyone seemed agitated as Joan began to talk anxiously.

JOAN: *(Angrily)* I can't believe how James reacted to something real important happening in my life! He forgets all the times in our marriage that I had to accommodate to his job changes. I just got a really great job promotion, and he only thinks about how it's going to affect him.

JAMES: It's not me I'm thinking about. It's the kids. How do you think they'll function with you traveling five days a week?! We finally worked out a great custody arrangement, and now you want to change everything.

JOAN: The difference is, James, that you have a wife at home to take care of things. I don't! This job means much more money for me and a big step up the corporate ladder. It's a huge opportunity for me. And you don't even want to listen to how we can work things out with the children.

NANCY: Why don't you both calm down so that we can try to do that. I don't even know what it is that you want to work out, Joan.

BARBARA: I'm in the dark, too. Perhaps each of you, Joan and James, can clarify your perceptions of this new situation.

JOAN: Well, you know I just went back to my old job a few months ago. And when I went to work yesterday, my boss called me in and offered me a major promotion. It would involve more responsibility, more money, and a few days a week of traveling. Since my boss, Joanne, knows I have children, she said they would try to be somewhat flexible about the traveling. When I told James this, he became angry and defensive and never even recognized the importance of this to me and the children.

JAMES: All I know is that you flatly stated that custody arrangements would have to be changed and that Nancy and I would get the kids most of the time. We can't just revolve our lives around you. And have you even thought about how this would affect the kids?

BARBARA: The possibility of this new job presents a big challenge to all of you. How do you kids see the situation?

PATTY: Well, it sounds great for Mom. But I'm not sure how it'll be for Jeremy and me.

JEREMY: We'll be fine. We're in school most of the time anyway.

JOAN: I've figured out two different ways to go that would work, but so far no one seems to be interested in what I have to say.

BARBARA: Tell us what your thoughts are.

JOAN: With the extra money I'll be making, I can pay a housekeeper to stay from Monday to Friday. Or they can stay with you and Nancy, James, when I'm gone during the week. Then I'd have them from Friday until Monday morning.

BARBARA: What you're possibly talking about is renegotiating a new or modified custody arrangement.

The next two sessions with the Wilder family focused upon modification of their previous custody arrangement. What has occurred with the Wilders is a systemic reaction to change in one individual. Barbara suggested, and the family agreed, that the children not be present for these particular sessions. Joan's differentiation of self and newfound strength have upset the homeostasis of the family. The distribution of power has obviously shifted. Cultural overtones, previously unspoken, now emerge.

JAMES: Barbara, I have thought a lot about what you said last session about renegotiating our custody arrangement. Nancy and I agree that it probably is time to do that.

JOAN: I thought we could work it out verbally. Are you talking about a written agreement?

NANCY: James and I agree that it is probably best to have it in writing so that it is clear for all of us.

BARBARA: Apparently you and James have talked about this issue since our last session. Can you tell us about your decision-making process?

JAMES: Well, it started with us both not wanting Joan to take the children every Friday night. You see, Nancy and I are Jewish, and we have a Friday night ritual of observing the Sabbath at dinner time. Joan and I were different religions, and we never could agree on how we wanted the kids to be raised in the area of religion.

JOAN: And we really still don't agree. I sometimes take the children to church, but James was never interested in taking them to temple. I was pretty surprised when I heard the kids say they were lighting candles on Friday night. When I asked James about it, he told me that Nancy was observant, and he thought it was a good idea for him to become more active with the children. I have no problem with Patty and Jeremy learning about Christianity and Judaism.

NANCY: By exposing them to both religions, they will be able to make a more educated choice for themselves. But in order to do this we need them at our house on Friday nights to be part of this family tradition.

JOAN: I guess I would have appreciated hearing this from both of you rather than from the children. Then I would have understood your points of view. I feel as if I'm working against a team.

BARBARA: Part of the work of the therapy has been to have the three of you learn to work as a parental team. So let's continue to see how you can make this happen as you reconstruct the custody arrangement. Sometimes a crisis situation brings unspoken issues to the fore. And with this situation an opportunity is created to work it all out. The differences in culture and power have not been talked about before, and I think it's important that we address them now.

NANCY: *(Angrily, voice somewhat raised)* I wasn't so aware of it before, but I think one of the reasons I want a signed agreement is so that my voice will be heard equally. As a stepmother, I often feel like I'm odd mom out even though I wind up spending more time with Patty and Jeremy than they spend with their mother or father.

JOAN: Well, we both work, and you've always said how you love being an at-home mom.

NANCY: I do love it, but I don't feel like I get enough credit for it.

JAMES: Look, we all try hard to be good parents, and I think we are. Let's just try to work out an agreement that we all can live with. Joan, not only does the agreement involve custody, but we also have to work out a new financial arrangement since you are making more money.

JOAN: Yes I am, but that money may need to go toward a housekeeper.

NANCY: Let's suppose we decided to take the kids more. Then you would-n't need a housekeeper.

JOAN: But since you want them Friday night, that would mean you'd have them an entire school week. Are you willing to do that?

JAMES: You mentioned your boss understood the situation with the chil-dren and would be flexible about your traveling. Could you possibly arrange to travel Tuesday through Friday so that the kids could be with you from Saturday morning through Tuesday morning? Then you'd have them for three nights and we'd have them the other four nights.

JOAN: That's a possibility I hadn't thought about. I could certainly check it out and get back to you on it. The money issue is something else. We need to talk more about that.

Many new topics were brought up in these negotiating sessions. Money, power, and religious issues had emerged and were acknowledged and then addressed. After the initial crisis session, the family cautiously resumed its functioning. The parental team restabilized, reorganized, and renegoti-ated. This process is ongoing in all families.

The Blending of Therapists' and Clients' Cultures

Since Barbara is in a blended family herself and is closely connected to the issues involved in remarriage and stepparenting, she knows firsthand the challenges that the Wilders have faced and will continue to face. Her inti-mate involvement on a personal level led to a depth of understanding that enhanced the therapeutic work. However, a therapist who is not in a blended family can certainly work effectively with remarried families. As differences in cultures are explored, the therapist must be actively curious and work with awareness and sensitivity. As long as there is an openness and awareness of differences, in both self and others, an ongoing, respect-ful dialogue will take place.

Remarriage: The Blending of Multiple Cultures

Every family is a culture that has assimilated the traditions, rituals, pat-terns, and history inherited from earlier generations. Understanding the family's culture is, indeed, a complex experience, one that necessitates looking at the multiple subgroups that affect each individual. Celia Falicov (1995, p. 376) writes about syncretism, the blending of cultural influences, stating:

Many families have two or more cultures represented within them, because parents or children grew up in different settings or because the spouses belong to different races, religions, or ethnic groups.

Given this enormous complexity, one readily understands the unique challenge of the remarried family. It is natural for these families to experience a state of profound disequilibrium because family formation cannot occur spontaneously. It takes time for the parental system to develop a new culture and to reorganize (Goldner, 1982). The case of the Wilder family was certainly an illustration of this process.

We have found the developmental perspective to be extremely helpful in our experiences with remarried families. Of course, the attitude of the therapist is of paramount importance, whatever one's theoretical orientation. The clinician's recognition of similarities and differences of the multiple contexts or cultures of families brings forth a conversation of respect, curiosity, and increased understanding. The tasks in Table 16-1 are those that we believe are necessary for families to address and negotiate as they move through the life cycle stage of separation, divorce, and remarriage.

TABLE 16-1. *Tasks of Life Cycle Stage of Separation, Divorce, and Remarriage*

1. Mourn the loss of original family.
2. Build new support systems and maintain present supports.
3. Develop a working relationship as divorced parents.
4. Establish a strong parental subsystem.
5. Clarify boundaries involving all parents in remarried system.
6. Recognize that the natural parent and child relationship predates the remarriage. This acknowledgment facilitates integration of newly formed family.

In spite of the fact that work with blended families is unique, with multiple layers of complexity, our treatment paradigm is nevertheless applicable. We strongly emphasize different aspects of the life cycle stages that are pertinent to this population. Greater flexibility on the part of the therapist parallels the flexibility needed by blended families to adapt and adjust to the merging of two completely different systems. This once again necessitates close self-examination of the therapist's own cultural biases, attitudes, values, and beliefs. Understanding oneself is of paramount importance with all families and especially salient when we work with the multiple cultures of blended families.

Generally, acknowledgment of loss and grief is a therapeutic issue throughout individual, couple, and family therapy. Although mourning any loss is a universal theme, it is often unexpressed in divorced families who are trying to get on with their lives. Couples who are rejoicing in new marriages are reluctant to grieve at such a happy time. When they enter therapy, however, the honeymoon is over, and feelings of loss and grief emerge. The psychological healing will unfold as the therapist works with families as they move through this life-cycle stage.

Chapter 17

Couples Facing Aging, Illness, and Death

Aging, illness, and death are taboo subjects in our society. None of us wants to face this final life-cycle stage. And yet, it is inevitable. Both the birth and death processes are traumatic. Different religions and cultures have specific rituals that are associated with each. The joy of birth and the sadness of death represent the polarity of emotions in the life cycle of man.

In our society the fear of death is universal. In his Pulitzer-Prize-winning book, *The Denial of Death*, Ernest Becker referred to this universality as the "terror" of death. Elizabeth Kübler-Ross wrote about the negative cultural attitudes from the past surrounding death. Dead bodies were seen as unclean and not to be touched by the ancient Hebrews. Evil spirits needed to be driven away by the early American Indians. Kübler-Ross states that the issues and history related to death and dying remain unchanged today. She writes: "Death is still a fearful, frightening happening, and the fear of death is a universal fear even if we think we have mastered it on many levels" (1969, p. 5).

Traditionally, our society has viewed death as an individual's physical process. This led to an acceptance of the loneliness and sense of isolation of individuals who die alone. Psychiatric theory reinforced the focus of death as an intrapsychic process. Murray Bowen's family systems theory broadened our perspective of death to incorporate the interpersonal realm (1976). Death is no longer viewed as an isolated event. It is now seen in a family context. Froma Walsh and Monica McGoldrick expanded Bowen's work in their more recent view on the subject of death in *Living*

Beyond Loss. Chapters by other well-known therapists make this work a significant contribution to the field.

Clients come to therapy experiencing some degree of loss in their lives. Certainly all of them have experienced grief at some time in their past. Each individual client, couple, or family is going through a developmental stage, which inevitably involves transition and change. The stage may involve leaving home, getting married, becoming parents, or any event that can be described as a beginning or an ending. Sometimes the loss is traumatic and obvious, such as the death of a person, job, or relationship. Sometimes the loss may be subtle, because it is associated with a gain. For example, a job promotion, with all outward appearances of a positive experience, may involve the loss of a comfortable support system. The joy of a remarriage often masks the mourning following a divorce.

Death represents the ultimate separation. Other losses may not be as traumatic. Clients must be encouraged to identify all losses, however, and share the circumstances surrounding them in order to experience relief during the grieving process. Only then can they begin the journey of healing. In order to facilitate this process, therapists must help clients understand what grief is and what is experienced as they attempt to cope with it. Grieving involves the process of acknowledging and experiencing the full range and intensity of emotions. At this time there is often a fear of losing control and "going crazy." Mourning is a normal reaction to loss and serves to restore the ability to love and interact. Shock, denial, numbness, and disbelief serve an important defensive function. Such numbness protects us for a time, but if it persists it can be a signal that professional help is needed.

During the next stage of painful longing, clients begin to experience wave-like episodes of tearfulness, sad memories, and painful images. These episodes tend to be especially intense at night and often remain intense for several months and sometimes longer. Gradually, interest in ordinary activities returns, and we are able to remember and talk about the loss with less pain. These emotional states recur periodically and not necessarily in a well-defined progression (Jacobs, 1988).

People who are unable to grieve, in an effort to protect themselves from pain, often cut themselves off from the joy of living. White and Epston (1990, p. 103) validate full expression of emotion by their law of grief: "Crying on the outside means that you are no longer crying on the inside. And crying on the inside drowns your strength." All of us have the potential for healing; the work of the therapist is to facilitate and encourage the unfolding of this natural human process.

In order to enable our clients to deal with tragedy and loss, we need to have the courage, honesty, and integrity to examine the wounds of our own losses. Without a personal understanding of our grief processes, we are unlikely to hear or recognize our clients' pain and conflict. The attempt to protect oneself from the anguish and pain of separation and loss is understandable. A conscious acknowledgment of the disorganization, depression, fear, sadness, and anger is required before resolution, acceptance, or adjustment is possible. We, as professionals, can help our clients achieve a better level of emotional functioning by directly facing the anxiety of loss—with them and with ourselves personally.

A Personal Examination of Loss

The fact that we both had severely ill mothers when we were young children drew us together. In a training group for therapists, we recognized during an experiential exercise that we equated illness with death. Therefore, illness was always terrifying for both of us. Writing this book has propelled us to continue this self-examination. As we revealed the depth of our pain to one another, we further clarified our own family beliefs and attitudes. The following is a dialogue that occurred between us as we wrote this chapter.

TOBY: I was so overly involved with my mother. It wasn't until I started doing this work that I realized how our entire family was affected. My dad was extremely concerned about Mom. In fact, he was totally devoted to taking care of her, which often left Elaine and me out of the picture.

BARBARA: My dad reacted very differently. He couldn't acknowledge and deal with my mom's illness and so he became very distanced from her. Since my brother and I allied with her pain, my dad was often odd man out in the family.

TOBY: Even though I've done a lot of work on this in therapy, the old feelings and images loom large as we talk. I always worried that my children would be burdened by my early family issues.

BARBARA: My mom's illness made me hypervigilant, overly responsible, a caretaker, and terrified of illness.

TOBY: You just gave words to my early terror and the beliefs about life that came out of it. I'm a caretaker, too. Is it any wonder that we both became therapists?

BARBARA: And we both wound up in therapy ourselves. Caretaking plus our own therapeutic journeys have brought us to where we are today.

TOBY: I guess it's not a coincidence that I married a doctor. Norm calmed my terror and made my present world safer than my early world. We've worked hard on our relationship. Our marriage has been a long-term one, and yet it's so different today than when we first married that it almost seems like a second marriage within the first. Now we often exchange the roles of caretaker.

BARBARA: That's certainly a good description of how I see you both. I guess I needed a first marriage to get it right the second time.

TOBY: I was always concerned that I would burden my three daughters with my anxieties and vulnerabilities. In my family, vulnerability meant weakness. Today, though, we now seem to be able to tolerate the intensity and the ups and downs of emotional life. But it sure took a lot of hard work. So, now, I feel scared but ready to face the issues of aging.

BARBARA: I guess Bernie's battle with cancer ten years ago brought up issues of illness and possible death long before we thought we'd have to deal with them. It was definitely a wake-up call for us. And I think that has forced us to look at things differently. Illness distanced my parents, but it brought Bernie and me closer together.

TOBY: From going through the experience of Bernie's illness with you, I have certainly seen you become stronger over the years.

BARBARA: I also wanted to be strong for my children. By denying the fragile part of myself I felt I'd be totally different from my mom. Through therapy I was able to stop trying to be a super strong mom. That allowed me to become more flexible with my own kids and stepchildren. My grandchildren seem to be flourishing and of course in their grandmother's eyes they are absolutely perfect!

Reflections about Self-Disclosure

Personal disclosure is an issue for all of us in our relationships with others. Some people choose to "let it all hang out," while others "play it closer to the vest." The issue of self-disclosure relates to the messages we learned in our families of origin, our own personal styles, and to how much we trust ourselves and others.

While our personal styles strongly influence who we are as therapists, the issue of self-disclosure in a clinical setting must adhere to boundaries that are respectful of our clients. The pivotal question therapists must ask themselves is, Whose needs are being served by my self-disclosure—my clients' needs or my own?

We pondered this question as we revealed ourselves in the above dialogue. Whose needs were being served by our self-disclosures? Would we burden our readers with our personal stories? Or, would our revelations serve to model the disclosure we ask of our students? Would the expression of our own wounds detract from our writing and teaching? Since we value authenticity, openness, and congruency, we felt the benefits of our self-disclosures outweighed the possible fallout. Our intention is to model what we are teaching by writing about our own family beliefs and attitudes.

Family Beliefs and Attitudes about Illness and Death

What we learn in our families of origin has a profound impact upon our later reactions to loss, illness, and death. Some of the questions we ask clients to consider are ones that elicit information about these early belief systems. As these early stories are brought forth, the listening partner develops greater empathy and understanding. The following are some of the questions we ask. Please add your own questions to this list.

1. What stories and beliefs about illness, loss, or death did you learn in your family of origin?
2. If you have children, how have these stories and beliefs affected them?
3. How might these beliefs affect your relationship with your partner?
4. How do you think your loved ones would eulogize you? How do you want to be remembered?
5. What would you want your obituary to say about you?
6. Is there any unfinished business with family members that you want to attend to before you die?

Issues of illness, loss, and death are particularly relevant within the gay community today. AIDS has become the epidemic of our time. The terror and horror of prolonged suffering—total loss of bodily control leading to dependency and a painful death—is everyone's nightmare. Clinicians are not immune to these fears, and often we dissociate and distance ourselves from our own deepest fears. In so doing, we dissociate and distance ourselves from our clients. Only after facing our own terror of suffering, total dependency, and eventual death, can we be truly emotionally present and available to our clients.

Vignette

Mark, 45, and Glen, 63, originally entered therapy when they learned that Mark had tested HIV positive. Their family physician referred them to

Toby for couple work. They were devastated. During the following year they addressed the presenting issue, worked on family attitudes toward illness and sexuality, and strengthened their coupleship. When they returned to therapy six years later, Mark had developed AIDS symptoms. He had recently been discharged from the hospital after a bout with pneumonia. Over the course of the next year and a half, he deteriorated physically, and Glen's anguish was palpable.

During the original work with this couple, Kübler-Ross's early stages of denial and anger were examined. Upon their return to therapy, the bargaining phase had ended, and their depression was apparent. This preparatory depression is an important stage that helped to prepare the couple for the acceptance of Mark's inevitable death.

Members of both families of origin were willing to come in for several sessions to support Mark and Glen. Often such a crisis is an opportunity for distanced families to reconcile and to reverse long-standing patterns of emotional cut-off. The impending loss of a son or daughter often fosters healing in the entire family and leads to the last stage of acceptance. Our observations have led to the belief that the acceptance phase has two parts: (1) total acceptance of the illness, and (2) total acceptance of death. Kübler-Ross's (1969) five "stages of dying" (denial, anger, bargaining, depression, acceptance) provide a useful conceptual tool for understanding dying patients, although not everyone goes through these phases in a predictable order.

During her grief work with Mark and Glen, Toby was aware of her own feelings of vulnerability. Her terror of dependency and prolonged suffering heightened her sensitivity and empathy. Her willingness to tolerate her own anxiety and intensity enabled her to remain emotionally present throughout the work. During this time, she used the support of colleagues to help her separate her own pain from the emotions of her clients.

Assumptions Underpinning Our Work With Grief and Loss

There are important underlying issues for therapists to understand when treating clients who are having difficulty dealing with loss:

1. Unresolved grief is often a barrier to intimacy and to optimal family functioning at any stage of the life cycle.
2. Signs of loss, whether overt, subtle, or simply unacknowledged, may intersect with family life-cycle issues (Walsh & McGoldrick, 1991).

3. Loss usually leads to a need for a major life change; a developmental shift will inevitably occur as the process evolves.
4. The life-cycle perspective is interwoven with the systems model and theory. The universal theme of loss affects the entire family system as well as its individual members throughout the life cycle.
5. Since loss is a cumulative process, grief experienced at one stage of the life cycle may not be consciously felt until much later. Some individuals are overwhelmed by unresolved past grief, which greatly affects their ability to grieve in the present.
6. The family or couple attributes particular meanings and beliefs to the handling of loss. These meanings must be clarified and understood as patterns of loss throughout the life cycle are identified.

Since pressure points are inevitable for all of us during life's journey, therapists must honor their own limitations. Therapists in the throes of loss and painful transitions of their own may be so personally overwhelmed that grief work with clients is precluded. Once the therapist's wounds are closed, space opens to resume grief work with others. When we continually place clients' needs above our own, the imbalance often leads to therapist burnout.

Along with the denial of death in our society goes the aversion to getting old. Since old age is typically associated with physical deterioration and loss of independence, enormous fear accompanies thoughts of aging. Our personal view of older people has more to do with how they continue to connect to life than with their numerical age. Interpersonal connections, meaningful pursuits, fulfilling mental and physical activity, and capacity to reach out to others are elements that contribute to a greater acceptance of one's aging process. An ability to laugh at oneself also helps. For ourselves, personally, letting go of the "need to get it right" has relieved us of many self-imposed expectations. As you learn to face the issues of aging, loss, and death, you will experience life in the present more fully.

Chapter 18

Couples Experiencing Domestic Violence

You are probably wondering by now about applying this treatment model to other populations, including those who have lived with the turmoil and pain of domestic violence. Here we address indications and contraindications of our model for couples therapy with this population. In addition, we look at the differences among therapists and the controversial personal and clinical issues surrounding domestic violence.

Overview of Domestic Violence

Have any of you ever experienced violence in your own family? The thoughts, emotions, and fears associated with domestic violence are so terrifying that people instinctively avoid talking or thinking about such incidents. They evoke feelings of rage, helplessness, hopelessness, and the ultimate fear of total loss of control. Emotionally laden themes are often avoided by clients and therapists alike. Issues of suicide, homicide, and domestic violence usually lie below the content being presented. In assessing an individual, couple, or family, it is the therapist's job to ask the kinds of questions that will elicit information in these areas. Novice and seasoned therapists alike must be trained in the specific skills necessary for assessment of this growing population. Effective assessment is of paramount importance, since active domestic violence is a contraindication for couples therapy.

Underlying all violence are issues of power and control. These issues manifest themselves in obvious and subtle ways. Using coercion, threats, and intimidation are the more blatant manifestations of power and control. The more subtle destructive behaviors are emotional abuse, economic control, and male domination. Figures 18-1 and 18-2 provide a comprehensive view of these issues.[1] The first depicts a relationship based upon power and control, while the second represents a relationship built upon equality.

Theoretical considerations and methods of therapy are particularly pertinent issues when examining the differences among therapists who work with couples involved in domestic violence. Feminists argue that the field of family therapy fails to include the sociocultural context in its assessment and understanding of abusive behavior. Feminist family therapists disagree with a family systems approach conceptually when it applies to domestic violence. Their central argument is that family theorists have not addressed the differences and inequality between men and women. In fact, Marsali Hansen (1995, p. 72) writes: "Feminist scholars contend that the 'context-free, gender-free' orientation of many current approaches to family therapy promotes inequality among the sexes." Indeed, if therapists do not acknowledge the sociocultural context and power differential in relationships in cases of domestic violence, one can understand how the therapeutic system actually contributes to the notion of "co-responsibility" for the battering or blame for the victim (Hansen, 1995; Jenkins, 1990). Whereas one of the objectives in couple therapy is often to empower both partners, we feel this is clearly contraindicated in the early stages of therapy involving domestic violence. We are both strongly influenced by the Domestic Violence Program of the Southern California Counseling Center and follow its structure when working with couples experiencing family violence.

Discomfort, lack of skill, issues of countertransference, and societal prejudice all interfere with openly addressing the subject of abuse and

---

[1]The Domestic Abuse Intervention Project of the Minnesota Program Development, Inc., has generously given us permission to use their "Power and Control" and "Equality" wheels. They requested that we include their position statement on couples counseling:

Many people are interested in working on relationship issues through the use of couples counseling. While couples counseling can be very beneficial, it is the policy of the Domestic Abuse Intervention Project that persons involved in the nonviolence classes *complete those classes prior to participating in couples counseling*. It is essential that people have dealt with their use of violence and abusive behavior and have made the commitment to remain nonviolent before starting couples counseling. Couples counseling is hard work and can be stressful and painful. Couples counseling *must* be a safe place for both parties involved. A woman may not be free to discuss what she needs to bring up in a couples counseling situation and her safety may be jeopardized if she reveals certain private information.

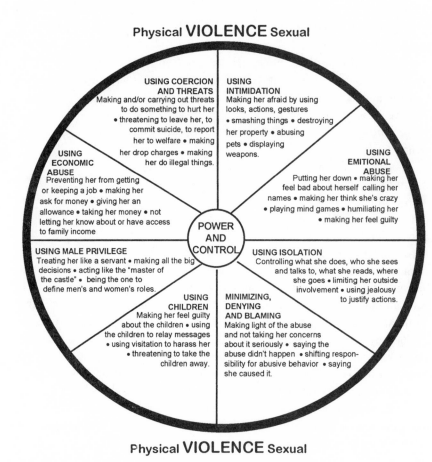

FIGURE 18-1. *Power and Control Wheel*
Reprinted with permission of the Domestic Abuse Intervention Project, 206 West Fourth St., Duluth, MN 55806.

violence. Even experienced counselors have difficulty asking about it. While the effectiveness of couple therapy depends upon the quality of the therapeutic relationship, adequate training and skills are also essential ingredients of therapist competence. The therapist's empathy, respect, and the ability to join are of major importance, but the creative use of questions is a necessary skill that leads to appropriate assessment and treatment. Special questions must be formulated and considered when assessing for the presence of domestic violence. Of critical importance is the issue of safety for all family members. If clients feel safe and supported in the therapeutic environment, it is more likely that they will talk about

NON VIOLENCE

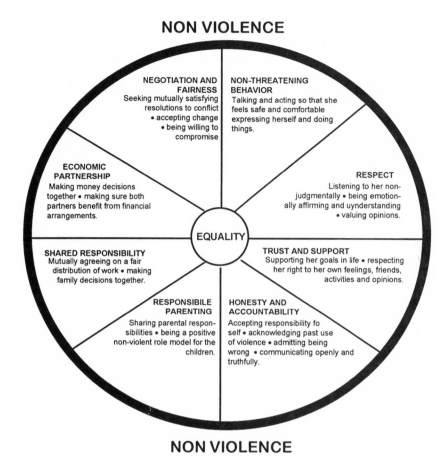

NEGOTIATION AND FAIRNESS
Seeking mutually satisfying resolutions to conflict • accepting change • being willing to compromise

NON-THREATENING BEHAVIOR
Talking and acting so that she feels safe and comfortable expressing herself and doing things.

ECONOMIC PARTNERSHIP
Making money decisions together • making sure both partners benefit from financial arrangements.

RESPECT
Listening to her non-judgmentally • being emotion-ally affirming and uynderstanding • valuing opinions.

EQUALITY

SHARED RESPONSIBILITY
Mutually agreeing on a fair distribution of work • making family decisions together.

TRUST AND SUPPORT
Supporting her goals in life • respecting her right to her own feelings, friends, activities and opinions.

RESPONSIBILE PARENTING
Sharing parental respon-sibilities • being a positive non-violent role model for the children.

HONESTY AND ACCOUNTABILITY
Accepting responsibility fo self • acknowledging past use of violence • admitting being wrong • communicating openly and truthfully.

NON VIOLENCE

FIGURE 18-2. *Equality Wheel*
Reprinted with permission of the Domestic Abuse Intervention Project, 206 West Fourth St., Duluth, MN 55806.

the violence. Before this occurs, however, the therapist must know the right questions to ask and must also be open to the answers.

Let us now turn our attention to the specific skills necessary for thera-pists to get beyond these barriers. The following are some statements and questions to introduce the topic:

- Many of the women we see today are in relationships in which there is an inequality of power. Do you ever feel controlled by your partner?
- It sounds like there is a lot of tension in your relationship. Can you tell me some more about it?

- How do you and your partner handle conflict? When you disagree and your partner doesn't get his way, what happens?
- You say that your husband's temper often gets out of hand. Can you tell me more specifically what you mean? What does he do? How do you respond?
- All couples fight. How do you two fight? Do these fights ever become physical? Does he ever hurt you?
- You say that your partner drinks a lot. Do you fight more or less when he drinks? Do you worry that he will hurt you?
- Does your partner ever get jealous? Does he ever threaten you, control you, humiliate you, or restrict your freedom in any way?

Many women will not acknowledge or talk about the violence they are experiencing at home. Some feel that they are to blame for the abuse. Others feel frightened for their own lives as well as for the lives of their children and/or other family members. Exposure of the truth could lead to life-threatening consequences. However, by asking the right questions, the therapist opens the door to later revelations. The therapist conveys to the client that he or she is available to help handle any situation that may arise from revealing the violence.

A Supervision Session

Jane, one of our supervisees at the Southern California Counseling Center, had been seeing her client, Maureen, for several months. During a routine case presentation, Jane stated that Maureen reported that she and her husband had been in a big fight and might need couple counseling. Further questions about the fight during the counseling session revealed the use of substances, physical threats, and pushing and shoving. When the supervisor asked for more details about the present situation, Jane acknowledged that she had retreated from further questioning of her client because of her own discomfort. Tearing up, she stated, "After hearing about the fight, I felt lost, spacey, and very anxious. I didn't know what to do."

Further discussion in the supervision group revealed strong reactions to this clinical situation. One supervisee thought the case should be reported but did not know about the correct procedures. Another thought an emergency conjoint session should be arranged immediately. As these suggestions were made, the anxiety in the room increased. Jane felt she had handled the session poorly and now worried that her client might be in danger.

Turning to Jane, the supervisor asked, "Do you have any idea what your intense reactions during the session were about?" Jane's reflections and responses led to revelations about abuse experienced in her own family of origin. The "lost, spacey, anxious" emotions she had felt during the session were similar to early childhood emotions. Not knowing what to do was a replication of her role as "lost child."

Once these early feelings were identified, and Jane's vulnerabilities were recognized, she began to look at the case more clearly. The supervisor asked other group members for their personal responses. After validating and normalizing the anxiety and concerns of the group members, the supervisor stated that a clinical assessment would require more information. As reactions were shared, the anxiety level diminished, and the group was then able to shift gears in order to discuss clinical assessment of the case.

Assessment and Treatment of Domestic Violence: The Model of the Southern California Counseling Center

The first therapeutic task in cases of domestic violence is assessment of issues of safety and danger. An appropriate treatment plan cannot be developed until this assessment has been made. Let us return to the case of Maureen. When Jane presented her individual client to the supervision group, the countertransference was identified. The multiple resources of the Southern California Counseling Center were immediately put into motion. The supervisor suggested a case consultation with George Thomas[2] and Connie Shafran, Co-directors of TAPP, The Abuse Prevention Program. Following the Center's philosophy of collaboration, Connie and George joined the next supervision session. A spirit of teamwork guaranteed that everyone's voices and suggestions were heard. Connie and George recommended the following:

1. The first step is for Jane to assess for the existence of violence and the degree of risk and lethality for her client.
2. Jane must educate Maureen about battering and domestic violence and validate her experience. If lethality is present, she will develop a danger management plan with the client.
3. The next step is for Jane to ask Maureen to bring Rick in for a consultation.
4. George will call Rick to make personal contact and invite him to the session.

---

[2] Since we completed this chapter, George Thomas, age 54, died. He was a true pioneer in the field of domestic violence. We appreciate all that he taught us and will deeply miss a wonderful friend.

5. George will then sit in as a consultant with Jane and the couple while Connie joins the supervision group behind the mirror.

It was decided that further recommendations would be made once the level of danger was assessed. Jane was reminded that denial on the part of both partners is often present in cases of domestic violence. The couple must be educated as to exactly what domestic violence means. The wheels in Figures 18-1 and 18-2 could be used to help the couple identify and articulate the specific destructive and violent behaviors.

After the recommendations were made for assessment of the couple, Jane voiced her relief and gratitude for the support she felt from the entire group. During the discussion following Jane's statement, other new counselors revealed their initial reluctance to ask for help. After experiencing this demonstration of teamwork, their anxiety regarding work with this population was greatly reduced. Even in private practice most of us ask for and count on the support of colleagues when handling difficult cases.

Since Jane's client, Maureen, knew about the Center's policy involving teamwork, she had already given permission for consultation and work behind the one-way mirror. This information was reiterated to Rick when he consented to come in for the conjoint consultation with Jane and George. Rick was anxious upon arrival with Maureen at the Center and stated this to Jane and George as they greeted the couple in the waiting room. Appropriate papers were gathered for clients to sign to give permission for viewing behind the one-way mirror. As they all walked up the stairs to the viewing room, Rick asked if he could meet the group who would be watching. Jane readily agreed and brief introductions were made. As is often the case, Maureen and Rick were visibly relieved in meeting the team. They then walked into the counseling room. After everyone was seated, George explained his role as consultant and then asked Jane to briefly describe the rationale for asking him to join the session. Jane talked about her concern for her client's safety. She also explained to George that she was reluctant to reply to Maureen's request for couple work without further assessment. Jane further informed them that during supervision it was decided that Rick's presence and voice were necessary to provide further information.

Dialogue of Consultation

GEORGE: Jane, let's start by bringing everybody up to date on our discussions about Maureen and Rick.

JANE: As you know, I've been meeting individually with Maureen for the past six months. At a recent session she talked about an incident of physical abuse between her and Rick. After talking about it in our supervision group, you and Connie were called in and indicated that further assessment was necessary.

GEORGE: That's right. Let's get to it. Are you guys both aware that the physical behavior that Maureen described is domestic violence?

RICK: Sometimes we do get physical in our fights, but I'd never call it violent. Maureen has never had to go to a hospital.

MAUREEN: Our last fight was pretty violent to me! You really hurt me.

GEORGE: So this just happened recently. When did the first incident of physical assault occur in your relationship?

MAUREEN: Well, we've been married for four years, and the first time he hit me was when we'd both had too much to drink.

GEORGE: When was that exactly?

MAUREEN: About one year after we were married. I stopped drinking before I became pregnant. Then I lost the baby. But the fighting continued anyway.

GEORGE: Rick, do you see it this way too?

RICK: Sure, once in a while we hassle. But it's not as bad as she describes it. Except the part about losing the baby.

GEORGE: Are you aware that what you call hassling is domestic violence, and it is illegal in California?

RICK: *(Defensively and with annoyance in his voice)* No way. Does Maureen look like she's been beat up to you?

After further questioning by George, each partner began to understand that the behaviors that were present in the relationship were acts of violence. These behaviors were then traced back to their respective families of origin. George and Connie concluded that Rick's inability to take responsibility for his acts indicated that couple therapy was inappropriate at this time. Rick was referred to a men's anger management group. Additionally, it became clear that Maureen would benefit from a women's support group. The fact that domestic violence had been acknowledged indicated that George could proceed with his recommendations:

1. Couple therapy was contraindicated until the couple could address future conflicts without violence.
2. Rick was referred to a men's anger management group.
3. Maureen was referred to a women's support group.
4. Skills and tools would be taught to the couple to ensure future safety and communication.

It should be noted that while the men's groups at the Southern California Counseling Center are referred to as anger management groups, at other agencies they may be called men's batterers groups. At some agencies women's support groups may be referred to as women survivors' groups.

Therapist's Biases, Prejudices, and Concerns Regarding the Subject of Domestic Violence

It is of utmost importance for therapists to address their own personal reactions as they work with all clients. In the case of domestic violence, the presence of danger is frightening for therapists and clients alike. The issues of safety, anxiety about the myriad of legal and ethical concerns, and inadequate training are factors that contribute to the complexity of therapist involvement in these cases. Domestic violence is not only a mental health issue; it is a societal crisis and a systemic problem of many dimensions. It occurs at all levels of society, regardless of age, culture, race, religion, socioeconomic class, or sexual orientation. Police are reluctant to intervene in domestic conflicts. Emergency room physicians often fail to ask appropriate questions that uncover violence and brutality. Many health-care providers also choose to look the other way, sometimes out of ignorance, sometimes out of fear.

Necessary Knowledge and Skills

To assess and to work with this population, therapists need:

- Comprehensive training in assessment and crises intervention
- Information on abuse and violence
- Knowledge of legal options and community resources
- Well-formulated questions that will elicit information
- Recognition of the enormity and seriousness of this life-threatening situation
- Competent supervision
- Awareness of one's own relationship to anger, rage, and violence

In summary, let us quote from the *Domestic Violence Training Manual* (Shafran & Thomas, 1997, p. 10):

Treatment issues include beginning with crisis intervention to ensure safety from abuse and stopping the violence. This may involve helping clients to connect with social and legal agencies. Treatment must be determined by the needs and violence characteristics of the clients. Couples or family work is not appropriate treatment, for example, when the violence has not stopped. Treatment for the trauma of domestic violence requires long-term intervention and requires motivated clients in an effort to restore esteem and personal resources and new ways of communication and conflict resolution. At best it is a slow process.

As we conclude this chapter let us ask you once again, Have you ever experienced violence in your own family? If so, (or, if not) how do you think your own experience will affect your clinical work?

Chapter 19

Working with Sexually Distressed Couples

Most couples present with the issues of money, sex, in-laws, and children. Early on in relationships, these presenting problems become the battleground. As the power struggle surfaces in therapy, the role of the therapist is to address the underlying significance of the interaction. Even if the presenting problem is not a sexual one, sexual issues are likely to emerge during the course of ongoing therapy. When sexual symptoms are presented, the therapist must first examine the partners' way of relating and the quality of their relationship. Is intimacy "the problem"? Does the sexual distress have organic aspects? Do medications, alcohol, or other substances play a part? What was going on in the relationship when the symptoms appeared?

Philosophically, we both view sexuality as a vital component of the total marital system. Each partner in the relationship must view him or herself as a complete person in order to feel good as a sexual being. People need to feel "at home" in their bodies and comfortable with their genders. Self-validation is a necessary component of a satisfying relationship and is certainly the cornerstone of a fulfilling sexual relationship. When we look to our mates to make us feel whole, we are headed for trouble. Work on oneself leads to clarity and reduced reactivity. This, in turn, leads to greater intimacy.

Evolving Paradigms in Human Sexuality

As with the early models of psychotherapy, beginning studies of human sexuality emanated from the medical model rather than the knowledge of healthy sexual functioning. The first scientific studies of human sexual behavior were conducted by Alfred Kinsey and his colleagues (Kinsey, Pomeroy, Martin, & Gebhard, 1948, 1953). The pioneering studies of William Masters and Virginia Johnson (1965) provided detailed descriptions of the human sexual response cycle. However, they paid little attention to the role of the psychosocial and psychological components in sexual functioning. In *The New Sex Therapy* (1974), Helen Singer Kaplan presented her biphasic model of the sexual response. Then, in *Disorders of Sexual Desire* (1979), she addressed the neglected concepts of erotic arousal and sexual desire. Although Kaplan made significant contributions to the development of a comprehensive model of human sexuality, David Schnarch (1991, p. 19) points out that her model failed to take into account "the human capacity for intimacy and attaching profound emotional meaning to sexual experience."

Schnarch's *Constructing the Sexual Crucible* (1991) integrates the multiple dimensions of sexuality: physiological, psychological, biological, and spiritual. Indeed, his contributions propel thinking forward and move therapists and laymen alike beyond symptomatology and dysfunction. His model emphasizes eroticism and intimacy, a focus philosophically aligned with the field's current inclination toward models of health and growth rather than dysfunction and pathology.

Taking a Sexual History

The partners' relationship and communication patterns are reflected in their sexual interaction. Robin Skynner (1976) refers to sexuality as a catalyst and "a touchstone for the quality of the total relationship." Whether the couple presents with a form of sexual distress or another relationship issue, our assumption is that there are correlations between the presenting problem and other relational interactions. Open communication is an important part of any relationship, and certainly a frank and straightforward discussion about sex in one's relationship is essential and, in our view, a goal of all couple therapy. Even when sexual issues are not the presenting problem, exploration of the couple's sexual relationship is an important part of the total therapeutic experience. Generally, what occurs in the sexual arena is part of the marital dance. The current interactional patterns of conflict, anger, and intimacy are indeed in the couple's crowded bed with them.

Taking a sexual history is an important part of the couple assessment. Of course, the therapist must be joined with and sensitive to the spouses to judge their readiness to discuss this topic. In some cases, feelings of shame and learned inhibitions must first be acknowledged as part of this process. Routinely, we ask the couple's permission to explore this subject. For example, we might begin by stating, "Many of us feel somewhat uncomfortable and inhibited when talking about sex. How does each of you feel about discussing this topic?" We raise the following questions at some point during the therapy, even when the presenting problem is not of a sexual nature.

1. What are the beliefs regarding sexuality in your family of origin? How are these beliefs similar to or different from your own beliefs today?
2. What are your early memories about your parents' sexual relationship? How do these memories impact your relationship today?
3. When did you first experience sexual feelings?
4. What was your first sexual experience like?
5. What did you learn in your family of origin about the way gender roles influence intimate relationships?
6. How do you think your parents felt about their gender roles? How do you feel about being a man or a woman?
7. How did you first learn about sex?
8. What were your parents' attitudes about sexuality?
9. Do you recall any early sexual fantasies? What feelings do you associate with them?
10. What are your long-held assumptions and beliefs about men? About women?
11. What associations do you have to the terms homosexuality and heterosexuality?
12. What did you learn in your family of origin about same-sex and opposite-sex relating?
13. How is your sexual relationship today different from when you first met? What are your memories about your early pleasurable times together?
14. Do you want your sexual relationship to change? If so, how?
15. What do you need from your partner to flourish? What do you want more of from your partner? What do you want less of from your partner?
16. Do you perceive yourself as worthy of pleasure?
17. When were your most pleasurable times with one another?
18. The "sexual miracle" question: Suppose you had the "perfect" sexual encounter with your partner before tomorrow morning. When you awakened, how would you feel? What would the relationship look like? What would you and your partner be saying to one another?

Mike and Lynn

Lynn and Mike shared a truly crowded bed. Both sets of in-laws were dominant in their lives from the beginning of their relationship. With a pregnancy during the first year of their marriage and debts from medical school, the couple welcomed their parents' financial help. Before long, however, they realized there were strings attached to this arrangement. After the arrival of the first grandchild, Lynn and Mike's small apartment was the scene of constant visits from the families. While boundaries needed to be set to ensure the young family's privacy, Lynn had a hard time limiting parental visits. When Mike had a rare weekend off, he was angry at his parents' and his in-laws' intrusions. Over time this constant intrusiveness became a source of friction for the couple. By the time their second child was born three years later, distance had developed between Lynn and Mike. Their early playfulness, warmth, and companionship were virtually nonexistent. Lynn began to spend even more time with her family, and Mike's patients became his priority. Each had triangulated another source to relieve the tension between them. Remember, a twosome is an unstable relationship; the status quo is maintained by bringing in a third party.

When Lynn and Mike entered therapy with Toby, this situation had taken its toll upon their relationship. Sex had become their battleground.

MIKE: You never want sex anymore. I may as well sleep at the hospital for all the attention I get at home.

LYNN: You're never around, and when you are, you're on the phone talking to your patients. The kids and I are not a priority.

TOBY: When did things change at home?

MIKE: It's hard to remember. It has been so long.

LYNN: I do remember a wonderful weekend the two of us had in Big Sur. It was only last year. Things felt wonderful then.

TOBY: So this shift seemed to happen about a year ago. What was going on at that time?

MIKE: Nothing unusual.

LYNN: But don't you remember a week after we returned from Big Sur my dad had a heart attack?

MIKE: Well, I do remember. But he's better now, so how does that affect us?

TOBY: Any illness, loss, or trauma in the family can have a profound effect upon a couple's relationship. Let's explore the possible effects upon you of Lynn's father's heart attack.

Further exploration revealed that the sexual distress experienced by this couple was directly related to the anxiety and unresolved grief surrounding Lynn's father's heart attack. Norman and Betty Paul (1990, p. 87) point out the importance of making connections between symptoms and earlier losses: "Previously hidden sources of anger and hurt are brought to the light of day, where their power to distort the present can be diminished." Partners who distance from each other in their present relationship are unconsciously reacting to previous anxiety and pain. It is, therefore, important for therapists to track what was going on in the couple's life when the relationship began to change. In the above dialogue we see that the symptom of sexual distress directly relates to anxiety and loss in Lynn's family of origin. Lynn and Mike experienced considerable relief as the sources of anger and hurt were identified and examined. Over time, Mike developed empathy for his wife as she began to openly experience the grief surrounding her father's brush with death.

Three Months Later

Lynn and Mike grew closer to each other during extensive family-of-origin work, as earlier hostilities were diffused. The pervasive distancing that had characterized their earlier interaction was replaced with a new-found respect and intimacy. A solid therapeutic alliance paved the way to address the couple's sexual relationship.

TOBY: Last week we talked about your sexual relationship. How do you feel about beginning to discuss it?

LYNN: I'm a bit scared about it. I realize it's the one issue we have been avoiding here.

MIKE: Well, our sex life is better than when we first started therapy. But we still have a long way to go.

TOBY: Your hard work in therapy these past few months reflects your strong commitment to each other. Talking about sex and intimacy is difficult for all of us. But it feels as if the time is right for us to do this now. What are some of your anxieties about this topic?

LYNN: Sex was something I never talked about with anyone. It was a taboo topic in my family, and it's embarrassing for me.

TOBY: So in your family, Lynn, you learned that sex was a forbidden subject. What about your family, Mike?

MIKE: As the youngest of four boys, I learned about sex at a real young age. My mom always railed at the foul language we used. And my dad just laughed with us.

TOBY: So what did you learn from all of that, Mike?

MIKE: I thought that men approved of sex and enjoyed it, and that all women were prudish and disapproving of it.

LYNN: I don't think I'm a prude but I'm certainly not as comfortable with sex as you are.

TOBY: How do you think these early beliefs that Mike learned at home affect you as a couple today?

LYNN: I think Mike sees me as disapproving and not much fun—especially in bed.

MIKE: I certainly didn't see you that way early in the relationship. But the stress of the last few years has taken its toll on us.

TOBY: How would each of you like to see your sexual relationship change?

MIKE: I'd like to see more of it!

LYNN: Would it surprise you to hear that I'd like more of it, too?

TOBY: *(Smiling)* Well, that seems to be something you both agree on. What do you need from each other to make that happen?

Because of the solid therapeutic foundation already provided, Lynn and Mike were responsive to addressing their sexual issues. This dialogue demonstrates how the therapist empowered them to make an agreement about change in their sexual relationship. The therapist was sensitive to and respectful of the couple's readiness and pacing. She obtained permission from the couple to proceed with questions, explored family-of-origin attitudes and beliefs, linked the past to the present, and collaborated with the couple to make a contract for change.

Sexual Intimacy: A Developmental Task

Couples connect on many different levels: emotional, spiritual, sexual, financial, social, cultural, historical, intellectual. These ways of connecting deepen the bonds of intimacy. These levels of relating must be addressed as couples navigate the life-cycle stages. Sexual attraction is often part of what draws a couple together. Keeping this part of a relationship alive and vital is one of the tasks of marriage. While often a pleasurable task, it is not an easy one. Judith Wallerstein and Sandra Blakeslee (1995, p. 183) capture the essence of this aspect of intimacy:

> The sixth task of marriage is to create a loving sexual relationship and to guard it well so that it will endure. A good sex life, however the couple defines that, is at the heart of a good marriage. This is the domain where intimacy is renewed and the excitement that first drew the couple together is kept alive. The bedroom is a privileged place for light-hearted play, laughter, adventure, passion, pleasure, where a couple can achieve freedom from childhood taboos. There is no better antidote to the pressures of living than a loving sex life.

David Schnarch (1991, p. xv) states that "eroticism and intimacy in marriage (and marriage itself) are adult developmental tasks." Building sexual intimacy requires open and ongoing communication, creativity, imagination, and energy. The lasting quality of the sexual relationship depends upon the interactional dance of the couple and the specialness of the passion they are able to create together.

Chapter 20

Working with the Lesbian and Gay Population: It Starts with Self-Examination

We have struggled with how to write about gay and lesbian clients in a way that would be authentic and true to our own experience. When we went to graduate school in the mid-seventies, programs paid little, if any, attention to same-sex couple relationships. Instructors and supervisors reassured us that the treatment of heterosexual and homosexual relationships was the same. We did not realize at the time that this advice represented avoidance and denial of our prejudices. In our culture, being gay meant invisibility, secrecy, denial, and shame. Not only were we unaware of the actual issues relevant to understanding homosexual clients, but we had little basis for relating to their subjective experiences. In the intervening years, gay people have become more visible. As John Patten (1992) writes, "Gay people have suddenly become visible. Their lives, relationships, and families are now an integral part of the urban and suburban landscape." At conferences more workshops are offered on gay and lesbian treatment issues, and there are more opportunities for graduate students to acknowledge their personal reactions to emotionally laden issues in general.

Our richest learning experience in diversity took place in the classroom, not as students but as instructors at Antioch University Los Angeles. The curriculum encouraged us to "teach" diversity, to acknowledge differences across all cultures. How were we to accomplish this? We began to look more sharply at our own prejudices, biases, and stereotypical thinking. We were struck by what had been buried beneath the surface. We also felt a sense of shame with the enormity and intensity of the feelings. We had been proud of our history of self-examination. But lo and behold! Look into those cobwebby corners and see what you find! A close look at our attitudes, prejudices, and discomforts is absolutely essential for therapists, especially when it comes to the issues of gender identity, sexuality, and homophobia.

A sense of gender identity is established very early in childhood, perhaps even in the womb. We are less likely to be confused or anxious about our gender identity if we have as models individuals with a strong sense of self-worth and secure gender identity. When we talk about a secure sense of identities we are not talking about the old rigid roles of male and female. What we are talking about is a family situation in which parents exchange roles. Both can be nurturers; both can set limits; cooking and cleaning may be shared responsibilities. Thus, traditional stereotypical roles are challenged. In opposite-sex coupleships, the exchange of roles is difficult enough. In same-sex couples, the task may seem overwhelming and confusing. Laura Markowitz (1991) states this dilemma well:

> The fact that same-sex couples have to balance stress in so many systems at once—their own families-of-origin, their relationship, the gay/lesbian community, their ethnic or religious communities, and mainstream society—makes their efforts at forming a family an impressive juggling act. And the complexity of a relationship between people with the same gender socialization can create further confusion and conflict, yet the problem may not be evident to the straight therapist.

In 1973 the American Psychiatric Association decreed that homosexuality was no longer a pathological condition (Markowitz, 1991). This did not, however, lead to automatic acceptance and understanding of gays and lesbians. Many of us consider ourselves sensitive to homosexual issues, and on the surface we probably are. However, we are all subject to the internalized beliefs, images, and societal attitudes that characterize homophobia. The terms racism, sexism, bigotry, and prejudice bring up feelings of shame and defensiveness in all of us. Homophobia also evokes shame.

What does the term "homophobia" mean to you? What thoughts or feelings are you aware of when the topic of homosexuality is raised? These are questions we all need to ask ourselves. When we bring these questions up with our students, they are initially uncomfortable. However, as the spirit of learning about oneself prevails, class members begin to share and reveal their innermost thoughts and vulnerabilities while exploring the issue of homophobia. When we are willing to disclose some of our personal fantasies and prejudices, the students are willing to reveal theirs.

Dealing with the sexual component in relationships can sometimes feel like walking through a minefield. You never know when there will be an explosion or an eruption. Saying the unsayable in the area of sexuality is akin to disrobing in a room of fully dressed people. Through open and intimate classroom discussions, however, the topic of sexuality becomes less frightening and emotional. Classes that are limited in size, of course, are most conducive to these kinds of discussions. When the group is large, we often structure smaller subgroups to encourage more openness and spontaneity. The following dialogue, a composite of our experiences, represents a typical classroom discussion.

INSTRUCTOR: As I mentioned last week, today we will be talking about the issues of our own sexuality and how this impacts our work with clients. Just as I always ask permission from my clients for such a discussion, I'm wondering where all of you are as you consider this topic.

SALLY: I guess I'm really anxious about any discussion of sex. It was hardly ever mentioned in my family, and I can't imagine ever bringing it up with clients.

ANDY: In my internship I'm starting to see a few couples. Since I'm gay, I feel more knowledgeable about same-sex couples. But I'm not as comfortable with heterosexual clients.

SALLY: With me it's just the opposite. I always wonder if I'll know enough to work with gay couples.

INSTRUCTOR: Whatever our own sexual orientation, we learn attitudes and prejudices from our families of origin and from our culture and society at large. I learned early on in this work that in order to be effective I had to openly and honestly examine my own sexuality. The first time I was attracted to a client, I was confused, ashamed, and even found it difficult to bring up the subject in supervision.

DEREK: I'd be embarrassed to reveal that too. How did you bring it up?

INSTRUCTOR: With great difficulty. But once I did summon up my courage, other people in my supervision group talked about similar experiences. As we opened up the subject, it seemed everyone was relieved to talk about it. Since the group had been meeting for several months, it felt safe to expose ourselves.

SUE ANN: I wouldn't have felt safe enough here at our first class meeting or two. But now that we've gotten to know each other better, it feels OK.

INSTRUCTOR: The same holds true in clinical work. You must be joined with clients for them to feel safe enough to reveal on a deeper level.

ANDY: I thought I was safe enough in my family, but it sure took a lot for me to reveal that I was gay to my parents. And I'm still not sure they can deal with it. They always introduce my lover as my good friend from college.

WENDY: How do you handle that?

ANDY: My siblings are real supportive and have encouraged me to confront my folks. I'm not sure I'm ready for that yet.

INSTRUCTOR: The fact that you're able to discuss this here is a big step and shows a lot of courage.

What we've demonstrated here is a dialogue that will invite more conversations. The issues of sexuality, gender identity, and homophobia no longer seem to be taboo topics. In order to do this work it is necessary to acknowledge shame, liberate one's own silenced voices, and face longstanding inhibitions and prejudices.

Working with Oppressed Populations

The legacy of oppression cannot be underestimated in terms of its impact upon clinical work with couples and families. We saw in the case of Laura and Michael how the horror of the Holocaust imprinted generations of a family. Slavery left wounds that still fester in the relationships of African Americans and white Americans. Prejudice still exists. Gay and lesbian couples are still perceived by many heterosexuals as abnormal. Homophobia runs rampant. Therapists who are not aware of such oppression are doing their clients a great disservice.

As therapists, how do we handle specific clinical situations in which there is a background of oppression? First and foremost, we must examine our internal responses. Our own political values and prejudices must be acknowledged. For example, if our grandparents were Nazi sympathizers, can we work with a Holocaust family? If we are frightened by the aggression associated with the stereotype of black male power, how effective can we be with a black couple experiencing domestic violence? If our parents have rejected a sister and her lesbian lover, how will our own emotions affect how we work with a young lesbian couple? These are obvious clinical dilemmas for the couple and family therapist. In order to work effectively and ethically we must seek out consultation and/or supervision with colleagues. If we cannot suspend our prejudices and judgments, a referral is indicated. Even when our own prejudices do not strongly interfere, we must invite our clients to educate us. They are our best teachers. In this way we can work collaboratively to understand and appreciate the effect of the oppression upon them. When our clients' wounds are fully acknowledged and understood, our work together will be effective and powerful.

Meeting the Challenge: Developing Culturally Sensitive Training Contexts

More attention must be devoted to training therapists to become both culturally aware and culturally sensitive. Awareness and sensitivity are key ingredients in an effective response to couples and families. Training programs tend to emphasize promotion of cultural awareness and underemphasize the affective component of cultural sensitivity. Kenneth Hardy and Tracey Laszloffy (1995, p. 227) write:

> The content-focused approach to multicultural education overemphasizes the characteristics of various cultural groups while ignoring the importance of the trainees' perceptions of and feelings toward their respective cultural backgrounds. As a result, trainees are rarely challenged to examine how their respective cultural identities influence understanding and acceptance of those who are both culturally similar and dissimilar.

They describe the distinction between awareness and sensitivity. Basically, the former is a cognitive function; the latter is an affective function. While awareness involves an intellectual process, sensitivity "is primarily an affective function: an individual responds emotionally to stimuli with delicacy and respectfulness."

How can trainers and trainees work together to create contexts that will promote the awareness and sensitivity necessary for training competent therapists? We believe that learning occurs through creation of contexts that are respectful, collaborative, and sensitive to exploration of personal reactions, multicultural experiences, biases, and prejudices. Trainers and trainees alike must be willing to examine their cultural identities in classroom, supervision, and other training settings.

Personal Reflections

Endings and anticipated separations have a way of producing incredible intensity and reactivity. Nearing the end of our collaborative efforts in writing this book propelled us to further examine our own issues of loss, separation, and abandonment. With one of us (Toby) moving from Los Angeles and the other (Barbara) dealing with her children's move to other states and her husband's working commute to Canada, issues of separation and abandonment loomed large. Both of us continually worked at sorting out the reality of present separation from our own childhood feelings of abandonment. We reminded ourselves that separation and abandonment have different meanings. We distinguished today's reality from yesterday's pain. The poignancy of this occurrence in our own relationship further clarified and enabled us to understand this important dynamic in the couples with whom we work.

Throughout our writing together our personal lives were continually evolving. During this two-year period we moved through a number of life-cycle transitions. Several very close friends and colleagues died suddenly, leaving us bereft and putting us in touch with our own mortality. Children were married, grandchildren were born, parents became aged and infirm, family crises erupted, and careers shifted. These developmental changes provided opportunities to reexamine our lives.

At various times in our writing, sibling rivalry produced competitive emotions, which were often difficult to acknowledge. We felt profound shame. As two first-borns, each having one sibling, we became competitive with each other. Our "sistership" was definitely a reworking of early family-of-origin positions. The old yearnings to be "Mom's favorite" increased as the book progressed. At times we competed with ideas, and at other times we competed to be the favorite with our editor, Susan Munro. When tension mounted in the writing room, exploration and processing cleared the air and moved us to a new level in our relationship. We are well aware that this sorting out is an ongoing process. As first-born children, we are not likely to relinquish our need to be stars! Perhaps this is what propelled us to write this book together in the first place.

The rituals that emerged in the writing process became part of our collaborative relationship. Our lunches together, brisk walks, nightly telephone calls with new additions and deletions all added to the richness and intimacy of our relationship. In a parallel way, our writing also moved to a deeper level. Our conversations generated more conversations. Our questions generated more questions.

As *The Crowded Bed* progressed, our confidence in ourselves as women, therapists, and competent writers increased. At times, however, we still needed to quiet those old nagging voices that told us to stay in our familiar places without rocking the boat. The motto, "A woman's place is in the House—and the Senate," expressed our internal conflict and ambivalence about our use of power in the world. Writing this book is, indeed, a declaration of our emerging beliefs and convictions. We are privileged to share this experience with you.

Glossary

alcoholic system Couple or family system in which one or more members abuses a substance. The couple or family then organizes interactions and patterns around the symptom.

blended marriage A new form of family structure that emerges with remarriage.

boundaries The demarcation of a part from the larger whole. In terms of family systems theory, it marks off a particular subsystem (individual, couple, children) from the larger family and/or community system. There are boundaries within the self, between self and other, as well as between the couple or family and the outside world (Scarf, 1995; Solomon, 1989).

Bowen Theory A theory which conceptualizes the family as a network of interlocking relationships. Bowen theory conceptualizes the family as an emotional unit or as a network of interlocking relationships, not only among the family members, but also among biological, psychological, and sociological processes. The originator of family systems theory and pioneer of family therapy, Murray Bowen, introduced eight interlocking concepts that are central to his theory and pivotal for deepening one's understanding of human behavior: differentiation of self, triangles, nuclear family emotional system, family projection process, multigenerational transmission process, sibling position, emotional cutoff, and societal regression (Kerr & Bowen, 1988).

circular questioning A manner of questioning that is exploratory and that stimulates clients to consider new meanings to their life circumstances. As questions are asked, clients move from a linear to a more expansive view of their situation, thus opening new possibilities.

circularity Process or way of thinking in which the therapist attends to patterns of interaction and the connection and interplay of perceptions, events, feelings, and persons.

collaborative language systems theory A postmodern approach to therapy that focuses upon language and the dialogical conversation between therapist and clients as the major instruments of change. The therapist maintains a "not-knowing," curious, respectful attitude and is the guide for the therapeutic conversation and process.

communication The exchange and interaction of ideas, thoughts, and feelings that occur on a conscious and/or unconscious level. A message between people that may be expressed verbally or nonverbally.

complementary relationship A pattern of communication between two people in which differences are maximized and unequal. For example, aggressive/submissive, superior/inferior.

complementarity The polarity of differences in a couple's interaction. Like children on a see-saw in a playground, when one is up the other is down. Partners alternate such positions. One overfunctions while the other underfunctions. One is emotional while the other is rational.

conjoint therapy Therapy conducted with two or more people in sessions.

constructionism Concept that focuses on "how people interact with one another to construct, modify, and maintain what their society holds to be true, real, and meaningful." This interactional view is distinguished from constructivism, which emphasizes how an individual constructs reality (Freedman & Combs, 1996, p. 27).

constructivism Concept that focuses "on how an individual person constructs a model of reality from his or her individual experience." This is distinguished from the more interactional view of social constructionism (Freedman & Combs, 1996, p. 27).

containment The ability to tolerate and contain internally the full range and intensity of emotion. This skill is critical for couple therapists to maintain their professional role as primitive emotions emerge in both clients and therapists.

contextual influences The threads that run through the various theoretical frameworks: race, gender, culture, class, religion, ethnicity, and sexuality.

co-therapy Couple or family therapy conducted by two therapists.

countertransference The sum total of the therapist's emotional responses toward the client which may be conscious or unconscious. The therapist's understanding of his or her own reactions is the cornerstone for doing effective clinical work.

culture "a broad multidimensional concept that includes but is not limited to ethnicity, gender, social class, and so forth" (Hardy & Laszloffy, 1995, p. 228).

cybernetics The study and operation of feedback loops and mechanisms that have the ability to self-regulate systems. In first-order cybernetics the system being observed is separate from the observer. In second-order cybernetics the therapist is no longer an outside observer but is part of the system that is being observed and modified.

dance of a couple The way partners interact over time so that patterns become a repetitive sequence.

defense mechanisms Mechanisms that develop in early childhood to protect a person's ego from anxiety-producing thoughts. This is generally an unconscious process.

developmental stages Series of longitudinal events that mark an individual's or a family's life and enable it to be seen as a system evolving through time.

developmental tasks At each stage in the family life cycle there are specific jobs that must be accomplished successfully in order to move on to the next stage.

dialogical conversations A shared inquiry between therapist and clients, which includes internal and external dialogue. This generative conversation is central to the collaborative language systems approach to therapy and involves a collaboration and crisscrossing of ideas among participants (Anderson, 1997, p. 112).

didactic Communication that reflects text material in contrast to experiential expression.

differentiation of self The cornerstone of Bowen theory and therapy. This concept refers to the ability of the individual to distinguish internally between the rational and emotional parts of self. This process enables family members to break free from long-standing reflexive responses and to become more objective and rational. "The ability to be in emotional contact with others yet still autonomous in one's emotional functioning is the essence of the concept of differentiation" (Kerr & Bowen, 1988, p. 145).

disengaged system A family or couple in which members feel unconnected, isolated, and uninvolved with each other.

domestic violence An interaction in a couple relationship in which emotional and physical intensity escalates, with destructive, even life-threatening, consequences.

double bind A type of communication in which two conflicting messages are expressed simultaneously. One is verbal; the other is nonverbal, thus placing the recipient in a conflicted situation.

dyad A relationship between any two persons.

dysfunctional system A couple or family that is impaired in the ability to cope with stressful situations.

empathy The ability "to feel what the other feels while maintaining psychological separateness" (Givelber, 1990, p. 176).

enmeshed system A family or couple in which members are overinvolved in each others' lives, boundaries are blurred, and healthy differentiation is difficult to achieve.

emotional cutoff Murray Bowen's concept describing the process by which people distance themselves from their families of origin by separating physically and/or emotionally.

epistemology The study of knowledge as it applies to a specific body of information.

ethnicity Those "unique characteristics of a cultural group" that are transmitted by the family over many generations (Goldenberg & Goldenberg, 1996, p. 36).

experiential Active use of self as a vehicle in learning.

externalization The symptom or problem is seen as occurring outside the individual, couple, or family rather than within. In this way forces may be mobilized to fight this outside "intruder."

externalizing conversations An intervention technique pioneered by Michael White and David Epston in which there is a linguistic separation between the person experiencing the problem and the problem itself.

family dynamics The various patterns that operate in the family system.

family legacies A tangible or intangible emotional inheritance that is handed down from the past. This may take the form of beliefs, myths, traditions, or tangible gifts.

family life cycle A view that focuses upon the developmental stages, tasks, and transitions through which individuals, couples, and family members move from birth to death (McGoldrick, 1995, p. 31).

family myths Beliefs that are deeply embedded in the family system and that often influence how people interpret life events. These beliefs are generally handed down from generation to generation.

family projection process The process by which undifferentiated parents unconsciously focus upon the most vulnerable child. One of the eight concepts that is central to Bowen theory.

family role A position assumed early in life by an individual, generally on an unconscious level. It often continues into adult life. Examples are caretaker, scapegoat, savior.

family secrets The concealment of family information often involving deception. This has a profound effect upon relationships. Boundaries are created by secrecy which controls the processes of togetherness and separateness (Lerner, 1993).

family systems theory This theory, pioneered by Murray Bowen, is based on the idea of the family as a complex system in which the complete unit is greater than the sum of its parts. Bowen viewed the family as a natural system that could only be understood in terms of the repetitive interactions of its members.

family of origin Refers to an individual's original family.

functional family system A couple or family in which the members have found satisfactory ways to cope with life situations.

gender The male/female identification of an individual.

genogram A graphic representation of a multigenerational family constellation. The therapeutic activity of drawing a genogram is a tangible way to punctuate systemic patterns, reframe and normalize situations, and explore how present issues are connected to a broader generational context.

homeostasis The maintenance of a steady state in a system.

homophobia Fear and hatred of same-sex relationships (Brown & Zimmer, 1986). Ignorance, insensitivity, stereotyped thinking, prejudice, discrimination and other negative attitudes are often used synonymously with this concept (Markowitz, 1991).

identified patient The individual designated by the family as the one who has "the problem."

individuality "refers to the capacity to be an individual while part of a group" (Kerr & Bowen, 1988, p. 63).

internal family relationships The internal models of family members that are inside each of us and are based upon our original direct experiences with parents and other significant people. Also called objects or images, these are powerful forces that shape our perceptions and interactions in all relationships.

internalization The process of "taking in" experiences of interactions with others, which then become part of an individual's internal world.

internalized-other interviewing An experiential mode of questioning created by Karl Tomm which elicits empathy and understanding as each partner moves into the other's experience. Partners learn how to differentiate their "internalized partner" from their "actual partner."

intimacy The expression of vulnerability of self with one's partner. It is "a multisystemic process—intrapersonal and interpersonal—involving both the discloser's relationship with the partner and his/her relationship with himself/herself" (Schnarch, 1991).

isomorphism The correspondence or parallel process that occurs at different levels of a system. For example, the client/therapist interaction may mirror aspects of the interactional process that occurs between therapist and supervisor. (See parallel process.)

joining The process by which the therapist enters the couple system through empathic understanding, acceptance, and recognition of each partner's perception of reality. It is an ongoing therapeutic task that facilitates change in the system.

linear questioning A manner of questioning that is investigative and enables therapists to gather information as they orient themselves to their client's situation. These basic questions ("Who did what?" "Where?" "When?" and "Why?") are often necessary to facilitate the joining process (Tomm, 1988a). Since these kinds of questions may stimulate clients to be critical of themselves or others, the therapist must track clients' responses closely.

language The primary vehicle through which we communicate and give understanding, order, and meaning to our lives by use of spoken and unspoken words (Anderson, 1997, p. 201).

meta-communication Communication about communication.

modeling A process of learning in which people emulate the behavior of others.

multigenerational transmission process A central concept of Bowen theory that refers to the transmission of emotional processes, patterns, and behaviors over the generations.

narrative theory and therapy A postmodern constructivist approach formulated by Michael White in Australia and David Epston in New Zealand. The central theory is that "the problem" is placed outside the family (externalized) rather than within an individual. The problem is viewed in a nonpathological manner, and the family is empowered to co-construct a new story (narrative) with the therapist in order to generate new stories and perspectives into their lives (Goldenberg & Goldenberg, 1996).

neutrality The therapist's ability to define and acknowledge his or her own values, judgments, opinions, feelings, and prejudices without being emotionally or ego-invested in changing anyone else. The therapist must be free and clear of any intention for clients to be a particular way.

normalizing The process of validating and acknowledging clients' feelings and circumstances. It is a way of letting clients know they are not crazy, and, in fact, that other people in these circumstances behave similarly. This is conveyed not only by the therapists' words but by his or her accepting, nonjudgmental attitude. Most couple and family therapists use this type of intervention often, regardless of their theoretical orientation. Sometimes this technique is called "universalizing" (Berg, 1994).

nuclear family A family whose members live together as a unit.

nuclear family emotional system A key aspect of Murray Bowen's theory, this concept refers to the tendency of people to choose partners with similar levels of differentiation. They then produce a family with similar characteristics and patterns. The anxiety in a highly fused dyad may produce symptoms that result in marital conflict, dysfunction in one spouse, and/or psychological problems in a child.

object relations theory Theory that examines human behavior in terms of early relational experiences with primary caregivers. A basic premise of this theory is that all of us have internalized mental representations of people and relationships and that these internal experiences, formed in childhood, provide the framework for perceiving objective reality in adulthood (Scarf, 1987). This theory interweaves the intrapsychic with the interpersonal.

paradigm A model, philosophy, and/or set of assumptions that describes a particular perspective or school of thought.

parallel process A behavior, thought, or action that occurs simultaneously at different levels of a system. The client-therapist interaction may, for example, mirror the interaction of the therapist-supervisor pair. (See isomorphism.)

parental child A child who takes on the role of the parent in the family.

parental subsystem The parents in a nuclear family.

positive connotation A family therapy technique in which the therapist prescribes the symptom in relation to its social context and with respect for the family's need to protect its equilibrium and maintain homeostasis of the system (Boscolo, Cecchin, Hoffman, & Penn, 1987).

power differential The lack of total equality in relationships with regard to decision-making and all other processes of couple and family interactions.

primitive emotions Very early childhood feelings that are often evoked in adulthood. When these emotions occur in later life, the reactions are often out of proportion to the current stimulus.

projection Process of attributing one's own feelings, thoughts, and reactions to another person.

projective identification The process in which internal images or disowned aspects of an individual are projected unto another person; the other person unconsciously accepts the projection and behaves as if it were his or her own (Scharff & Scharff, 1981, p. 8). An intrapsychic and interpersonal concept of object relations theory. It is a framework of thinking that enables the therapist to understand the interplay of the internal subjectivity of each partner while simultaneously observing the external couple system.

psychodrama A powerful group therapy experience in which participants actually enact their situations through role reversals, doubling, and other methods that deepen perceptions, thoughts, and feelings, and increase spontaneity.

punctuation A therapeutic statement that emphasizes and highlights a particular process that has occurred.

reflecting team A technique for learning and thinking about human systems that is frequently used in family therapy training. The supervision team generally views a live clinical session through the one-way mirror. At some point during or following the session, the team exchanges rooms with the therapist and client couple or family. The therapist and client watch and listen to the team reflect upon their session. At the conclusion of the comments, all participants return to their original rooms. The therapist then reviews with the couple the impact of the experience upon them. Tom Andersen (1991) is the creator of this technique.

reflexive questioning Questions that are facilitative and that are designed to enable change in couples and families by stimulating them to give new meaning to their actions, perceptions, and behaviors. These questions encourage people to reconsider preexisting belief systems. They frame current behaviors in a fashion that implies new ways to interpret old patterns of behavior (Tomm, 1987, 1988a).

reframing A therapy technique that enables clients to conceptualize the meaning of their situation differently. The setting or viewpoint of a situation is placed in "another frame which fits the 'facts' of the same concrete situation equally well or even better, and thereby changes its entire meaning" (Watzlawick, Weakland, & Fisch, 1974, p. 95).

ripple effect of change The process by which change that occurs in one area of interaction filters out and is experienced at all other levels of a system.

rituals "Rituals are coevolved symbolic acts that include not only the ceremonial aspects of the actual presentation of the ritual, but the process of preparing for it as well. It may or may not include words, but does have both open and closed parts which are 'held' together by a guiding metaphor. Repetition can be a part of rituals through either the content, the form, or the occasion. There should be enough space in therapeutic rituals for the incorporation of multiple meanings by various family members and clinicians, as well as a variety of levels of participation" (Roberts, 1988, p. 8).

role reversal A change in family positions that may take place unconsciously (a child acts like a responsible parent) or be prescribed by the therapist during the therapeutic process (have the husband answer as his wife would).

scapegoat A role assumed by a family member who is the object of the system's conflict and tension. Other family members avoid intensity by displacing tension upon this person, who is usually the identified patient.

see-saw syndrome Describes the polarities in the couple system. Like children on a see-saw in a playground, when one is up, the other is down. Partners alternate such complementary positions: One overfunctions while the other underfunctions; one is emotional while the other is rational. (See complementarity.)

self-disclosure Revelation of some personal information or reaction between people.

sexual history An interviewing tool that is useful to explore the developmental history and context of a couple's sexual relationship.

sibling position The birth order of children in a family, which often influences their place of power in the family as well as their marital interactions in adult life.

sibling subsystem The alliance of the children in a nuclear or a blended family.

solution-focused brief therapy An approach to therapy that focuses on the positive, the solution, the future, and upon the client as expert (Walter & Peller, 1992). The main therapeutic activities are asking "miracle" and scaling questions and helping clients shape a future without the problem.

stepfamily A form of family structure that emerges with remarriage and that includes the parents and children of two systems. See blended marriage.

structural family therapy An approach to therapy formulated by Salvador Minuchin that emphasizes a family's structure, subsystems, and boundaries. The focus is upon the here-and-now interactions of families, and altering the structure underlying interactions is a central component of change.

subsystem A unit or part of a larger system.

survival mechanisms Ways of coping learned in one's family of origin that enable the child to protect him or herself in difficult situations. These are often continued into adult life.

systemic hypothesis Tentative ideas and possibilities about a clinical case that are based upon systems principles.

systemic patterns A sequence of interactions of a couple or family that becomes repetitive over time.

system Any entity with interacting parts that behaves in a predictable way and maintains patterned responses.

systems theory A comprehensive way of conceptualizing human behavior that provides a valuable framework for understanding couples and families. The focus is upon interpersonal patterns of connection and interactional processes that make up the whole.

therapeutic crisis A critical interruption in the therapeutic process between therapist and couple or family. This situation provides an opportunity to model the process of repairing interactions of the relationship.

therapeutic contract or therapeutic frame The ground rules or boundaries that form the agreement between the therapist and client, couple, or family. Covers fees, time and length of sessions, policy concerning phone contact, etc.

transference Conscious or unconscious process in which emotional responses originating in one's family of origin are displaced onto other current relationships.

transgenerational issues Patterns that are passed down through the generations of a family.

triangle (triad) A three-person system that is the smallest stable relationship in families. See triangulation.

triangulation The process whereby any two-party relationship that is experiencing great intensity will naturally involve a third party to reduce anxiety. This third party can be a person, issue, substance, or any entity that takes the focus off the relationship and thereby reduces the tension.

unconscious The realm of the individual's personality which contains the emotions, thoughts, images, memories, fantasies, attitudes, and all subjective responses.

undifferentiated family ego mass A term created by Murray Bowen that refers to a family whose members are fused, overinvolved, and emotionally "stuck together."

Bibliography

Andersen, T. (Ed.) (1991). *The reflecting team: Dialogues and dialogues about the dialogues*. New York: Norton.

Anderson, H., & Goolishian, H. A. (1990). Beyond cybernetics: Comments on Atkinson and Heath's "Further thoughts on second-order family therapy." *Family Process, 29*, 157–163.

Anderson, H. (1997). *Conversation, language and possibilities: A postmodern approach to therapy*. New York: Basic Books.

Balcom, D., Lee, R. G., & Tager, J. (1995). The systemic treatment of shame in couples. *Journal of Marital & Family Therapy, 21*, 1, 55–65.

Barbach, L. (1982). *For each other*. New York: Anchor.

Becker, E. (1973). *The denial of death*. New York: Free Press.

Berg, I. (1994). *Family-based services*. New York: Norton.

Bobes, T., & Rothman, B. (1996). Meeting the challenge: Providing effective couple therapy in the age of managed care. *The California Therapist*, September/October, *8* (5).

Bograd, M. (1990). Women treating men confronting our gender assumptions. *The Family Therapy Networker*, May/June, 54–58.

Boscolo, L., Cecchin, G., Hoffman, L., & Penn, P. (1987). *Milan systemic family therapy: Conversations in theory and practice*. New York: Basic Books.

Bowen, M. (1991). Family reaction to death. In F. Walsh & M. McGoldrick (Eds.), *Living beyond loss: death in the family* (pp. 79–92). New York: Norton.

Bowen, M. (1978). *Family therapy in clinical practice*. Northvale, NJ: Aronson.

Brown, L., & Zimmer, D. (1986). An introduction to therapy issues of lesbian and gay male couples. In N. S. Jacobson & A. S. Gurman, *Clinical handbook of marital therapy*. New York: Guilford.

Carter, B., & McGoldrick, M. (1989). *The changing family life cycle. A framework for family therapy*, 2nd ed. Boston: Allyn & Bacon.

Chasin, R., Grunebaum, H., & Herzig, M. (Eds.) (1990). *One couple four realities: Multiple perspectives on couple therapy*. New York: Guilford.

Davidson, J., Lax, W. D., Lussardi, D., Miller, D., & Ratheau, M. (1988). The reflecting team. *Family Therapy Networker*, *12*(5), 44–47.

DiNicola, V. (1997). *A stranger in the family: Culture, families, and therapy*. New York: Norton.

Duvall, E. (1977). *Marriage and family development* (5th edition). Philadelphia: Lippincott. (Original work published 1957.)

Efran, J. S., Lukens, R. J., & Lukens, M. D. (1988). Constructivism: What's in it for you? *Family Therapy Networker, 12*(5), 27–35.

Epston, D. (1993). Internalized other questioning with couples: The New Zealand version. In S. Gilligan & R. Price (Eds.), *Therapeutic conversations* (pp. 183–189*)*. New York: Norton.

Epston, D., & Roth, S. (1996, May). Working with plot and alternative plot. Workshop handout, Ann Arbor, MI. Copyright David Epston and Sallyann Roth. Contact: Sallyann Roth, Family Institute of Cambridge, 51 Kondazian St., Cambridge, MA 02172.

Erikson, E. (1950). *Childhood and society*. New York: Norton.

Erikson, E. (1964). *Insight and responsibility*. New York: Norton.

Erikson, E. (1968). *Identity: Youth and crisis*. New York: Norton.

Falicov, C. J. (1995). Training to think culturally: A multidimensional comparative framework. *Family Process, 34,* 373–388.

Freedman, J., & Combs, G. (1996). *Narrative therapy: The social construction of preferred realities*. New York: Norton.

Garcia-Preto, N. (1994). On the bridge. *The Family Therapy Networker,* July/August, *18* (4), 35–37.

Garfield, R. (1982). Mourning and its resolution for spouses in marital separation. In J. C. Hansen (Ed.), *Therapy with remarriage families*. Gaithersburg, MD: Aspen.

Gilligan, C. (1992). *In a different voice: Psychological theory and women's development*. Cambridge: Harvard University Press.

Givelber, F. (1990). Object relations and the couple: Separation, individuation, intimacy, and marriage. In R. Chasin, H. Grunebaum, & M. Herzig (Eds.), *One couple four realities: Multiple perspectives on couple therapy*. New York: Guilford.

Goldenberg, I., & Goldenberg, H. (1996). *Family therapy: An overview*. 4th ed. Pacific Grove, CA: Brooks/Cole.

Goldner, V. (1982). Remarriage family: Structure, system, future. In J. C. Hansen (Ed.), *Therapy with remarriage families*. Gaithersburg, MD: Aspen.

Hansen, M. (1995). Feminism and family therapy: A review of feminist critiques of approaches to family violence. In M. Hansen & M. Harway (Eds.), *Battering and family therapy: A feminist perspective* (pp. 69–81). Newbury Park: Sage.

Hardy, K. V., & Laszloffy, T. A. (1995). The cultural genogram: Key to training culturally competent family therapists. *Journal of Marital and Family Therapy, 21* (3), 227–237.

Harway, M., & Hansen, M. (1994). *Spouse abuse: Assessing and treating battered women, batterers, and their children.* Sarasota, FL: Professional Resource Press.

Hoyt, M. F. (Ed.) (1994). *Constructive therapies.* New York: Guildford Press.

Imber-Black, E., & Roberts, J. (Ed.) (1992). *Rituals for our times: Celebrating, healing, and changing our lives and our relationships.* New York: Harper-Collins.

Imber-Black, E. (1991). Rituals and the healing process. In F. Walsh & M. McGoldrick (Eds.), *Living beyond loss: Death in the family* (pp. 207–223). New York: Norton.

Imber-Black, E., Roberts, J., & Whiting, R.A. (1988). *Rituals in families and family therapy.* New York: Norton.

Jacobs, Marsha (1988). *The use of family dynamics for the establishment of a shared grieving process.* Thesis submission, Sierra University.

Jenkins, A. (1990). *Invitations to responsibility: The therapeutic engagement of men who are violent and abusive.* Adelaide, South Australia: Dulwich Centre Publications.

Kaplan, H. S. (1974). *The new sex therapy.* New York: Brunner/Mazel.

Kaplan, H. S. (1979). *Disorders of sexual desire.* New York: Brunner/Mazel.

Kerr, M., & Bowen, M. (1988). *Family evaluation.* New York: Norton.

Killian, K. D. (1998). Interracial couples and therapists: Challenging "the hype." Presentation at 1998 meeting of TAMFT (Texas Association of Marriage and Family Therapy).

Kinsey, C., Pomeroy, W. B., Martin, C.R., & Gebhard, P. H. (1948). *Sexual behavior in the human male.* Philadelphia: W. B. Saunders.

Kinsey, C., Pomeroy, W. B., Martin, C.R., & Gebhard, P. H. (1953). *Sexual behavior in the human female.* Philadelphia: W. B. Saunders.

Knudson-Martin, C. (1997). The politics of gender in family therapy. *Journal of Marital and Family Therapy. 23* (4), 421–437.

Kübler-Ross, E. (1969). *On death and dying.* New York: Macmillan.

Lerner, H. (1993). *The dance of deception: Pretending and truth-telling in women's lives.* New York: HarperCollins.

Liddle, H. A. (1988). Systemic supervision: Conceptual overlays and pragmatic guidelines. In H. A. Liddle, D. C. Breunlin, & R. C. Schwartz (Eds.), *Handbook of family therapy training and supervision.* New York: Guilford.

Liddle, H. A., Breunlin, D. C., & Schwartz, R.C. (Eds.) (1988). *Handbook of family therapy training and supervision.* New York: Guilford.

Liddle, H. A., & Saba, G. W. (1985). The isomorphic nature of training and therapy: epistemologic foundation for a structural-strategic training paradigm. In J. Schwartzman (Ed.), *Families and other systems.* New York: Guilford.

Low, N. (1990). Women in couples: How their experience of relationships differs from men's. In R. Chasin, H. Grunebaum, & M. Herzig (Eds.), *One couple four realities: Multiple perspectives on couple therapy*. New York: Guilford.

Margolin, G. (1986). Ethical issues in marital therapy. In N. J. Jacobson & A. S. Gurman (Eds.), *Clinical handbook of marital therapy*. New York: Guilford.

Markowitz, L. (1991). Homosexuality: Are we still in the dark? *Family Therapy Networker, 15* (1), 27–35.

Martin, M., & Martin, D., with the assistance of P. Jeffers (1992). *Stepfamilies in therapy: Understanding systems, assessment, and intervention*. San Francisco: Jossey-Bass.

Masters, W., & Johnson, V. (1965). *The human sexual response*. Boston: Little, Brown and Co.

McGoldrick, M. (1995). *You can go home again: Reconnecting with your family*. New York: Norton.

McGoldrick, M., Garcia Preto, N., Hines, P.M., & Lee, E. (1991). Ethnicity and family therapy. In A. S. Gurman & D. P. Kniskern (Eds.), *Handbook of family therapy*, Vol. 2. New York: Brunner/Mazel.

McGoldrick, M., & Gerson, R. (1985). *Genograms in family assessment*. New York: Norton.

Minuchin, S. (1974). *Families and family therapy*. Cambridge: Harvard University Press.

Minuchin, S., & Fishman, C. H. (1981). *Family therapy techniques*. Cambridge: Harvard University Press.

Napier, A. Y., & Whitaker, C. A. (1978). *The family crucible*. New York: Harper & Row.

Nichols, M., & Schwartz, R. (1997). *Family therapy: Concepts and methods*. Boston: Allyn & Bacon.

Nichols, W. C. (1988). *Marital therapy: An integrative approach*. New York: Guilford.

O'Hanlon, B. (1994). The third wave. *Family Therapy Networker, 18* (6),19–29.

Papp, P. (1990). The use of structured fantasy in couple therapy. In R. Chasin, H. Grunebaum, & M. Herzig (Eds.), *One couple four realities: Multiple perspectives on couple therapy*. New York: Guilford.

Patten, J. (1992). Gay and lesbian families. *Family Therapy News,* October.

Paul, N., & Paul, B. (1990). Enhancing empathy in couples, a transgenerational approach. In R. Chasin, H. Grunebaum, & M. Herzig (Eds.), *One couple four realities: Multiple perspectives on couple therapy*. New York: Guilford.

Roberts, J. (1988). Setting the frame: Definitions, functions, and typology of rituals. In E. Imber-Black, J. Roberts, & R. Whiting (Eds.), *Rituals in families and family therapy* (pp. 3–46). New York: Norton.

Roth, S., & Epston, D. (1996). Consulting the problem about the problematic relationship, an exercise for experiencing a relationship with an externalized problem. In M. F. Hoyt (Ed.), *Constructive therapies*, Vol. 2. New York: Guilford.

Satir, V. (1967). *Conjoint family therapy*. Palo Alto: Science & Behavior Books.

Satir, V. (1972). *Peoplemaking*. Palo Alto: Science & Behavior Books.

Scarf, M. (1995). *Intimate worlds: Life inside the family*. New York: Random House.

Scarf, M. (1987). *Intimate partners: Patterns in love and marriage*. New York: Ballantine.

Scharff, D. E., & Scharff, J. S. (1991). *Object relations couple therapy*. Northvale, NJ: Aronson.

Scharff, D. E., & Scharff, J. S. (1987). *Object relations family therapy*. Northvale, NJ: Aronson.

Scharff, D. E., & Scharff, J. S. (1992). *Scharff notes. A primer of object relations therapy*. Northvale, NJ: Aronson.

Schnarch, D. (1991). *Constructing the sexual crucible*. New York: Norton.

Shafran, C., & Thomas, G. (1997). *The domestic violence training manual*. Los Angeles: TAPP, The Abuse Prevention Program of The Southern California Counseling Center.

Schwartz, R. C., Liddle, H. A., & Breunlin, D. C. (1988). Muddles in live supervision. In H. A. Liddle, D. C. Breunlin, & R. C. Schwartz (Eds.), *Handbook of family therapy training and supervision*. New York: Guilford.

Siegel, J. (1992). *Repairing intimacy: An object relations approach to couples therapy*. Northvale, NJ: Aronson.

Skynner, A. C. R. (1976). *Systems of family and marital psychotherapy*. New York: Brunner/Mazel.

Solomon, M. F. (1989). *Narcissism and intimacy: Love and marriage in an age of confusion*. New York: Norton.

St. Clair, M. (1986). *Object relations and self psychology: An introduction*. Belmont, CA: Brooks/Cole.

Steiny, N. (1988). Director's message. *The Southern California Counseling Center Dialogue*, Los Angeles, CA.

Stern, D. N. (1985). *The interpersonal world of the infant*. New York: Basic Books.

The Ethical Standards for Marriage and Family Therapists Part I and Part II, published by the California Association of Marriage and Family Therapists; May/June, Vol. 9, Issue 3.

Tomm, K. (1987). Interventive interviewing: Part II. Reflexive questioning as a means to enable self-healing. *Family Process, 26*, 167–183.

Tomm, K. (1988a). Interventive interviewing Part III. Intending to ask lineal, circular, strategic, or reflexive questions? *Family Process, 27*, 1–15.

Tomm, K. (1988b). Questions as interventions. *Family Therapy Networker, 12* (5), 38–41.

Treadway, D. C. (1989). *Before it's too late: Working with substance abuse in the family*. New York: Norton.

Wallerstein, J. S., & Blakeslee, S. (1995). *The good marriage: How and why love lasts*. New York: Warner Books.

Walsh, F., & McGoldrick, M., (Eds.) (1995). *Living beyond loss: Death in the family*. New York: Norton.

Walter, J. L., & Peller, J. E. (1992). *Becoming solution-focused in brief therapy.* New York: Brunner/Mazel.

Warshaw, C., Ganley, A. L., & Salber, P. R. (1995). Identification, assessment and intervention with victims of domestic violence. Excerpted from the publication entitled *Improving your community clinic's response to domestic violence: A training manual for California clinicians,* by Debbie Lee and Lisa Fries Anderson. Produced by the Family Violence Prevention Fund and Education Programs Associates, Inc. In collaboration with Physicians for a Violence-Free Society, San Francisco Injury Center for Research and Prevention.

Watzlawick, P., Beavin Bavelas, J., & Jackson, D. (1967). *Pragmatics of human communication: A study of interactional patterns, pathologies, and paradoxes.* New York: Norton.

Watzlawick, P., Weakland, J., & Fisch, R. (1974). *Change: Principles of problem formation and problem resolution.* New York: Norton.

Weingarten, K. (1994). *The mother's voice: Strengthening intimacy in families.* New York: Guilford.

Whitaker, C. A., & Keith, D.V. (1981). Symbolic-experiential family therapy. In A. S. Gurman & D. P. Kniskern (Eds.), *Handbook of family therapy.* New York: Brunner/Mazel.

White, M., & Epston, D. (1990). *Narrative means to therapeutic ends.* New York: Norton.

Zimmerman, J. L. & Dickerson, V. C. (1993). Separating couples from restraining patterns and the relationship discourse that supports them. *Journal of Marital and Family Therapy, 19,* 4, 403–413.

Index

aging, illness, and death, 151–53
    assumptions underpinning grief and loss, 156–57
    family beliefs and attitudes about illness and death, 155
    personal examination of loss, 153–54
    reflections about self-disclosure, 154–55
    vignette, 155–56
AIDS, 155–56
American Association for Marriage and Family Therapy (AAMFT), 5
American Psychiatric Association, 176
Anderson, Harlene, 4, 10, 12, 78
anger management groups, men's, 165, 166
Antioch University Los Angeles, 175

Balcom, D., 97
basic treatment framework
    Bowen theory, 7–8
    collaborative language systems approach, 12
    comparing and contrasting earlier models with postmodern thinking, 18–19
    contextual influences, 16–17
    developmental family life-cycle paradigm, 12–15
    narrative theory, 11
    object relations theory, 8–10
    philosophical stance, 3–6
    postmodern constructivism, 10–12
    systems theory, 6–7
batterers groups, men's, 166
Beavin Bavelas, J., 99

Becker, Ernest, 151
beginning stage of couple therapy
    subsequent sessions in, 27
    therapeutic tasks in, 24–25, 27–28, 56
Blakeslee, Sandra, 173
blended marriage, a, 140–44
    the blending of therapists' and clients' cultures, 148
    continuation of therapy with the Wilder family, 144–48
    remarriage: the blending of multiple cultures, 148–50
    the ruptured bond, 144
Bobes, Toby, 125
    the art of questioning, 78
    countertransference, 30–31
    grief and loss, 153–54, 156
    mixed marriages, 122, 125
    personal reflections, 180–81
    reframing, 44
    sexually distressed couples, 171–73
Bograd, Michele, 89
Boscolo, Luigi, 4
boundary issues
    boundaries between self and other, 64, 68
    boundaries and the couple system, 63–64
    concept of boundaries and reframing, 18
    setting the frame and boundaries of therapy, 56
Bowen, Murray, 4, 12, 18, 49, 70
    Bowen theory, 7–8, 19, 23, 24, 55, 56, 70, 151
Breunlin, D. C., 124, 125

199

California Association of Marriage and
  Family Therapists, 34
caretaker role, 31
Carter, Betty, 13, 14–15, 140
case study of Laura and Michael
  the couple's dance, 69–82
  crowded "marital bed", 62–68
  endings and new beginnings, 110–16
  family secrets exposed, 57–61
  the first session, 48–56
  the initial contact, 41–47
  ripple effect of change, 104–9
  unconscious agendas, 83–92
  the untouchable wound, 93–103
children
  in couple therapy, 37
  developmental tasks of, 64
  effects of couple therapy upon, 104–6
  Hispanic couple with teenage children,
    127–34
  object relations theory and, 65
  secrets and, 57, 97
circular questioning, 26, 61, 78–79, 82
circular thinking, 35
collaborative language systems theory, 12
Combs, G., 10
communication, nonverbal, 98–99, 100–103
confidentiality, 34–35
conjoint therapy, 37, 38
Constructing the Sexual Crucible (Schnarch),
    169
constructivism, 5, 18–19
  postmodern, 10–12
conversations
  externalizing, 76–77
  therapeutic, 24
countertransference, 30–31, 86–87, 92
  impact of countertransference disclosure,
    87–88
  in termination process, 115–16
couple's dance, the (Laura and Michael),
    69–70
  art of questioning, 78
  circular questioning, 78–79, 82
  externalizing conversations, 76–77
  guidelines for crafting questions that
    generate change, 80–82
  internalized-other interviewing, 76
  loops, patterns, and circularity, 73–75
  punctuating strengths of couple, 70
  reflexive questions, 79–80, 82
  triangular patterns, 70–73
crisis situations, 135–39
cross-referential questioning, 74
crowded marital bed (Laura and Michael),
    62–63
  boundaries between self and other, 64, 68
  boundaries and the couple system, 63–64
  object relations theory, 65–67
  planning the next steps of therapy, 63
  projective identification, 67–68

cybernetic epistemology, 10
cybernetics, first-order/second-order, 10, 18

*Dance of Deception: Pretending and Truth-
    telling in Women's Lives, The*
    (Lerner), 57, 97
Davidson, J., 122
death, *see* aging, illness, and death
Denial of Death, The (Becker), 151
developmental tasks
  of children, 64
  sexual intimacy, 173–74
diagnosis and labeling, 35–37
*Diagnostic and Statistical Manual of Mental
    Disorders, Fourth Edition* (DSM-IV),
    35
diagnostic thinkers, 35
Dickerson, V. C., 50
DiNicola, Vincenzo, 130, 132
disclosure
  containment vs., 85–87
  countertransference, 87–88
  personal, 154
  self-disclosure, 154–55
Disorders of Sexual Desire (Kaplan), 169
divorce, 140, 142–44, 149, 150
Domestic Abuse Intervention Project, 159,
    160, 161
domestic violence
  assessment and treatment of, 163–64
  dialogue of consultation, 164–66
  necessary knowledge and skills to treat,
    166–67
  overview of, 158–62
  a supervision session, 162–63
  therapist's biases, prejudices, and con-
    cerns regarding, 166
  using conjoint therapy in treating, 38
Domestic Violence Training Manual, The
    (Shafran and Thomas), 166–67
DSM-IV, 35
Duvall, Evelyn, 14

Efran, J. S., 5, 18
emotions
  identifying the therapist's own emo-
    tional responses, 30–31
  managing reactivity of clients, 31–32, 84
Epston, David, 11, 74, 77, 80–81, 96, 152
Erikson, Erik, 13–14
*Ethical Standards for Marriage and Family
    Therapists, The* Part I and II, 34-35
ethical and therapeutic dilemmas
  diagnosis and labeling, 35–37
  indications and contraindications for
    couple therapy, 37–39
  therapeutic responsibility, ethical and
    legal considerations, 33–35
ethnic and cultural considerations, 132–34
ethnicity and religious influences, 89–90
externalizing coversations, 76–77

Falicov, Celia J., 17, 148–49
family-of-origin issues
    in case study of Laura and Michael,
        50–51, 55–56, 95, 106–8
    effects of couple therapy upon family-
        of-origin, 106–8
    power of family-of-origin influences,
        50–51
    unresolved, 95
family tree, drawing a, 23–24
first session, guidelines for, 26
first session (Laura and Michael), 48–49
    clarifying each partner's perception of
        problem, 55
    connect presenting problem to family-
        of-origin, 55–56
    the couple's attraction, 51–52
    focus on strengths and instilling hope,
        52–54
    joining the couple system, 54
    power of family-of-origin influences,
        50–51
    setting the frame and boundaries of
        therapy, 56
Framo, James, 4
Freedman, J., 10

Garfield, Robert, 144
gay population, *see* lesbian and gay popula-
    tion
Gebhard, P. H., 169
gender
    gendercentric questions, 61
    gender influences, 88–89
    identity, 176
    and power differences, 61, 73
genograms, 18
    in beginning stage of treatment, 27
    in case study of Laura and Michael,
        55–56, 59–61
    construction of, 23–24
    of the Wilder family, 141
Gerson, R., 24, 145
Gilligan, Carol, 73
Goldner, V., 149
Goolishian, Harry, 12
Greene, Robert, 141
grief, loss
    assumptions underpinning grief and loss,
        156–57
    and divorce and remarriage, 140, 142–43,
        144, 150, 152
    and the family life cycle, 129–31
    grieving process, 152
    and healing, 97
guidelines for assessment and evaluation of
    the couple system, 25–30

*Handbook of Family Therapy Training and
    Supervision, The* (Liddle, Breunlin,
    and Schwartz), 125

Hansen, Marsali, 159
Hardy, Kenneth, 179
Hardy, K. V., 16
Hill, Reuben, 14
Hispanic couple with teenage children,
    127–29
    ethnic and cultural considerations, 132–34
    grief, loss, and the family life cycle, 129–31
Holocaust families, 93–95, 107, 178
homophobia, 176, 178
homosexuality, 176

illness, *see* aging, illness, and death
Imber-Black, Evan, 109
initial contact, the (Laura and Michael),
    43–44
    first telephone call, 44
    individual or couple work, 45–47
    reframing, 44–45
inner models, 65
internal family relationships, 31, 65–66
internalized-other interviewing, 61, 74–76
intervention, methods of, 21–25
    step-by-step treatment format, 21–22
isomorphism, 124, 125

Jackson, D., 99
Jacobs, Marsha, 152
Jenkins, A., 159
Johnson, Virginia, 169

Kaplan, Helen Singer, 169
Keith, D. V., 9
Kerr, M., 70
Killian, K. D., 16
Kinsey, Alfred, 169
Knudson-Martin, Carmen, 61
Kübler-Ross, Elizabeth, 151, 156

labeling, diagnosis and, 35–37
Laszloffy, Tracey A., 16, 179
later stages of couple therapy, therapeutic
    tasks in, 28–29
Lax, W. D., 122
Lee, R. G., 97
Lerner, Harriet, 57, 97
lesbian and gay population, 175–78
    developing culturally sensitive training
        contexts, 179
    illness, loss, and death issues in gay com-
        munity, 155–56
    working with oppressed populations, 178
Liddle, H. A., 124, 125
life cycle issues
    developmental family life-cycle para-
        digm, 12–15
    grief, loss, and the family life cycle, 129–31
    rituals relating to the life cycle, 109
    tasks of life-cycle stage of separation,
        divorce, and remarriage, 149
    therapeutic life cycle, 24–25
linear questions, 82

linear thinking, 35
Living Beyond Loss: Death in the Family
(Walsh and McGoldrick), 151–52
Low, Natalie, 73
Lukens, M. D. and R. J., 5, 18
Lussardi, D., 122

McGoldrick, Monica, 24, 137
    death, 151–52
    family life-cycle framework, 13, 14–15
    grief and loss, 156
    remarried families, 140, 144, 145
managed care, 6, 110
Markowitz, Laura, 176
Marriage and Family Development (Duvall),
    14
Martin, C. R., 169
Martin, Don and Maggie, 141
Masters, William, 169
men's anger management groups, 165, 166
men's batterers groups, 166
middle stage of couple therapy, therapeutic
    tasks in, 25, 28, 92
midlife, couple encountering multiple losses
    at, 135–39
Milan group, 18
Miller, D., 122
Minuchin, Salvador, 4, 12, 18
mixed marriages, 119–24
    the interconnection of interactions at
        different levels of a system, 124–26
mourning, 152

Napier, Augustus Y., 4, 6, 44, 84–85
narrative theory, 11
New Sex Therapy, The (Kaplan), 169
nontraditional households, 140
normalizing, 24
nuclear families, 140, 141

object relations theory, 4, 7, 8–10, 19, 23, 55,
    65–68
O'Hanlon, Bill, 77
oppressed populations, working with, 178

Patten, John, 175
Paul, Norman and Betty, 172
personal disclosure, 154
Pomeroy, W. B., 169
positive connotation, concept of, 18
postmodern constructivism, 10–12
postmodern thinking, 18–19
power
    gender and power differences, 61, 73
    Power and Control Wheel, 160
projective identification, concept of, 9, 67–68
psychodrama, 99–103
psychotherapy, 33

questioning
    art of, 78
    circular, 26, 61, 78–79, 82
    cross-referential, 74
    gendercentric questions, 61
    guidelines for crafting questions that
        generate change, 80–82
    linear questions, 82
    reflexive questions, 79–80, 82, 102

Ratheau, M., 122
reciprocal behaviors, 73–74
reflecting process, 122–24
reflecting teams, 121–22
reflexive questions, 79–80, 82, 102
reframing, 18, 23
    in case study of Laura and Michael,
        44–45, 50
relabeling, 23
religious influences, ethnicity and, 89–90
remarried families, 140–50
    ripple effect of change (Laura and Michael),
        104–6
    effects of couple therapy upon the chil-
        dren, 104–6
    effects of couple therapy upon family-
        of-origin, 106–8
    rituals relating to the life cycle, 109
Rothman, Barbara, 78
    the art of questioning, 78
    grief and loss, 153–54
    mixed marriages, 122–23, 125
    personal reflections, 180–81
    reframing, 44
    remarried families, 141–43, 145–48
Roth, Sallyann, 4, 77, 80–81

Saba, G. W., 125
St. Clair, Michael, 9
same-sex couples, 176
Satir, Virginia, 4, 18
Scarf, Maggie, 8, 45, 64, 65
Scharff, David E. and Jill S., 4, 8, 9, 30, 55,
    56, 129
Schnarch, David, 60, 169, 174
Schwartz, R. C., 124, 125
secrets
    confidentiality and, 34
    as deep wounds, 93
    family secrets in case study of Laura and
        Michael, 57–61
    impact of stories, secrets, and myths,
        96–97
    secrecy and shame, 97–98
see-saw syndrome, 89
self-disclosure, 154–55
separation, marital, 144, 149
sex-role issues, 34

sexually distressed couples, 168
  evolving paradigms in human sexuality, 168–69
  Mike and Lynn, 171–73
  sexual intimacy, 173–74
  taking a sexual history, 169–70
Shafran, Connie, 163–64, 165, 166–67
shame, secrecy and, 97–98
Siegel, J., 67
Skynner, Robin, 169
slavery, 178
social constructionism and social constructivism, 10
Solomon, M. F., 64
Southern California Counseling Center (Los Angeles), 3, 5
  Domestic Violence Program, 159, 162–64, 166
Steiny, Nancy, 3, 35
stepfamilies, 140–50
Stepfamilies in Therapy: Understanding Systems, Assessment, and Intervention (Martin and Martin), 141
Stern, Daniel, 64
support groups, women's, 165, 166
syncretism, 148–49
systems theory, 6–7, 35

Tager, J., 97
TAPP, The Abuse Prevention Program of the Southern California Counseling Center, 163
telephone contact, initial
  in case study of Laura and Michael, 44
  guidelines, 25–26
terminating stage of therapy
  tasks in, 111
  termination process in case study of Laura and Michael, 108, 110–14
  therapeutic tasks in, 25, 29–30
  varieties of endings in therapy, 114–16
therapeutic conversations, 24
therapeutic life cycle, 24–25
therapists
  beginning, xv-xvi, xvii
  the blending of therapists' and clients' cultures, 148
  countertransference, 30–31, 86–88, 92, 115–16
  feminist family, 159

guidelines for assessment and evaluation of the couple system, 25–30
identifying and managing intense reactivity of clients, 31–32
methods of intervention, 21–25
necessary knowledge and skills for domestic violence training, 166–67
postmodern, 18
therapist competency and confidentiality, 33–35
therapist's biases, prejudices, and concerns regarding domestic violence, 166
what the therapist does, 20–21
see also unconcious agendas
Thomas, George, 163–66, 167
threshold therapy, 130
Tomm, Karl, 4, 24, 74, 77, 80, 81–82
Treadway, David, 27, 45, 50, 55
triangulation, 70–73

unconscious agendas (Laura and Michael), 83–84
  belief systems of Jennifer Reed, 85
  containment vs. disclosure, 85–87
  ethnicity and religious influences, 89–90
  gender influences, 88–89
  impact of countertransference disclosure, 87–88
  internal processing and musings of Jennifer Reed, 90–92
  Jennifer Reed's crowded bed, 84–85
untouchable wound, the (Laura and Michael), 93–95
  exploring the nonverbal realm, 98–99
  grief, loss, and healing, 97
  impact of stories, secrets, and myths, 96–97
  opening windows of vulnerability, 95–96
  psychodramatic journey, 99–103
  secrecy and shame, 97–98

Wallerstein, Judith, 173
Walsh, Froma, 144, 151–52, 156
Watzlawick, P., 99
Whitaker, Carl A., 4, 6, 9, 44, 84
White, Michael, 11, 77, 96, 152
Wilder family, the, 141–48, 149
women's support groups, 165, 166
women survivors' groups, 166

Zimmerman, J. L., 50